The Culture Builders

*Of course, this book is dedicated to my Mum and Dad who,
through the support they've given me, my husband and my daughter,
have made it possible for me to bring this work to you.*

The Culture Builders

Leadership Strategies for Employee Performance

JANE SPARROW

Routledge
Taylor & Francis Group

LONDON AND NEW YORK

First published 2012 by Ashgate Publishing

Published 2016 by Routledge

2 Park Square, Milton Park, Abingdon, Oxon OX14 4RN

711 Third Avenue, New York, NY 10017, USA

Routledge is an imprint of the Taylor & Francis Group, an informa business

British Library Cataloguing in Publication Data
Sparrow, Jane.
    The culture builders : leadership strategies for employee performance.
    1. Employee motivation. 2. Corporate culture.
    I. Title
    658.3'14–dc23

Library of Congress Cataloging-in-Publication Data
Sparrow, Jane.
    The culture builders : leadership strategies for employee performance / by Jane Sparrow.
        p. cm.
    Includes bibliographical references and index.
    ISBN 978-1-4094-3724-6 (hardback : alk. paper) – ISBN 978-1-4094-3725-3 (ebook)
  1. Employee motivation. 2. Corporate culture. I. Title.
    HF5549.5.M63S663 2012
    658.3'14–dc23
                                                           2012011068

ISBN 9781409437246 (pbk)

Contents

List of Figures

List of Tables

About the Author

Jane Sparrow uses her passion, capability and drive to enable others to maximise their potential, build capacity and implement behavioural change programmes within different cultures and a changing business environment. She has worked as special adviser to some of the world's largest and most respected brands to enable people to sustain high performance by nurturing culture and engaging people. Her work across the globe has attracted much acclaim, and she continues to use her experience across leadership development, culture change and employee engagement to work with leaders and managers of all levels. She is an expert facilitator, consultant, performance coach and impactful speaker who has held board-level positions in a variety of organisations.

For further insight, visit www.theculturebuilders.com and join the group on Facebook at www.facebook.com/TheCultureBuilders. You can also see more about Jane at www.jane-sparrow.com.

Preface

Tens of millions of pounds are spent each year on leadership communication events, roadshows and values programmes. Most of these are a waste of money and don't provide adequate return on investment. Why? Not because the leaders aren't compelling or trustworthy (although this is sometimes the case), but because after the rah-rah events, middle and senior managers are expected to sustain the momentum with gusto, yet are rarely equipped with the content, skills and capability to do so. They also don't have the time – when their 'day job' takes up 99 per cent of their energy.

I have a strong belief that the organisations that will truly sustain high performance in the long term, are those that best equip their middle managers to engage their people to deliver. The focus and responsibility is threefold: on the senior executives, on line managers, and thus on the organisation as a whole. The organisations that get this right are the companies that will ride the economic waves and be with us in the future.

Middle managers are the key to achieving employee engagement for performance. The challenge is that most of them are under so much time pressure that it's hard for them to take on this role fully. Managers need all the help they can get so they can sustain their own performance, be happier and healthier, and deliver more in their roles as people managers.

Throughout my career, my passion has always been to share my knowledge and experience with others. My goal with this book is to do just that. By combining my own experiences and those of other unique people around the globe, the pages that follow should enable leaders and managers across the world to truly shine.

The books that have given me the most powerful and sustainable value are those that bring together theory and practice. My aim is to give you, the reader, a strategic view, but also practical tips, hints and inspiration that you'll be able to use every day. Further tips, templates and tools will continually be added to the website at www.TheCultureBuilders.com.

There are many people who have been part of my life tapestry and helped me gain the experiences, confidence and skills to progress a career that includes writing this book. My family is the most incredible source of encouragement, enablement and wisdom. As a child, my wonderful parents, David and Penny Sparrow, gave me the gift of their time and wisdom. They continue to do this in every way, and have made it possible for me to write this book by caring for my darling daughter. 'Thank you' isn't powerful enough for everything I owe them.

I have also had the good fortune to work with many extraordinary people throughout my career. Jo Moore gave me the coaching, space and encouragement to grow during my first management role at IBM. She is a fabulous friend and colleague, and I thank her deeply for her influence, mentoring and for believing in me. Tony Field and Diane Turpin both gave me huge opportunities to excel at the very start of my career. My progression was as a result of great learning and sponsorship from both of you.

Other people in my early career at IBM played a huge part in my personal and professional development. Thanks to you all, and in particular to Patrick O'Connor, Helen Swannell and Chris Phillips.

My time at MCA was a huge inspiration and springboard. My thanks to all of you, in particular Kevin Thomson, Kathy Whitwell, Adrian Lenard and Fiona Rogers.

A huge thank you to Jeremy Keeley for his wisdom and for connecting me to so many of the outstanding people I interviewed in preparing this book.

My work leading The Energy Project Europe and with Jean and Sally-Ann Gomes was some of the most rewarding of my career.

Sony was the place where I tried new approaches and was given the freedom to implement innovative approaches to people and engagement. Thank you to everyone who was part of that experience.

I'd particularly like to thank every leader and manager who gave me the opportunity to interview them and gain such powerful insights to share in the pages that follow. I can honestly say that every one of you left me feeling energised and inspired. Thank you to David McClements, David Bush, Jo Huddie and Judy Goldberg for sharing such first-class work and deep insight. Thanks to Kirstin Furber, Val Elliott, Anthony Cerquone and Janet Markwick for the breadth of examples that bring so many of the Culture Builder roles to life. You have given plenty from which others can learn, and I know you will continue to do so through your work. Emma Berry and Nick Green, you are both leaders in your field. Your beliefs, married with your experience, will go on to make a difference everywhere you work. Heather Golding, your creative inspiration was priceless – thank you!

Simon Ashby, you have always been a pleasure to work with. You are one of the most grounded, intelligent, practical and special people I have met, and I know your unique leadership style will continue to add value to every business that has the good fortune to come into contact with you.

Kai Boschmann, your ability to focus on the business by never losing sight of the importance of people will always amaze and delight. Your experience is deep, and your approach to life, leadership and engagement is a great model from which others can learn.

Darren Childs, my work with you has been some of the most significant in recent years. You are a spectacular individual, and your transformational leadership style is unique. Thank you for your openness in giving to this book and for the opportunity to work together.

Naomi Climer, the impact you have on those around you in business is immense. As a leader, you are a true role model, and the focus you place on people and engagement is something many can learn from.

Andreas Ditter, our work together at Sony features as some of the most pivotal in my career. Your passion, focus, transformation and determination as a leader are truly unique, and I admire you in so many ways.

Nigel Edwards, your experience across so many fields of communication and engagement has already been shared through your intense contribution to Melcrum and other professional bodies. You are an 'all-star' in your field, and I thank you enormously for sharing such great examples for this text.

Stuart Fletcher, I thank you for your passion, openness and wisdom. Your approach to leadership will continue to inspire and enrich others' lives, while also having a lasting impact on the businesses you lead.

Sarah Henbrey, your beliefs, wisdom and experience of implementation with organisational development provides many best practices from which others can learn. Thank you for the opportunity to work together and co-develop approaches so far in our careers.

Patrick Lewis, I feel privileged to have explored engagement and the meaning of 'partner' with you at the John Lewis Partnership. There is no doubt that your approach to leadership and engagement is one that other organisations strive to learn from and replicate. Your impact as a leader with strong personal purpose is admired. Thank you.

Gordon Lyle, your stories are incredible, and the learning others will gain is huge. Everything you have done has made a difference, and your ability to notice great people around you is outstanding.

Debra Nelson, I know that the work you have done so far in your career has been an inspiration to people at every level of the community and society. The international experience you shared with me provides great learning for others, and I look forward to following your award-winning work in diversity.

Derry Newman, when I first came into contact with you, others told me you were unique in your calm, wise and compassionate leadership style. I then worked with you and realised that was a real understatement! Your contribution to this text based on recent experiences at Solarcentury will be valuable to many readers, and yet it's only a small snippet of your experiences that make you such a role model of building cultures and good engagement.

Fujio Nishida, I feel honoured to have had the opportunity to work with a leader who absolutely 'gets' engagement and the importance of culture to make a business successful. You gave me the space to grow and the encouragement to try new ideas with people and culture. You are a direct and indirect inspiration to many people across the world. You're exceptional.

Steve Thorn, when I asked what had influenced your views about engagement and leadership, I never expected to hear a story that has remained with me every day since; the naval tale has already enabled others to boost the ways they lead and engage others. You are clearly an exceptional leader, and I thank you for your time and openness.

Gordon Watt, your infectious and intelligent approach to engagement and leadership was a delight to learn about. I feel sure that your ongoing work in this area will continue to add value to many. Your experiences that are captured in each part of this book will inspire and fuel others.

Roy White, you have a leadership style that is held in such high regard by all that have worked with you. Your ability to enable people to grow, while balancing the business pressures, is an art that many others can only dream about demonstrating. You have made leaps in my career possible and been supportive for my work across the globe – from New Orleans to Tokyo. A heartfelt thank you.

Finally, words cannot express my appreciation and gratitude to my husband, Christopher Preston. I made a commitment to myself that I would write this book while on maternity leave. On day one of our beautiful daughter arriving, I realised that writing a book might be quite difficult to squeeze in! Nonetheless, Chris helped me to keep that commitment to myself and did everything possible to create an environment that helped me write while also working with great clients and seeing the special moments of Elouisa's first year. Elouisa challenges me and adds to my personal growth every day. I hope this will continue, and that she is able to learn from the content in this book in future years.

Chris's wisdom, intelligence, experience, love and calm nature are like none other. He made it possible for me to bring this knowledge to you, while adding much of his great experience and talent to the mix, too. Thank you from the deepest part of my heart.

Introduction

On a hot summer's day during 2005, one of the world's largest cities was hit by a terrorist attack. Multiple bombs across its transport network brought horror to thousands, and chaos to millions of people.

The emergency services acted quickly, along with a wide range of government bodies, with the aim of getting everyone safely out of the city, taking aid to those most affected by the attack and bringing the transport system back into service as soon as possible. Office workers were given clear instructions – get out – the city wasn't deemed to be safe, and thousands of people started to walk home. Offices were deserted; business for many large corporations simply didn't happen that day.

Among this chaos, a number of heroes emerged. The incredible ones were the emergency responders who dashed into smoke-filled situations and the staff and commuters who assisted injured passengers. But there was one other group, again told to leave their work and find a place of safety, that ignored this clear instruction and stood firm. They kept the doors open and maintained a steady flow of drinks and snacks to the shellshocked, confused commuters who wandered past their coffee houses.

When the management realised their stores were still open and their staff were staying in the danger zones, direct calls were placed to the shop staff. The response was unequivocal – 'We are staying.' The city suffered terribly that day, but it didn't walk home thirsty. A group of service workers delivered on a company promise to provide for the community, they made a bad situation better, and demonstrated, like many other front line workers that day, in the most striking fashion, their commitment to the job.

Why is it that a barista working, on a moderate wage, for a global coffee house brand will defy orders from management and risk their wellbeing to, as one described it, 'provide somewhere safe for people', yet some of those on six-figure salaries, with a huge amount of responsibility to ensure the continued success of a company, will risk very little to see this work fulfilled?

The bombings in London highlighted a group of highly engaged employees, in a place where perhaps people would not expect to find them. My subsequent conversations with the former senior management at the coffee company brought to life the huge amount of work they undertake to make all employees feel part of the brand, to feel loyal to the aims of the organisation and live its values in practice.

They know the value of engagement and understand how to create it within the company. You'll see me refer to engagement a great deal because it's at the heart of positively shaping and sustaining culture in organisations, so to build a great culture, engagement is critical. My research in writing this book has given me insight to how some of the world's largest (and smallest) companies are building cultures and creating an engaged workforce and how they're linking this directly back to performance for the organisation. I've seen and heard CEOs, CFOs, founders and human resource vice presidents talk passionately about the work they've undertaken to build high states of inclusion, passion and action. This, coupled with my own experience, provides an incredibly rich mix.

Engagement, and the tools and approaches to build it within organisations, have only relatively recently appeared on the business agenda. It's an emerging science that is still attracting debate around what it is and isn't, how it supports performance, and how much emphasis organisations should place on building it. Some are even saying that it's already passé. Not all of what is being done under the banner of engagement is new – in this book, I cover organisations that have engaged their workforce from day one, and have intuitively undertaken activity that creates an engagement culture.

Part I looks at the evidence and case for engagement. It references how organisations are measuring and defining it. This is necessary to set the context, but on its own will not make a difference to performance in an organisation. For me, what is important is the components that go into creating a workforce who feel passionate about their work, their company and are able to deliver something they feel makes a difference. It's the practical approach and implementation that makes the difference, not talking about it. To do this requires a focus at three levels: an organisational engagement strategy, focus on managers as Culture Builders and engagers, and leaders who are both role models and create the space for managers to engage and motivate their people.

The early chapters in Part I look at the first component: how engagement happens in practice at an organisational level. They set out the activity needed and the impact we can expect as a result. You'll find elements that will form the basis for an engagement strategy, along with spectacular examples of companies that are getting it right. You'll read about the strong sense of purpose felt in the John Lewis Partnership, the importance Innocent places on values, how Sony has used visual metaphors to give context and strategic direction, and how MGM Resorts targets engagement strategies to the needs of specific employee groups.

Having an engagement strategy at an organisational level is one step. However, it all too often ends there, and leaders – despite numerous internal communication campaigns – are left working in organisations where values only feature on mousemats. These leaders look at people such as the London baristas and wonder why their own employees don't also go the extra mile. The answer is covered in Part II: 'Manager as Culture Builder'.

Middle managers are the people with the highest influence on the culture, on engagement levels and team and individual performance. You'll see that I put the case clearly for why more investment, support and focus is needed to better enable this community. The five roles a manager must adopt to shape culture and achieve engagement are shared and brought to life with practical examples and top tips.

No single person is a perfect Culture Builder and engager – my conversations put me in front of people who are fulfilling certain elements incredibly well, and mindfully tackling the elements that don't come as naturally. Planning what to do, when, and with what mindset is a vital step in the engagement process – the success hinges as much on the effort of managers as it does the central initiatives.

Engagement takes place within the containment of an organisation – which, as an entity, has an important bearing on the success, or otherwise, of building a culture of high performance. It is the senior leaders who have the most sway on how the organisation colours what happens. They have the strongest hand on the tiller and the loudest voice in the room. It is they who have an opportunity to set a culture where managers are supported and expected to truly engage their people beyond the basics.

Part III looks at what senior leaders should be doing within the engagement process – both to support wider company activity and to build their own platform of action – and how, to go about it. You'll read about how phenomenal leaders have excelled in engaging their organisations to deliver incredible results. To them, this game-changing approach is just business as usual: it's who they are and what they do.

Chapter 23 provides you with a collection of stories outlining approaches that have been proven to increase engagement levels and build the cultures that organisations desire to promote high performance. These are designed to inspire you – and may even give you goose bumps.

No single organisation, leader or manager I've met is doing all of what I suggest in this text, nor do I believe that this should be the case. What follows is a summary of the conversations and conclusions of best practice from organisations and individuals across the world. I'm sharing the highlights of a series of very rich examples, with my conclusions and own experience making it a practical guide to achieving a culture where engagement enables performance.

As engagers, we all face one reality – you can't hire engaged people, you have to create them. A strong brand and good compensation package will attract the interested and motivated, but they won't build within them the sense of loyalty, purpose and connection that high-performing individuals display. You have to work to create these – to understand what to do, when, and in what frame of mind. I hope you'll find guidance on how to do this in the pages that follow. Enjoy!

The Organisational Engagement Strategy

CHAPTER 1

What is Engagement?

Type the word 'engagement' into Google and it gives more than 312,000,000 results – probably even more by the time you read this text. It's a word used in a variety of contexts and active situations: *engage* customers, *engage* stakeholders, *engage* colleagues.

It's an increasingly frequent term that attracts a wide range of descriptions, so perhaps it's best to start with exploring what we mean by engagement and why it matters.

Within this book, engagement refers to employee, or colleague, engagement. This is, in itself, an industry in its own right, and there are numerous books, papers and research reports that talk about engagement. Consequently, as we see, there are hundreds of definitions. The essence may be the same in each, but the expression is affected by our experiences of being engaged and disengaged.

Let's look at some of the best definitions of engagement.

The *Management Competencies for Enhancing Employee Engagement* Research Insight report (CIPD 2011), defined employee engagement as:

Being focused in what you do (thinking), feeling good about yourself in your role and the organisation (feeling), and acting in a way that demonstrates commitment to the organisational values and objectives (acting).

Gatenby and colleagues add depth to the word, and define engagement as follows:

Engagement is about creating opportunities for employees to connect with their colleagues, managers, and wider organisation. It is also about creating an environment where employees are motivated to want to connect with their work and really care about doing a good job. It is a concept that places flexibility, change and continuous improvement at the heart of what it means to be an employee and an employer in a twenty-first century workplace.

(Gatenby et al. 2009, p. 4)

I like this definition, but many leaders tire of hearing Communications and HR professionals talk passionately about 'employee engagement' with no practical depth behind making it happen. What we're really talking about here is:

How do we boost individual and company performance by engaging people, through inclusion and participation, providing a framework of direction and unlocking the true potential in people to do extraordinary things?

Great leaders have an intuitive sense of how to engage people for performance. During my interviews for this book, great leaders didn't see the examples they gave me as 'best practices of engagement'; they are part of the way they get on and do things to create a culture that breeds success in their businesses. Great leaders engage naturally. However, for those of us still on the journey (and those who recognise that there is always room for improvement), let's look in more detail at why it's important and how we can achieve it.

2 *Why Engage People in Business?*

I have realised in the last six years what's possible when you get the right level of alignment of the organisation with a clear strategy. When leaders and the organisation are truly engaged, amazing things become possible.

Stuart Fletcher, former President of International Business at Diageo

Business cases for employee engagement have strengthened recently as more evidence has become available linking it to customer satisfaction and profit. However, the most powerful evidence of the need to engage employees to nurture culture and increase performance is when CEOs and leaders intuitively notice the benefits without needing to see a business case. During my time as Director of Employee Engagement and Change at Sony Europe, I worked closely with Fujio Nishida, Sony Europe's President. He used to say that he would instinctively feel the positive difference of an engaged workforce, and believed it was critical to sustain a culture of long-term innovation in the business.

Not every leader feels the difference so quickly, so let's capture some of the critical reasons to engage employees for a performance culture (see Figure 2.1). The first element is, quite rightly, the most focused upon – business performance. Beyond this, I've also covered the wider benefits, including confidence, reductions in sickness, and increased customer satisfaction and customer benefits.

Business Performance: Revenue, Profit, Earnings per Share

There are many studies that attribute an increase in revenues and profits/earnings per share to greater employee engagement. Public sector bodies have also seen positive outcomes connected to financial management and individual motivation. Here is a selection.

The report *Engaging for Success: Enhancing Performance through Employee Engagement* (MacLeod and Clarke 2009) concluded that engagement has tangible outcomes at an organisational and individual level. At an organisational level, it found better outcomes in the public sector: specifically, better financial performance and higher levels of innovation and advocacy. For the individual, it reported higher levels of wellbeing and a more satisfying workplace.

During 2006, Gallup examined almost 24,000 business units and compared top-quartile and bottom-quartile financial performance with engagement scores (Harter et al. 2006, Gallup Q12 meta-analysis, cited in MacLeod and Clarke 2009). It found that those with scores in the bottom quartile averaged 31–51 per cent more employee turnover, 51 per cent more inventory shrinkage and 62 per cent more accidents.

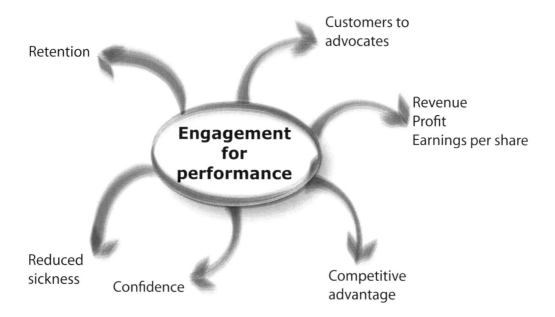

Figure 2.1   Engagement for Performance Model
Source: Copyright Best Companies LLP and reproduced with kind permission.

Those with engagement scores in the top quartile averaged 12 per cent higher customer advocacy, 18 per cent higher productivity and 12 per cent higher profitability.

Tower Perrins-ISR carried out a global survey in 2006 that included data gathered from opinion surveys of more than 664,000 employees from 50 companies around the world, representing a range of industries and sizes (Tower Perrins-ISR 2006). The survey compared the financial performance of organisations with a highly engaged workforce to their peers with a less engaged workforce over a 12-month period.

The conclusions indicated a significant difference in bottom-line results in companies with highly engaged employees compared with companies with low levels of employee engagement. Most noticeable was the near 52 per cent gap in the performance improvement in operating income over the year between companies with highly engaged employees versus companies whose employees had low engagement scores. Companies with high levels of employee engagement improved 19.2 per cent in operating income, while companies with low levels of employee engagement declined 32.7 per cent over the study period.

In evidence to the MacLeod review (MacLeod and Clarke 2009), Standard Chartered Bank reported that in 2007 it found that branches with a statistically significant increase in levels of employee engagement (0.2 or more on a scale of five) had a 16 per cent higher profit margin growth than branches with decreased levels of employee engagement.

A Watson Wyatt study of 115 companies suggested that a company with highly engaged employees achieves a financial performance four times greater than companies with poor engagement (Watson Wyatt 2009). They also reported that the highly engaged were more than twice as likely to be top performers – almost 60 per cent of them exceeded or far exceeded expectations for performance. Moreover, the highly engaged missed 43 per cent fewer days of work due to illness.

Hewitt reports that companies with a greater than 10 per cent profit growth had 39 per cent more engaged employees and 45 per cent fewer disengaged employees than those with less than 10 per cent growth (Hewitt Associates 2004).

A paper by Fleming, Coffman and Harter in the *Harvard Business Review* found that customer and employee engagement augment each other at the local level, creating an opportunity for accelerated improvement and growth of overall financial performance (Fleming, Coffman and Harter 2005). Analysis of the performance of 1,979 business units in ten companies revealed that those units that scored above the median on both employee and customer engagement were on average 3.4 times more effective financially (in terms of total sales and revenue performance to target and year over year gain in sales and revenue) than units in the bottom half of both measures.

The Best Companies to Work For survey[1] is conducted annually and attracts companies that are keen to benchmark their engagement levels against others. It has surveyed 3,270 companies since 2001.

Best Companies states that there is a direct correlation between companies which are featured on the Best Companies listing and increased profits. FTSE 100 companies that are high on the Best Companies listing have significantly higher profits than their peers in the index.

Moreover, organisations that have consistently featured in the Best Companies to Work For lists over the period 2005–2009 increased their turnover by 67 per cent and their profits by 64.2 per cent.

Jonathan Austin, Founder and CEO of Best Companies, says the evidence is clear that organisations paying attention to engaging their people are more successful. Here's how he explains it:

> Let's look at shareholder value. To do that, we're going to put you in a time machine and send you back to 2006. With you, you have a wallet containing £2,000 and copies of the 2011 Best Companies to Work For lists.
>
> Step out of the time machine, walk into a stockbroker's office and invest that money. Put £1,000 of it into the FTSE 100. Then take the other £1,000 and invest it in all publicly quoted companies that appear in this year's Best Companies To Work For lists.
>
> Done that? Good. Now, back into the time machine, return to the present day, and head for home …. At home, on the doormat, there's a letter from your stockbroker with some surprising news.
>
> Your overall FTSE 100 investment of £1,000 is now worth about … £1,000 …. Oh well.
>
> But your investment in the Best Companies portfolio selection? … That's now worth close to £2,000.

The point is clearly made by Jonathan. Best Companies goes further to report that over a five-year period, organisations that have consistently featured in the Best Companies to Work For lists, such as KPMG, Deloitte, Beaverbrooks and Haygarth, have seen a 67 per cent increase in turnover and a 64.2 per cent increase in profits (see Figure 2.2).

---

1   See Best Companies: www.bestcompanies.co.uk.

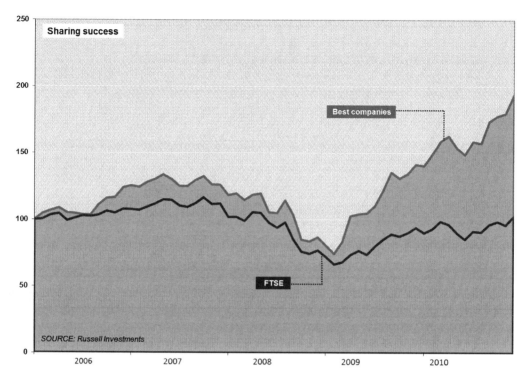

Figure 2.2   Why engagement matters

Source: Copyright Best Companies LLP and reproduced with kind permission. Produced by Russell Investments

The data about the value of employee engagement are vast, but the summary is that hard numbers exist, in many businesses, to support the logical case for a focus on engagement.

Competitive Advantage

On top of the evidence around business measures based on current data, organisations need a strong competitive advantage if growth is to be sustained. Employee engagement has a huge impact in this area, through routes such as innovation and the ability to make breakthroughs in process, operations and product design.

A highly engaged workforce is more likely to find ways to outsmart the competition and find creative ways to excel for customers.

As the MacLeod report commented:

> *In a world where most factors of production are increasingly standardised, where a production line or the goods on a supermarket shelf are much the same the world over, employee engagement is the difference that makes the difference – and could make all the difference as we face the realities of globalised competition and of the millions of graduates and even more skilled and committed workers that China, India and other economies are producing each year.*
>
> *(MacLeod and Clarke 2009)*

Given this context, can any organisation, leader or manager afford to ignore employee engagement?

Confidence

Employee engagement creates a more confident workforce. Confidence is a behaviour that many organisations are keen to encourage, particularly as studies show it leads to more successful businesses. As reported by Macleod and Clarke (2009), Towers Perrin found that broadly three-quarters of the highly engaged believe they can impact costs, quality and customer service, while only 25 per cent of the disengaged believe they can.

Sickness

According to the CBI, engaged employees in the UK take an average of 2.69 sick days per year; the disengaged take 6.19 (CBI-AXA 2007, cited in MacLeod and Clarke 2009). The CBI reports that sickness absence costs the UK economy £13.4 billion a year.

Running the maths on this statistic proves what a tremendous cost disengagement is, and it's even greater if we consider the emotional costs for colleagues that often cover work for their sick team members.

Gallup found that engagement levels can be predictors of sickness absence, with more highly engaged employees taking an average of 2.7 days per year, compared with disengaged employees taking an average of 6.2 days per year (Harter et al. 2006, Gallup Q12 meta-analysis, cited in MacLeod and Clarke 2009).

Attrition

We operate in a world where competitive advantage and performance is highly reliant on the talent organisations attract, recruit and retain. The cost of attracting great people is high, and it's critical that bright talent has the ability to flourish and add the most value to an organisation. Where engagement levels are high, people often stay in the company and give their best. In situations where engagement levels are low, employees will vote with their feet, or stay but consistently perform below their potential.

According to the Corporate Leadership Council (2004), engaged employees are 87 per cent less likely to leave the organisation than the disengaged. The cost of high turnover among disengaged employees is significant; some estimates put the cost of replacing each employee at equal to annual salary.

A low-engagement environment disempowers staff and tends to encourage silos. Trust is low, and leadership often becomes dictatorial to ensure that results are achieved. It will be hard to retain great talent unless there is a significant financial reason to stay. Even if this is the case, their ability and desire to bring their best talents to work each day will be questionable.

Customers/advocates

Highly engaged employees create rich, unique customer experiences, and thus influence business performance. Think of the last time you experienced an outstanding level of service from a company. What made it so great? The answer is usually that the person dealing with your requirements did so in a way that met or exceeded your expectations. Quite often a friendly face who actively listens and responds appropriately is all it takes for us to feel we've received great service. There's usually an emotional connection in some way, and we are made to feel valued. Such a feeling rarely comes from an employee who is disengaged.

Employees who are engaged care about the job they do. They have pride in their work and want to do the right thing for the company that they so readily advocate. Sony employees are huge brand advocates, and all own a wide range of company products. Favourable pricing contributes to this, but the company also does a fantastic job of building energy and focus within the organisation to help employees feel proud of the brand. Sony knows that its workforce is a significant part of building brand awareness and desire for its products.

The flip side – the impact of disengaged employees on customer relationships – can be catastrophic. The time and financial investment in attracting new customers is vast for most industries. Disengaged employees are unlikely to give an excellent customer experience, and customers will vote with their feet. Fundamentally, customer satisfaction results in profit.

This won't be a revelation to anyone reading this book; but consider the statistics below:

The CIPD (2006b) says that 70 per cent of engaged employees indicate they have a good understanding of how to meet customer needs; only 17 per cent of non-engaged employees say the same.

Research by Ipsos Mori on Audit Commission data showed that staff in councils rated as 'excellent' had much better results than those in weak or poor councils when asked about factors such as being informed and consulted, having confidence in senior managers and understanding the overall objectives of their organisation; they were also twice as likely to be advocates for their organisation than staff in weak or poor councils (Ipsos MORI and Improvement & Development Agency 2006).

These are powerful arguments for making engagement a core factor of customer service development. Organisations so often miss the point that giving customer-facing staff insight into the wider company directly improves how they feel and how they interact with customers.

The Unquantifiable Cost

Disengaged people are much less likely to make the right choices each day. Poor or wrong decisions impede progress and stifle success. At worst, they damage the reputation of a company beyond repair. It's often difficult to put a price on this, but the cost can be catastrophic: when staff don't value the company, their actions – such as rude customer letters, subversive content or leaking of information – reliably end up in the public domain.

Ultimately, an organisation where people don't feel engaged is an unpleasant place to be. Without engagement, the sense of loneliness and isolation among leaders and managers is high. For employees, it means that coming to work each day is a task rather than a pleasure. The cost in terms of emotional and mental wellbeing is potentially extreme.

We can see from these examples that the business case for employee engagement is clear. Put simply, engagement is a means to an end. The end is performance, which can be defined in different ways depending on whether the organisation is a commercial entity or a non-governmental or public sector organisation. Regardless of how it's defined, performance through high engagement clearly also draws in and improves the lives of employees and the experience of the customer.

Given the clear case for employee engagement, it is rarely enough for an organisation to have good intentions to engage. That's why a clear employee engagement strategy is important.

Such a strategy will ensure that effort and energy are directed where they are most needed, and that the kinds of levers used are appropriate for the levels of engagement required. For example, in some cases, such as health and safety information, it may be enough that people engage by having a clear understanding about what is required of them. In other cases, we may want to unlock creativity or discretionary effort, or to create an innovation-led approach to future-proof the business. The routes to achieving this will be very different to that for sharing health and safety information.

An engagement strategy also ensures consistent, long-term approaches from leaders to engage employees, and makes a stronger business case for investment in appropriate initiatives.

CHAPTER

3 *What Are the Factors that Drive Engagement?*

The case for engagement is clear, but what about the factors that really drive an engaged workforce. Let's not rush off to 'improve engagement' without truly understanding the levers that will have most impact.

A variety of factors have a positive and negative influence in engagement levels: culture, geography, organisational purpose, and industry and financial performance. However, there are some common levers that are proven to have the biggest impact on engagement levels and thus performance levels of individuals, teams and companies.

Best Companies believes there are eight factors that influence workplace engagement, as shown in Figure 3.1: 'My Manager', 'Leadership', 'My Company', 'Personal Growth', 'My Team', 'Fair Deal', 'Giving Something Back' and 'Wellbeing'. Figure 3.1 sets these out in order of impact on engagement, and Figure 3.2 explains the individual factors.

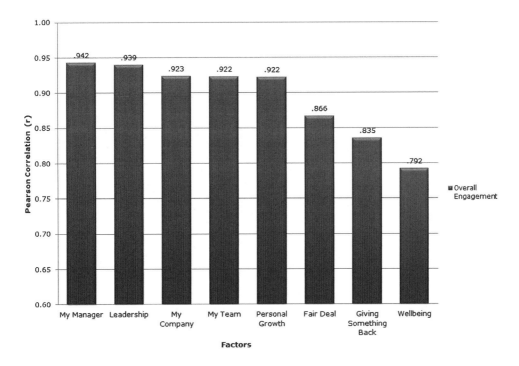

Figure 3.1   Workplace engagement factors

Source: Copyright Best Companies LLP and reproduced with kind permission.

My Manager
How employees feel
about and communicate
with their direct manager

My Company
How emotionally
connected employees
feel towards their
organisation

Leadership
How employees feel about the head of the
organisation, senior managers, and the
organisations values and principles

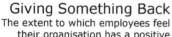

Personal Growth
How employees feel about
their job in terms of challenge,
using and developing their
skills, and opportunities to
advance

Fair Deal
How employees
perceive the fairness
of their rewards

Giving Something Back
The extent to which employees feel
their organisation has a positive
impact on society

Wellbeing
How employees feel
about their work-life
balance and pressure at
work

My Team
Employees feelings towards
their immediate colleagues
and how well they work
together

Figure 3.2   Eight factors of engagement
Source: Copyright Best Companies LLP and reproduced with kind permission.

In 2011, 'My Manager' became the factor with the highest influence on engagement levels; 'Leadership' closely followed it. This remained the case in 2012. In earlier years, leadership had been the primary factor; however, it's unsurprising that 'My Manager' has taken the top position of influence in today's turbulent and uncertain economic climate, when leadership is increasingly called to scrutiny. More positively, the data do suggest that work within organisations to bolster the role of managers is succeeding.

Towers Watson concludes that a similar set of factors influence engagement. Its global research on the levers that increase employee engagement has shown that high engagement results from an array of organisational elements. Its 2007–2008 Global Workforce Study (a worldwide survey of close to 90,000 employees in mid-size and large organisations) found that employee engagement rises when people experience a combination of effective and caring leadership, appealing development opportunities, interesting work, and fulfilling tangible and intangible rewards (Towers Perrin 2008).

Unlike the Best Companies data, Towers Watson doesn't explicitly reference the importance of manager in its factors. However, there is clearly a line-management role in ensuring interesting work, development opportunities and reward. To some degree, managers are also a component of the 'caring leadership' element – being the more direct and immediate face of the entire management structure.

Like Best Companies, MacLeod and Clarke's report concludes that leadership and management are strong influencing factors (MacLeod and Clarke 2009). It set out four enablers of engagement.

1. Leadership, providing a strong strategic narrative; showing alignment between roles and direction, painting a clear narrative of the past, present and future of the organisation.
2. Engaging managers who coach and stretch their people, trust their people as individuals, focus their people and offer scope for advancement.
3. Employee voice, where employees are well-informed because information is shared widely, early and often, employees' views are sought and followed up, explanations are given if ideas/views are not adopted, employees are involved in developing solutions early rather than being informed of the next initiative, and options for change are discussed.
4. Integrity, where company values are translated into behaviours.

Dwelling on the darker side of motivation for a moment, none of these factors mentions 'fear' as a driver for engagement. Yet it's a powerful lever that has been used successfully for centuries, and some may argue that it's worthy of consideration. The challenge is that a strategy driven by fear is not sustainable: an engagement strategy based on it makes people 'change-hardened', so each time it's used, a higher degree of fear is needed. It doesn't encourage an organisation to be agile and flexible, and is thus not an effective long-term strategy to consider.

Fear can also, conversely, positively skew the results of employee engagement surveys. That's why it's important that a survey isn't the only tool used to measure understanding, commitment and so forth. In some companies, the scores will show high engagement in areas where it's clear that performance is poor due to low engagement. The reason for this can be an underlying fear that prevents people from telling the truth about their feelings when completing the survey.

4 *An Introduction to the Organisational Engagement Strategy*

Having identified why engagement matters and explored the factors that influence engagement, the need for a strategy will be well understood. The obvious next step is to build an appropriate organisational engagement strategy. Although I say 'engagement strategy', I prefer to think of it more as a performance strategy. If an organisation effectively addresses each of the elements in the model outlined in the following chapters, increased performance will follow.

Fundamentally, there are basic hygiene factors that need to be in place before people can even approach high levels of engagement and performance. A good working environment is absolutely essential: clean kitchens and toilets, warmth, adequate space, lighting and furniture, pay and benefits. Although I'm assuming that these are in place in most organisations and that they are looking to engage at a higher level, it's worth asking yourself whether you're doing enough to ensure that the basics are in place. Are carpets bright and clean? Are there sufficient facilities for people to be able to work at their best? Do people have fair pay for the jobs they're doing?

This may sound trivial, and something outside the remit of most readers, but consider the importance of pride as a tool for performance. Shabby premises breed shabby attitudes. There's a reason why so many corporations invest money in dramatic, unique artworks, installations and sculptures – they help create dramatic, classic environments that people want to spend time in, want to show their friends and family, and want to preserve. There's a simple acid test for this – would you want your family to visit your offices? If not, why would any other employee? Paying attention to the basics is a core foundation for performance.

UKTV started to provide free breakfast to all employees when it moved to new offices in Hammersmith. This was partly in recognition that a number of employees had to leave home very early to reach the office, but also because the CEO wanted to ensure that people had the right facilities to enable them to bring their talents to life. It's also had an effect on bringing people closer together, breaking through silos and generally improving informal communication. Darren Childs, CEO of UKTV, said:

> *I know that an engaged team doesn't come from simply providing breakfast, however, it's one of the many fundamentals we've put in place in addition to the more sophisticated engagement drivers such as a focus on leadership, values, innovation and management skills.*

The 'basics' that companies must consider don't end here – the list is long, and includes access to equipment, transport considerations, site services and day care. The message is clear, though: don't walk out to the wicket with a broken bat.

Some of these are not easy fixes, and I don't propose to cover how to improve the fabric of your organisation. However, once the basics are in place, attention can begin to turn to the different areas of engagement. My experience, research and observation of many organisations over the last 15 years has led to the creation of a Four-stage Model of Engagement used extensively in my work (see Figure 4.1).

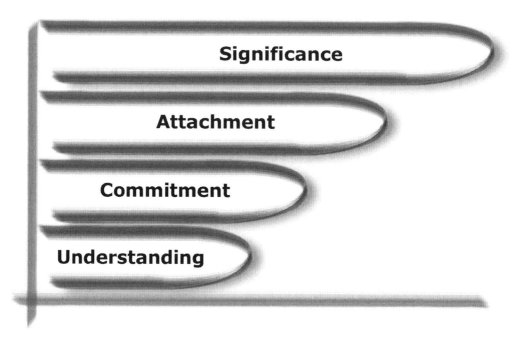

Figure 4.1   Four-stage Model of Engagement

Level 1: Understanding

I understand where we are going/what I need to do.

Employees' understanding of requirements, direction and information relevant to their roles and what's happening across the organisation is the essential lifeblood for any entity. A group whose members have little understanding of what is required of them will add limited value. This is the base level of any organisational strategy to engage employees for performance.

An organisation must have a reasonable level of understanding among its employees before it can move up the level of engagement to effectively achieve exceptional performance through emotional commitment, attachment and significance.

More locally, when engaging groups for specific change, this can be the most utilised and stressed level. Recognising that there are some things that people 'just have to do' is a healthy attitude, and one that leads to an adult conversation around the specifics to ensure compliance.

Level 2: Commitment

I feel and am committed to delivering for this organisation.

Individuals who have high emotional commitment will engage at a deeper level than those who simply understand a direction. This is therefore the second level of an organisational engagement strategy.

Emotional commitment comes from the heart of an employee, and requires them to give more to the organisation before this level of engagement can be achieved. This level moves away from the rational, logical elements of the first level and brings in colour, excitement and delight to create a fertile environment for people to form a bond with the ideas and initiatives in the organisation.

Level 3: Attachment

I have a positive emotional attachment with the organisation.

Attachment comes from a deeper relationship between an individual and the organisation than is achieved through emotional commitment alone. It's about people feeling attached at a financial and psychological level with their organisation. They genuinely feel shared ownership for success, positive outcomes, positive perceptions, and an overarching pride in what they deliver and achieve.

It is at this point that employees 'stick' with organisations, despite more appealing offers from elsewhere.

Level 4: Significance

I see significance in what I do each day as part of this organisation and it aligns with my personal values and what gives me meaning in my life.

An incredibly rich and powerful level of engagement happens when individuals see alignment between their role and what gives them meaning and significance in life. When this happens, exceptional performance is possible. People who operate from this level of engagement are true investors and contagious elements who bring others to a similar level. Later in the book you will read stories of where this is evident in a range of roles and companies – from Starbucks coffee shop managers to the leaders of multi-national divisions.

*   *   *

As employee groups progress up the stages of this model, their level of engagement increases, so business performance will improve. Where an individual understands the direction of the organisation and believes that their contribution aligns with it, where that individual feels emotionally committed to deliver and has developed an attachment with the company, and sees an alignment between what they do each day and what gives them meaning and significance, they will be in a position to bring their very best to the work. Just take a moment to re-read and digest that last long sentence. If every employee of your organisation were in this position, performance would be phenomenal.

At the heart of this organisational engagement strategy is the notion of creating *investors* – not savers. At the foundational level, employees who have a good degree of understanding and some emotional commitment to the organisation are well placed to be savers. They are able to place some of their talent in the right places to add value and create a return. Their risks are cautious – it's never 'all or nothing' for the organisation, emotional statements about their feelings for the work are muted, and their actions are 'within parameters'.

At the upper level of an exemplary organisational strategy, where employees from all levels are encouraged to take their talent, passion and energy to a deeper level, individuals invest more of themselves in the organisation. While risky, the gains offer a higher return in terms of fulfilment, satisfaction and experience. Investors play for higher stakes than savers by investing more of themselves daily. Sometimes this may mean behaving in very different ways to align their work and sense of purpose. It also involves taking personal responsibility and being accountable for making oneself and the business a success.

Organisations have to invest far more to create an environment of investors rather than savers. What's guaranteed is a higher return in performance terms than playing safe and just concentrating on creating understanding among colleagues. If we add these factors to my model, we arrive at the Full Four-stage Model of Engagement (see Figure 4.2).

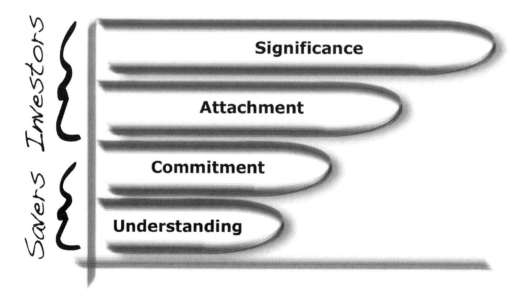

Figure 4.2   Full Four-stage Model of Engagement

Deep levels of emotional commitment, high attachment and alignment of individual significance to that of the organisation are key ways to turn employees from savers into investors.

John Lewis Partnership (JLP) is a good example. This UK retailer has been in existence since 1914, and consistently performs well in the market. JLP has a loyal customer following, but what makes it particularly successful is that it recruits people who want to be investors. Employees understand right from the beginning that they are expected to devote time, energy and effort to their work. As a result, they become a partner in the organisation and benefit from long-term investment aimed at nurturing people who want to remain loyal to the company.

The ultimate aim for organisations is to have large numbers of investors, in engagement terms. That said, it's also important to recognise that there are times when a community of savers may be sufficient or appropriate. This might be true of specific messages, when creating understanding for compliance purposes is enough. For example, when seeking to engage employees in a new IT policy change, a manager will need to ensure understanding, but it's not necessary for people to see a deep significance in how it connects with their personal purpose.

Any leader or manager who wants to engage people must consider what level of engagement is actually required so that energy can be focused on the areas that really matter (see Figure 4.3). It takes a great deal of time and energy to engage people by helping them see a connection with what gives them meaning and significance, so use the effort wisely. A manager who tries to achieve all four levels of engagement among their staff for everything they do may suffer from both exhaustion and frustration, because in some cases it just isn't possible! People can be investors overall, but savers when it comes to specific initiatives.

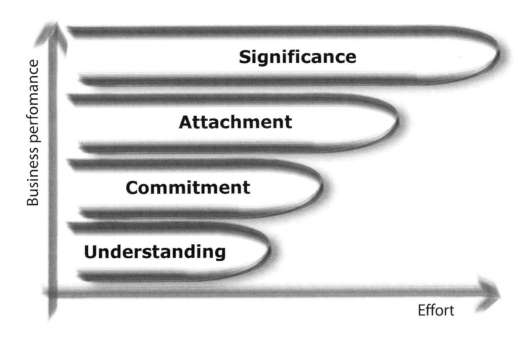

Figure 4.3   Four-stage Model – business performance/effort

In addition to individual managers considering to what level they wish to engage people, it's also important for the organisation to consider how much extraordinary performance the organisation is able to cope with – some will be happy to achieve 'on track' performance in most areas, and this will influence their engagement strategy.

High engagement levels come from high levels of involvement, where teams co-create direction. Their level of emotional connection will also be high if all four levels of engagement are addressed. It's therefore important to find ways to boost levels of involvement as a lever for advanced employee engagement. This involvement is required at all levels within the organisation. Where individuals are involved in finding solutions or generating new ideas, they will invest more of themselves, and will move from being savers to investors.

The deeper the emotional connection, the more investors are likely to be created (see Figure 4.4). This is partially a result of leaders and organisations demonstrating that they value their staff and finding ways to connect with them on a less rational level.

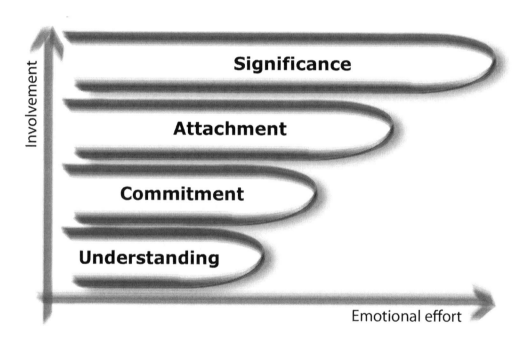

Figure 4.4   Four-stage Model – involvement/emotional effort

Diageo staged the Breakthrough Everywhere conference for its top 300 leaders during 2008. At the three-day conference, people participated in workshops and dialogue around the future of the business and how to best achieve the outcomes desired. On the third day of the conference, work at every warehouse and packaging operation was halted across the International Division, allowing every employee to join the leaders via conference call. Telephone lines connected people in offices and homes across the world, and Stuart Fletcher, former President of International Business at Diageo, talked to 6,500 people at the same time. He shared his heartfelt appreciation for what the business had achieved, and stated that every individual was vital to the continuing success of the Breakthrough Strategy. The feedback was so moving that Stuart has repeated the exercise every year from then on. In 2011, he asked 14 centres to contribute to the call by sharing what they were taking on and had delivered. In all, 8,500 people attended and witnessed their business placing importance on engaging with them to the point that it was willing to stop the whole company's operations so that people could attend. This sent a massive signal about the importance of people to the leadership team. Bilingual local staff members translated key messages where necessary, and Stuart used his tone of voice to stress key points and his passion.

Helping people see significance in what they do involves more fluid conversations and working practices than the fixed and structured way of working that happens when mere understanding is enough (see Figure 4.5).

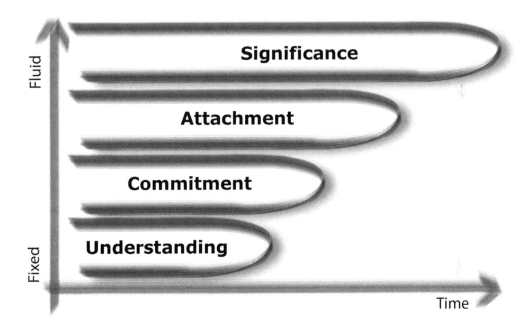

Figure 4.5   Four-stage Model – fluidity/time

People who succeed in more fluid organisations can very often see how their work aligns with their passion and what gives them significance in life. They are less concerned about being 'managed' by line managers, and their focus is on making great things happen using their skills. This can be wonderful for innovation and creativity, but it carries a risk that people may have high passion but not always devote time to understand the direction and goals of the organisation. Strategic understanding is important in channelling the passion and commitment in the right direction. Thus, in fluid organisations, more effort is often required at the base of the engagement model.

The production department in highly creative organisations, such as television companies, is often fluid. A structure with defined line managers is rare, so more effort is required from senior leadership to engage with people; showing them the direction in which the company is heading and the importance of their roles in making success happen. In the BskyB production areas, people are known for saying: 'I have the job I have always dreamed of.' Someone who loves sport who has a chance to spend every day working with their passion is hugely motivated. There is great pride among people working on the channel, and they desire high autonomy as a group. The role for leaders and managers here is to maintain alignment between this passion and direction. Performance then blossoms, rather than militant tendencies when activities that veer too wide of the mark are curtailed.

In a fluid organisation, the need for managers who excel at the significance level of engagement is therefore reduced. There is a bigger role for them in ensuring that the base levels of understanding and compliance are in existence so that output is aligned with company direction and complies with the law.

CHAPTER

5 *Generating Understanding*

Find a great company that outperforms its competitors and you'll see that its employees understand what is required of them. It's rare that this just happens without intention, focus and effort. So how do we get the base level right and create a community of *savers* in an organisation?

Understanding involves knowing what to do. It's about context and the answers to Rudyard Kipling's 'six wise men' (Kipling 1902):

1. What?
2. Why?
3. Who?
4. Where?
5. How?
6. When?

I have added a seventh to bring it closer to home for the individual:

7. What does it mean for me?

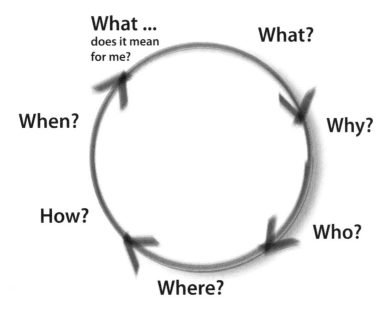

Figure 5.1 Creating understanding – the questions

People find it very difficult to be engaged in a business if they don't understand where the company is going, why it's heading there, what action is needed and what it means for them. Regular progress and excitement about those basics are also necessary.

At another level, engaging someone in a project or informing someone about a new procedure requires understanding to ensure that the task is performed appropriately and safely.

Good engagement at this level means that an employee would strongly agree with the statement 'I know where we are going/what I need to do.' This implies an understanding beyond 'what', expanding into 'what it means for me' and 'how I'm therefore aligned to the bigger picture'. Line of sight, so that an individual can see how their contribution affects the bigger picture, is a vital tool.

Ask most leaders whether understanding is an important component of engagement and you'll find that they think it is. However, it's an area that can often be neglected.

Accenture's 2008 High Performance Workplace study found that only around 40 per cent of those surveyed understand their organisation's strategy (unpublished Accenture study, cited in MacLeod and Clarke 2009).

In an ever-changing economic environment, it's easy for leaders to assume that their staff understand, yet if they haven't been taken on the journey, they will often be confused or frustrated. In fluid organisations, employees are more likely to cope with such factors. In more fixed organisations, this will lead to problems of disengagement quite quickly.

A classic example of this is shareholder value. So many listed companies spend a huge amount of time and effort engaging with shareholders, analysts and fund managers, but fail to encourage employees to make the link between this work and the success of the company. Ask an average employee how share price affects the company's performance and they will struggle to give a coherent answer.

In a commercial organisation, money can be lost, time and effort wasted or bad decisions taken as a result of poor understanding. However, the impact in other types of organisation can be even more dramatic. Imagine a military organisation that isn't clear about its direction and goals, or a charity with people in danger zones that doesn't have firm understanding about what is required and when. Understanding is therefore critical for reasons beyond engagement. This raises the 'what' to new levels of importance.

Increasingly, employees also want to understand the 'why', so that they can decide whether or not to engage. In a market where jobs for life are rare, individuals nowadays want to make informed choices about where they invest their time and effort.

In MacLeod and Clarke (2009), Admiral Sir Mark Stanhope, the Royal Navy's Commander-in-Chief Fleet, pointed out that even in the armed forces, young men and women putting their lives at risk will, at an appropriate moment, ask and expect to have answered the question 'Why?' Answering that question satisfactorily is the precondition for their being willing to obey orders unquestioningly when they are on the front line.

How to Create Understanding

There are three levels of understanding required for an employee to be an effective saver:

1. **Macro level** – strategic clarity and alignment, understanding of direction, the employee's role and how they are required to contribute

2. **Dynamic level** – the need to understand change and what it means for the employee;
3. **Micro level** – concerned with what is happening that affects the employee's work on a daily basis.

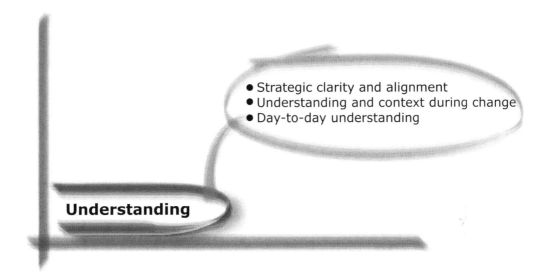

● Strategic clarity and alignment
● Understanding and context during change
● Day-to-day understanding

Understanding

Figure 5.2   Creating understanding

Strategic Clarity and Alignment

In MacLeod and Clarke (2009), the authors listed strategic clarity as one of the key drivers of engagement. At an organisational level, this comes from helping people understand the 'big picture' of strategy, direction and how the future looks. It involves creating context and helping to establish a line of sight from their role in the organisation through to the bigger goals and strategy.

The messaging to increase understanding about strategic clarity and context starts with simplicity. When working with organisations, I start by exploring five fundamental areas:

1. **Why do you exist?** – What is the organisation's purpose and reason for being?
2. **External environment** – What's going on in the wider world that influences or has an impact on the business right now? What will that context look like in the future?
3. **Vision of the future** – What is it for this organisation? What does success look like in three, five or ten years from now? How will it look and feel?
4. **Ambition(s)** – What are yours, and what are the key goals for the business?
5. **Building blocks** – What are the enablers to get there?

This insight helps to build the context for any work that I go on to do in a business. The same 'big picture' provides context for employees working in any organisation, and is a good starting point in ensuring that people are able to engage with the right content. In so many organisations, employees don't have sight of this macro level, therefore strategic clarity is missing. When people have visibility of this bigger picture, the next stage is to help them see where their role and contribution fit in.

A great way to do this is to paint a visual picture that encapsulates the direction, vision and key enablers in a way that is more memorable and emotive than words. Seeing the big picture in visual terms acts like the image on the jigsaw puzzle lid, and means that an employee can consider where their piece (their role or contribution) sits within the overall direction. The picture also acts as a decision-making tool: if an activity is undertaken that can't be tracked back to the visual direction, questions can be asked about whether it should be embarked upon at all.

The complexity of the organisation will dictate the most appropriate style of picture. Some organisations use a clear framework to show how all elements of the strategy fit together. This acts as a strategic map for its people. An example is the roundel used in UKTV to show how the vision, purpose, imperatives and strategy fit together (see Figure 5.3). Darren Childs, CEO of UKTV, explained:

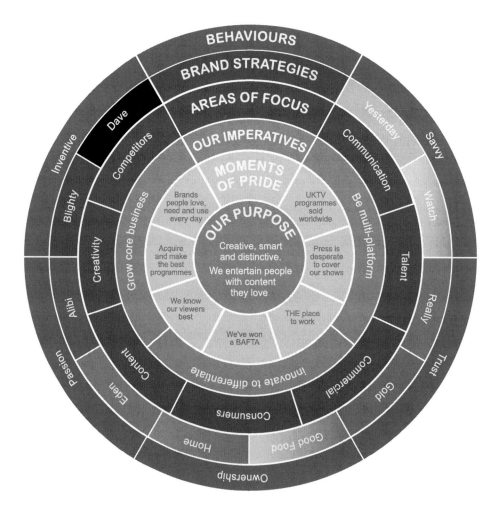

Figure 5.3   UKTV roundel

Source: Reproduced with kind permission.

The 'big picture' is deliberately a roundel because this fitted with our external brands. Our ten television channel brands all had a roundel, and so the strategy map became the 11th. There was something quite eloquent about developing a visual that fitted with our branding.

At every meeting, new announcements and progress updates are mapped back to the visual so that people can immediately see how the content they are hearing contributes to the whole. The vision is brought to life through 'moments of pride' articulated by employees when talking about how the business will feel when it truly lives its purpose. These moments of pride are represented on the roundel, but also in other innovative ways across the business.

Other organisations prefer a big picture that articulates the journey in other ways. A major consideration with the creative treatment is where the picture will be used – in which countries and cultures. Sony Professional Solutions Europe used a big picture to articulate its journey to implement key initiatives as building blocks to achieve its vision. As you can see in Figure 5.4, this is a visual metaphor that shows a journey and key milestones that need to be reached along the way. For them, it is a good fit for the diverse cultures using it.

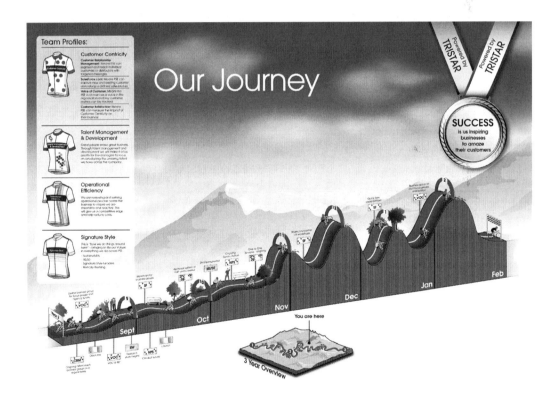

Figure 5.4   Sony Professional Solutions Europe journey story

Source: Sony PSE. Reproduced with kind permission.

For the executive team involved, the process of answering the basic questions leading to the creation of a visual big picture is a useful exercise in itself. It's not unusual for the articulation of direction to vary depending on the individual executive. The result is often a rich conversation at board level about the strategy and vision of the organisation. This can feel frustrating for a communication professional who wants to help create the visual map. However, it's a hugely valuable conversation for a board to have on a regular basis, as it keeps them consistent in their messaging to people. Making complex messages simple for everyone to understand is the name of the game. It's easy to build on examples and give colour once people have a basic understanding embedded in their minds.

Once the picture is created, engagement comes by using it in a variety of ways to generate understanding among employees, for example by:

- sharing it with all employees at all staff events;
- using the picture as a tool to generate dialogue about the future;
- involving employee groups in creating the big picture;
- incorporating the visual as a structure for induction programmes – a module in induction for each module of the picture;
- mapping all strategic initiatives onto the picture;
- using the visual as a structure for intranet communications or newsletters;
- drawing in elements, colours and styles to give other work a flavour of the big picture.

There are a variety of engagement methods that can be used to create ongoing understanding about key messages. Whichever is chosen, it's imperative that communicators use powerful language and are good at telling the story in an emotional, clear and consistent way.

At UKTV, the business is all situated in one building. It is approximately 200 people strong, and all work on the same floor. Every Tuesday morning all employees gather together for the Tuesday Morning Meeting (TMM) and hear about the company direction, performance and new shows on its television channels. It's a chance for people who are leaving, moving or starting to be recognised and given visibility. The agenda is owned by the internal communication team, with input from the CEO. Anyone can request an agenda slot. Colleagues cite TMM as a core way to ensure they understand what is happening in the business, and it's reduced the need for large emails. 'TMM is much more effective than my sending out an email update,' believes Darren Childs, CEO of UKTV. For larger organisations, the concept may be more challenging if people are spread across buildings and floors, but the principles could be replicated across business units or virtually: regular brief meetings that give people the information they need to understand in manageable, bite-size chunks.

Solarcentury relies on a similar approach. All employees gather monthly to hear about the business's performance and direction. Anyone can take a slot on the agenda, and the CEO will ask people to comment about their projects and progress without warning. Questions can be asked, and movers, leavers and new starters are announced. Even though the company's staff are not all based in one building, it uses webcasting and teleconferencing methods to link its offices in France and Italy.

Creating Understanding and Context Throughout Change

If the business is going through change, the level and type of understanding required are slightly different. People will want the answers to similar questions, but with much greater emphasis placed on 'why':

- What is happening?
- Why is it happening?
- How and when will it happen?
- When and how will it affect me/my team?
- Where will we see the impact?
- Who and where should I go to find out more?

The 'why' part of the story is often lost in the eagerness of the communicator to explain what is happening and what it means for the individual. However, the 'why' is the context, and can make the difference between acceptance or rejection of change among communities. Even in situations where change causes pain and unpleasant consequences, people will be more accepting if they understand the reasons why it must happen.

Where possible, it's a good idea to share this context before announcements about change are made. It helps to make the organisation 'change-ready'. During the beginnings of a decision to outsource an IT function, I seeded messages via the internal news announcement about outsourcing occurring within competitors. It was done very subtly, and was part of the external news update about competitors and customers. The aim was to create understanding of the reality in the market, so that if a decision were made to outsource IT, people would already have some context about 'why'. They would thus be more change-ready and positively engaged.

A basic standard for any organisation is to explain 'why' whenever a decision is made. Say it once, say it twice, and say it three times. Evidence suggests that a message about 'why' has to be delivered seven times in different ways to be sure it has been received. It's also critical to keep communicating throughout change, even if there is no new news. Saying that progress continues but there are no significant developments to report is an essential way to keep people from disengaging during the change process.

In larger organisations, managers play a key role in ensuring that employees understand the context and reasons 'why' during change. To be able to do this effectively, managers themselves need to be engaged and have a good understanding of what's happening and why. Manager briefings, face-to-face or via teleconferencing, are one way to share information early and give this community an opportunity to question and ensure a sufficiently deep degree of understanding. Only then are they best equipped to either spread the same news or answer questions and host dialogue after town hall or all-employee sessions.

Understanding can be embedded through use of communication or change champion networks. These consist of nominated talent from across the organisation, and each is given the tools to help embed key principles and messages. Where these networks work most effectively is alongside managers. Success will depend on the culture of the organisation, but where the right schemes are set up, they are a great way to develop deeper understanding, and have an extremely high impact on engagement levels.

More information about best practice within Pfizer and its change champions network can be found in Chapter 23.

Day-to-day Understanding and What's Required of Me

It's reassuring to have good strategic understanding about the direction of an organisation, but to do a great job, it's also vital that employees know what's happening in their area of the business and what's required of them. This responsibility largely sits with the team leader or manager. At an organisation-wide level, managers need the tools, support and systems to aid them. They'll need information about progress, new legislation and performance targets.

In parallel, managers need to consider the best ways to ensure understanding day-to-day. They need to be clear, consistent and regular with their communication so that colleagues are in no doubt about what is required. Performance objectives and measures need to be aligned to the strategic direction.

Many large organisations measure managers on a simple metric: number of team meetings per year. Regular face-to-face or virtual team meetings play a big factor in engagement and are a good way to ensure daily understanding.

But gatherings at a team level don't have to be formal. An impromptu team huddle that takes place when a news story breaks or after a big employee meeting is a great way to check and clarify understanding of key messages and developments. Within these, teams can explore what information means to them and what individuals may need to start, stop or review in their work. These are not as easy to measure, but arguably add far more to the engagement process.

Understanding starts with being clear about the message and tailoring it to different employee groups where possible.

At Sky, Internal Communications Director Nick Green is passionate about providing people with communication 'they can set their watch by'. He believes it critical that managers and employees know when they are going to receive or be involved in communication. Doing this reduces suspicion and frustration that can often arise from people feeling that they don't know about a new development or that information is being held back from them. The intranet at Sky is always updated at midnight each day, so people know when they can expect to see new content. Managers are provided with a business information update every Monday, and a deeper business review pack is issued once a month.

6 *Commitment*

Let's think about great companies again. The organisations that outperform others on multiple levels don't just have high levels of understanding. They're also intentional about building emotional connections and commitment among employees. Think about it from your own experience: when have you been a 'baseline' saver, and when have you been looking to 'invest more for a higher rate of savings return'? Knowing what's required is important, but in many cases, we need the next level to become a more serious saver.

Commitment is about a desire to execute and deliver. It's about feelings, passion and an emotional connection:

> *I feel and am committed to delivering for this organisation.*

People who are emotionally connected and committed are more likely to make discretionary efforts. High passion often leads to great innovation and imagination. It creates an energy that's infectious and engaging. It's hugely positive when it goes hand in hand with high levels of understanding among individuals. Without strong understanding, there's a high risk of a group of loose cannons who have a huge desire for success but no framework around which to innovate and execute:

> *You can be engaged in the company but that doesn't mean that you are fully aligned – you can have engaged people that are loose cannons if there is not clear alignment of direction.*
> *(Nigel Edwards, Pfizer)*

Organisations with strong employee commitment levels have higher business performance. In its 1999 study *From People to Profits*, the Institute for Employment Studies (IES) found a link between employee satisfaction, customer satisfaction and increases in sales, based on a study of 65,000 employees and 25,000 customers from 100 stores, over two years (Barber, Hayday and Bevan 1999, cited in MacLeod and Clarke 2009). Employee commitment had an impact on sales through three routes: directly on sales, mediated through customer satisfaction, and through reduction in staff absence. The IES concluded that a one per cent increase in employee commitment (using a five-point scale) could lead to a monthly increase of nine per cent in sales.

Similarly, the Corporate Leadership Council's *Driving Performance and Retention through Employee Engagement* report (CLC 2004) states that companies with above-average employee commitment were, in 71 per cent of cases, achieving above-average company performance for their sectors. Companies with below-average employee commitment found only 40 per cent of their organisations achieving above-average company performance.

In addition to the tangible business benefits of emotionally committed employees, there are also positive outcomes for the individual. The Chartered Institute for Professional Development (CIPD 2006a) found that those who were absorbed in their work (cognitively engaged) were almost three times as likely to have six key positive emotions at work (enthusiasm, cheerfulness, optimism, contentment, feeling calm and relaxed) as negative ones (miserable, worried, depressed, gloomy, tense or uneasy). Those who were physically engaged (committed to completing work tasks) were more than ten times likelier to feel those positive emotions than the negative ones.

The link between emotional commitment and performance through discretionary effort is further highlighted by MacLeod and Clarke (2009) in evidence from the Corporate Leadership Council. It concludes that:

> emotional commitment drives effort, it is four times as valuable as rational commitment in producing discretionary effort. Indeed the search for a high performance workforce is synonymous with the search for emotional commitment. Rational commitment is based around financial, developmental and professional issues while emotional commitment is the extent to which employees value, enjoy and believe in their jobs, managers, teams or organisations.

It's clear, then, that emotional commitment is a strong engagement driver and has the ability to convert savers into investors. The next area to explore is how to achieve it.

How to Increase Levels of Commitment

There is a raft of activities that influence levels of commitment. As with understanding, the basic environmental factors have to be covered before we can build emotional commitment. For example, appropriate pay and benefits affect individuals deeply and have a profound effect on emotional commitment to an organisation. If people don't believe that they're getting a fair deal, their propensity to be open to positive emotional levers is low. Organisations can offer pay and benefits at lower than the market rate and still have high emotional commitment. This is particularly the case where people see great significance in what they do: for example, people working in a charity or caring profession. However, if pay and benefits feel unfair, emotional commitment is hard to build, or tends to be directed to those who benefit from organisation's activities (the clients, patients, or those experiencing discrimination, persecution or hardship).

With the basic hygiene factors in place, here are the seven focus areas that I believe have the biggest impact at an organisational level.

1. Define and Communicate a Clear Purpose and Direction

For people to feel committed to the organisation for which they work, there needs to be a clear purpose and reason to exist. Once this in place, it must be communicated – not only to ensure understanding, but also so that hearts are involved as well as minds.

It's hard for people to form a strong emotional commitment to their company if there is no clear reason for its existence. It's important that people don't feel like they're just working for a business that could be any company that exists to make money, but a business that has more meaning, and one that they can believe in.

Consider for a moment: what is the purpose of your organisation? What is its core reason for being?

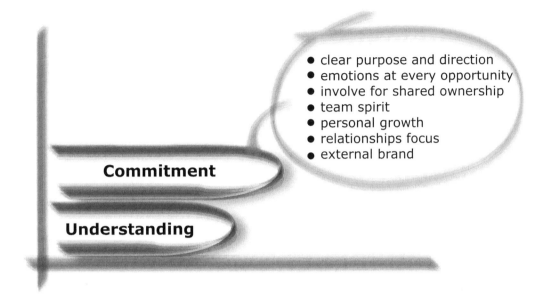

- clear purpose and direction
- emotions at every opportunity
- involve for shared ownership
- team spirit
- personal growth
- relationships focus
- external brand

Commitment

Understanding

Figure 6.1   Increasing commitment

Many organisations have vision or mission statements, but fewer are really clear about their purpose. For an organisation that wants to increase performance, it's crucial that it has this element clearly defined, and in a way that employees can identify with. Without it, individuals will find it extremely hard to find high levels of significance in what they do.

A clear purpose helps organisations to be true to their reason for existing. It also provides the basis for decision-making, value judgements and discretion, and provides a framework for employees to identify how their contribution makes a higher level of difference than making more money for shareholders.

In the late 2000s, police forces in the UK were challenged to re-connect serving officers with 'discretion' – seen as a key enabler in the fulfilment of their duties. For the last decade, the UK police as an entity has struggled to re-connect with its purpose in a rapidly changing social, technological and economic landscape.

Having a clear purpose isn't enough unless it's communicated effectively so that employees can engage their hearts and minds. This requires a robust and emotive set of communication tactics to ensure that people truly buy in.

Sony Europe is an example of a company that engaged people through purpose, and the full details are highlighted in Chapter 23. Senior leaders were involved in defining the purpose and what it meant to them. This ensured that they were highly committed to it and were better placed to communicate and gain buy-in further down the organisation.

The same vehicles can be used to communicate purpose as are commonly utilised to generate understanding about strategy. The difference is that the way messages are delivered needs to tap into the human emotions of happiness, joy, pride, fear and anxiety.

Starbucks has a clear purpose and six stated principles. Gordon Lyle, former Human Resources Director for Starbucks UK, says that its induction and communication is geared to ensuring that all employees understand them and live each one in everything they do. The first five principles are about the coffee, partners, customers, stores and neighbourhood communities. The sixth is about shareholders, and understanding that profit allows Starbucks to grow. Gordon explains:

> *Profit is the last principle because the company believes that if they live the top five extensively, the profit will follow. All partners in the business are given a clear line of sight that shows how their roles and contribution fit to deliver the vision and purpose. Huge amounts are invested to fly partners to Seattle to meet the Starbucks leaders and feel part of what it means to be part of the company that brings great coffee to the world.*

I'm often asked for examples of companies that are clear about why they exist and carry this through everything they do. The most powerful example that I've found is where I've seen employees understand, live, breathe and feel proud of their purpose as an entity rather than just having a brilliant statement. John Lewis Partnership is a great example.

The purpose of the John Lewis Partnership is extremely clear for all partners (a term that in this organisation refers to all company workers, all of whom are shareholders) within the organisation, and great emphasis is placed on ensuring that it's at the heart of every decision taken across the two operating companies, Waitrose and John Lewis. It's also lived daily by people at all levels, leading to a strong purpose in action – found in decision-making, direction-setting, day-to-day support of colleagues and customer service. 'Fulfilling employment for all, by running a successful business is a thread that runs through everything we do,' says Patrick Lewis, JLP's Partners' Counsellor. It's the rock that underpins every decision in the business, and Patrick believes that it can be seen every day in behaviour across the partnership: 'To deliver this, we constantly talk about our purpose and link decisions, news and announcements back to it.'

2. Tap into Emotions at Every Opportunity

Understanding is created around strategy in a variety of ways, and savers are secured. That's not enough in most cases, so the stories need to be richly told to tap into the emotions of people. This is achieved through using emotive language and methods of delivery.

In 2006, Pfizer embarked on a major restructure of its UK organisation. Nigel Edwards, then Communications Head for the UK, used a 'viral change' approach to ensure people were taken on the journey and could look to the future with a positive mindset. He led a series of interventions to take people through the change, and is still using many of the successful techniques in his wider European remit today.

With the new structure in place, Nigel planned a sales conference for the following September where the entire organisation would come together for the first time in history. This was to be a defining moment where people could look to the future and be excited about working together in a new way. The conference would communicate the context, direction and goals for the coming years.

Two months before the conference, a photographer visited Pfizer sites and other locations where groups of colleagues met across the UK. All employees had been asked to have their photograph taken, and invited to do so with an object or outfit that illustrated what they were passionate about. People brought everything from gardening gloves to football shirts; one lady proudly showed her latest tattoo! Some people had their photos taken as individuals – others chose to have theirs taken in groups. Nigel was astounded by the passion and energy this simple exercise unlocked. As a result, they used the photographs to dress the room for the sales conference, and for the 1,200 people who attended, it acted as a genuinely human connection of strategy, change and people. It made people feel valued for being themselves, and showed that Pfizer saw its people as the future of its business.

Three months before the conference, ten people in the field force were selected to be involved in sharing their experiences. The ten were chosen from the parts of the UK where most change in job roles had occurred. They were each given a tripod and camcorder and asked to record a video diary capturing what they had done that day, how they felt, what progress they had made, new connections, what had worked well, and what they felt less positive about. Every two weeks, they sent their tapes to Nigel and his team to edit. There was no censoring of the balance between positive and negative.

Each episode was sent to employees on a DVD, and the total picture was shared at the conference. Nigel said:

> *This really helped people to see the future and charted progress on our journey. The result was that people felt empowered to talk about their emotions and were more likely to question and challenge in the business as a result.*

Defining moments like this are important because they live in the memories of the organisation well after the event. If employees leave feeling they've had 'goose bump' moments, that feeling lives on.

At conferences, it's easy to explain strategy and direction rationally. This is the focus for many organisations that want to outline their story and create understanding. However, to take that one step further and build emotional commitment, the story has to come to life and appeal to individuals' feelings – passion and pride.

In August 2011, UKTV assembled the entire company at an off-site meeting to provide strategic clarity and accelerate emotional commitment. A 'big picture' was built to show people how the purpose, ambition, strategic imperatives and direction fitted together (see Figure 5.3). The emotional connection came from conversations about how the future would *feel* when it was reached. Once UKTV was truly living its purpose, how would it manifest for employees, talent, consumers and partners. The Leadership Team talked about their anticipated 'moments of pride' and how it would look and feel in the future for them. Groups then started to explore their own moments of pride – the energy in the room was intense, and an emotional connection with the strategy immediately followed. The direction went from understanding a rational framework to a memorable emotional journey with an exciting and enticing destination.

In the 1990s, Tesco ran the 'Every Little Helps' campaign. It was hugely motivational for employees, who could see a connection with the fact their work was helping families to save money and thus helping others. The motivation came from an emotional, rather than rational, line of sight. Strong external brand promises, if delivered upon consistently, have an enormous impact on the staff making them happen.

3. Involve People to Achieve Shared Ownership

Emotional commitment comes when people feel they have invested in the outcome or experience. This can come from involving people in defining direction and strategy to give them some drive and accountability for successful implementation.

Some companies involve talent pools to work on addressing considerable problem areas in the business. This is a great way to boost emotional commitment among key people. It's also important to involve other talent too – next time your organisation is facing a challenge, take the collegiate step of involving employees in finding the solution. Creative ideas often come from the most unexpected places. Making problem-solving a skill and part of the day job is a great way to encourage people to invest more of their intellectual effort into the organisation. Toyota is a world leader in doing this – its employees produce far more solutions and ideas than most of the competition.

4. Foster a Strong Team Spirit

'My team' is one of the Best Companies to Work For survey's eight factors of engagement. Think of a time when you have worked with great people and the team dynamic was on fire. This type of environment is incredibly motivating and helps us perform at our very best. The organisation can encourage positive team dynamics through investment and by providing space for team-building events, social calendars and valuing those people who take time to talk and build relationships with each other: for example, managers can embrace the idea of co-workers taking a coffee break together rather than perceiving it as slacking.

Managers have a significant role to play in steering the team dynamic, hiring individuals that will fit into or extend the team in new ways, encouraging shared understanding, transparency, and common understanding of goals and roles. They must also see the importance of building relationships with team members. High-performing teams are often filled with great talents who have both a competitive *and* collaborative spirit.

5. Enable Personal Growth

The Best Companies to Work For survey highlights 'personal growth' as one of the eight factors influencing engagement levels. People are more likely to be emotionally committed to the organisation if they are given opportunities for career and personal development. This starts with well-defined career and development plans for all employees. Some of these will consist of roadmaps to increase competency for the individual to move to the next level. In other cases, individuals may not be looking to move role or level in the hierarchy, but still appreciate development to widen their skills and add value to the organisation. Some organisations invest in extracurricular activities for employees that have no direct link with their work yet make them feel more committed to the company.

Personal growth is also influenced by the ability of a manager to help individuals see how far they have travelled and grown during set periods of time. It's often easy to forget how far we have developed as individuals, and a great manager will encourage us to reflect and take stock of our achievements. This is important because feeling that we are growing acts as a motivator and influencer of engagement.

6. Focus on Relationships between Leaders/managers and their People

Transactional-based organisations find it much harder to build emotional commitment than enterprises that value relationships. It's not hard to imagine why, yet the pressures on most managers mean that interactions are increasingly becoming transactional, or at allotted times when managers schedule the regular 'How are you?' chat to maintain connection.

This trend must be reversed if emotional commitment is to be used effectively as a performance level.

A CEO who takes time to walk around the office and talk to people in the corridors makes a big difference to levels of emotional commitment in a company. Similarly, the line manager who talks to a colleague about his family with genuine interest and at the appropriate time will strike a different level of relationship with staff.

Trust is a major contributor to levels of emotional commitment, and this comes from building relationships with others. CEOs and senior leaders who are good at spending time talking with colleagues at all levels are critical. 'Managing by walking around' is a good way to do this. Other techniques are equally powerful, such as holding regular breakfast sessions with a small cluster of people, or a handwritten letter of appreciation for a job well done or a risk worth taking

7. Utilise a Strong External Brand Proposition

The power of a brand also influences levels of emotional commitment and connection. If the brand has strong positive values, employees will feel a deeper connection with the organisation. In Diageo, people take great pride in working for brands such as Smirnoff and Guinness. This creates an emotional connection that can be built upon to engage people more deeply in the business.

Emotional commitment is largely influenced by the relationship individuals have with their organisation, their leaders and managers. It's the latter who have most influence over emotional engagement levels, and this will be dealt with in greater depth in Parts II, III and IV, where specific best practices and tools for the job are presented.

Emotional language is a key tool for the manager as Storyteller, as explained in Chapter 13.

CHAPTER 7 *Attachment*

Do you feel an attachment to the place where you spend most of your time? Do others around you feel any kind of deep attachment to their organisation? Are those around you savers with good understanding and commitment, or are they investors who have a deeper sense of a mutual value with their organisation?

Where individuals feel deeply attached to the people and organisation in which they work, they will deliver performance in a more sustained way than if they simply understand the direction.

I have a positive emotional attachment with the organisation.

Attachment comes from an individual feeling a deep sense of value from the relationship with their employer – a deep psychological contract. Individuals with strong levels of attachment invest more of themselves in the organisation and their work. They are investors, and therefore tend to outperform their saver colleagues. Where this happens, a series of tangible benefits results for both the organisation and individual. For example, when people feel attached to the organisation in which they work, they are more likely to be an advocate.

MGM Resorts has a customer loyalty programme called 'M Life'. This gives special privileges to regular customers visiting and enjoying its resorts. It has recently introduced an M Life Insider scheme to encourage engagement among employees. This gives discounts for shows and hotel stays for friends and family. It's creating advocates among its 75,000-employee base.

Sony is another example of an organisation that sees the value of advocacy. In Sony UK, Managing Director Gildas Pelliet positively engages his people in product launches. The company launches a variety of products each year, but Gildas focuses on its 'hero' products and finds ways to excite people to encourage them to become brand ambassadors and advocates. It reminds people that they work for Sony, and not any other company.

During the introduction of the Sony tablet, Gildas offered every employee the opportunity to be trained as an ambassador and then to work in Dixons and share their knowledge with the public. Anyone participating was also entitled to a discount on the product.

Back in 1888, William Hesketh Lever (later Viscount Leverhulme) built Port Sunlight to house his soap factory workers at Lever Brothers. In a similar vein, Marks & Spencer (M&S) was originally renowned for treating its people as members of the family. A generation ago, employers assumed that their people would be with the company for life and that they had a responsibility to look after both them and their families.

Employees had the security of regular employment, and with it all of Maslow's basic hygiene factors. In Port Sunlight, housing was provided, together with community facilities. Even as recently as the 1970s and 1980s, Marks & Spencer offered a similar contract for its people. Emma Berry, former Internal Communications Manager at M&S, recalls:

I remember we felt a real sense of job security. We had share ownership options, a non-contributory pension scheme, staff shops, discounts, hairdressers and chiropodists in-store for employees. The result was high levels of employee attachment – people felt a high degree of attachment to their employer and its success because there was a high level of investment in individuals. High proportions of employees were shareholders in the organisation and had a desire to perform and ensure business success. The employment contract was different back then.

Those contracts between employer and employee rarely exist in the Western world today. Individuals realise that a 'job for life' is unlikely and that experience in a variety of organisations is expected for promotion and career advancement. We therefore have to find new ways to help people to feel a deep attachment to an organisation.

One way to do this is to create a culture that is full of investors that 'feels like a family'. An example is UKTV – a highly successful organisation that is full of passionate and creative people. There is an incredibly strong sense of 'family' within the culture, and as such, people give a huge amount of discretionary effort. This results in high levels of attachment.

It's also worth considering the differences in country culture when we think about attachment and the importance of the psychological contract and whether it is strong or weak. In many Japanese organisation headquarters, emphasis is placed upon career planning and performance management. Most members of organisations feel they will have a job with their employer for life, so their levels of commitment and attachment differ from their colleagues in other countries and cultures. Career planning is central to their way of operating, and thus has a high impact on engagement levels. Performance reviews are often carried out twice a year, and bonuses form a higher part of total salary than in the UK or USA. However, despite this deeper psychological contract, there is little evidence to suggest that mental engagement levels and performance are higher than colleagues in the same companies situated in other countries. Attachment alone, therefore, is not enough to create high levels of engagement.

Generally, organisations and cultures that place a higher emphasis on longer-term business performance may have higher levels of attachment than those driven by annual shareholder returns. In Germany, the recession didn't bite as hard as in the UK, Japan and USA. Some analysts believe that the high number of family-owned businesses that strive for long-term success is a contributing factor to the minimal impact on the German economy. Rather than having an economy that totally values shareholder return, there are thousands of small to medium-size family businesses that are able to make decisions based on the long-term success of their operations, rather than being driven by short-term shareholder pressure.

How to Increase Levels of Attachment

There are many levers that can be used to increase attachment. Although few enterprises have the desire or capability to replicate Port Sunlight-style contracts, there is still much to be learned from organisations that have strong attachment levels.

In the current economic reality, I believe there are eight strong levels to consider.

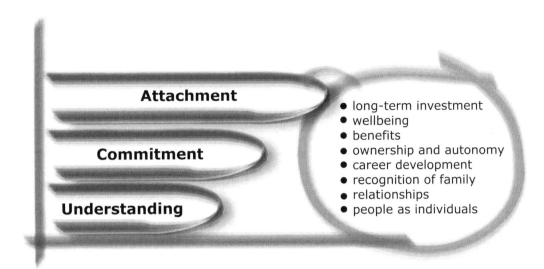

Figure 7.1   Increasing attachment

1. LONG-TERM INVESTMENT

Helping employees to see the long-term strategy and return balanced with annual shareholder value is a big lever to increase employee engagement.

In most businesses, shareholders want to see a yearly return. That's the reality we are dealing with in most global businesses today. In smaller businesses where the ownership structure is different, it can be easier to show how some decisions are made for the long-term good of the business rather than for annual shareholder return. This is incredibly powerful in keeping people engaged.

Even in a business that is driven by annual targets, there are ways to ensure that employees see that there is a long-term future. Communicating clearly about these investments is one easy way to do this. It's also important to share information if decisions are made that reflect the desire to see longer-term return. For example, if the performance hasn't been great in a particular year but investment still continues in projects that won't see a return for another five to ten years, it is important to say so.

Similarly, demonstrate that you are willing to invest in people so that they can give more to the organisation. This could be through career development or through a more fundamental attitude change that attracts key talent and encourages those individuals to stay for at least a medium-term career in the business. This might involve offering sabbaticals or career breaks, but will create long-term attachment and sustained performance levels.

The John Lewis Partnership recruits people with a specific view to their becoming long-term investors in the organisation. It makes it clear to candidates that more will be required of them than in similar organisations. However, the return is higher too.

2. PAY ATTENTION TO THE WELLBEING OF EMPLOYEES

Reduced sickness and absenteeism is good for business. In addition to reducing the costs associated with both, providing services to improve employee wellbeing also adds to the level of attachment people have with their organisation. If I and those who matter most to me in my life are well looked after by my employer, I'll give more than if I am seen as a commodity. I will also think twice before going somewhere else that doesn't offer the same benefits.

Wellbeing is one of the Best Companies to Work For survey factors for employee engagement. Where companies pay attention to the wellbeing of employees, the result is a healthier workforce with less absenteeism. Sony UK in Pencoed, Wales, proved exactly this when the management team invested in its wellbeing programme. The site had medical professionals on hand to help deal with stress and sickness issues, yet the need for them disappeared after the company paid more attention to the employees' wellbeing and gave them the tools to take control of the way they lived and worked.

3. MEANINGFUL BENEFITS PACKAGES

Companies across the world offer a variety of benefits packages to employees to attract and retain great talent. The quality and relevance of these can go a long way to creating higher levels of attachment. If I have benefits that are worth a great deal to me, I'm much less likely to leave and more likely to give discretionary effort. The less positive side of this can be a feeling of employee entitlement concerning these packages, rather than them being seen as privileges, but if handled well, it can make a big difference.

Former Human Resources Director at Starbucks Gordon Lyle remembers that Starbucks made healthcare available to all US employees right at the beginning of its growth because its founder wanted to ensure he was doing the right thing for his employees. Free healthcare provision created high levels of attachment and engagement with the company, and ensured that even when people left Starbucks, they were ambassadors of the brand because it did the right thing.

Staff discount schemes are a component of some successful benefits packages. The type of business one is in often governs the discounts available. For example, Sony UK has a staff sales scheme where employees can purchase goods at reduced rates. They are often offered extra special offers and are able to purchase for close friends and family. The result is brand loyalty, advocacy and attachment. On their own, such schemes aren't enough to keep people engaged because, again, they start to be seen as an assumed benefit over time. However, such schemes do contribute to engagement levels and pay back to the business by having more brand ambassadors in the market.

Hilton Hotels used to run a £15 per night scheme for employees in the UK. During feedback sessions, employees would often cite the scheme as hugely important. However, few actually used it. The critical factor was that people felt an attachment to Hilton because they'd been sufficiently valued that such a scheme had been made available to them.

These discount schemes can be fairly easy to administer for many businesses. However, in some countries there are tax implications to consider. For businesses or not-for-profit organisations that don't have goods or services to offer their employees, negotiated discounts with other providers or suppliers can make a difference to engagement levels and give you a competitive advantage in the war for talent.

Looking at benefits packages and keeping them relevant to employees is key. It's also important for managers to have flexibility to offer different benefits to individual employees. For example, an additional day a month working from home could be extremely meaningful to a working parent who races home each day to fit in with childcare timetables. For another individual, being able to start work at 7 a.m. and leave at 4 p.m. may be an easy-to-accommodate benefit, yet create high levels of goodwill and attachment. The benefits don't always have to be formal and part of the legally binding employment contract to have an impact. However, the organisational culture must be one that gives managers and individuals freedom to find and accommodate these different benefits. It's often easier in a high-trust culture or more fluid organisation than ones where 'working to rule' prevails.

4. SHARE OWNERSHIP AND AUTONOMY

Employees who are also owners in the business are definite investors. That's why share schemes are another powerful lever to create attachment and thus increase engagement levels.

At Stakis Hotels, employees were given shares through the Employee Share Scheme. When asked, they would often comment upon how important the shares were to them as part of their package. However, when probed further about how much they were worth, managers would often receive blank looks and comments such as: 'I have no idea how much they are worth, but I know I have them.' The attachment came from feeling sufficiently valued to be given the shares, not the monetary value of the shares themselves.

Engagement from 'ownership' isn't just about having shares. It also comes from feeling a sense of autonomy and an ability to be involved. Having a feeling that 'I have skin in the game' counts for a huge amount with many individuals, and leads to higher levels of performance and thus engagement. I've always encouraged those I've managed to ask themselves 'What would I do if this were my business?' when faced with a decision or dilemma. This is a powerful technique, but not as powerful as when it really is that person's business, either because they own shares or feel a sense of ownership for the success of a project. Equally, such ownership might be felt as a result of coming up with an idea and being able to continue seeing it through to fruition; with the investment backing and leadership support required. Often, great ideas are born from the most unlikely places and get subsumed into the bigger organisation, so the teams that created the idea and initial work aren't given the chance to see the project through. In companies where the person coming up with the breakthrough is then supported to be involved right through to delivery, engagement levels of that individual are extremely high because they have such a high degree of ownership.

The John Lewis Partnership provides a high level of autonomy to managers and partners. Managers are expected to involve their teams in finding solutions to challenges on a regular basis. Partners' Counsellor Patrick Lewis explains:

It's not necessarily the fastest way of making decisions. It's easy to look at tangible measures that would show the cost of the time involved. What's priceless is the less quantifiable yet substantial benefits that come from highly engaged partners, bringing the best of themselves to work each day. We also have better quality of solutions than if managers alone were to work on cracking problems.

5. CAREER DEVELOPMENT

Personal growth is another one of Best Companies to Work For's eight factors of engagement, and was mentioned earlier as being an important component of gaining emotional commitment. Career development is also a way to build greater attachment.

The more tailored and personal a development plan feels, the more attached individuals will be to their employer. This is particularly the case where development goes beyond the immediate role and includes the wider 'me' – for example, taking into account where people might want to be in ten years from now or what life skills they'll need for the future.

A good career development conversation is often down to the quality of a manager or coach. This is covered in much more depth in Part II, 'Manager as Culture Builder.

6. RECOGNITION OF THE FAMILY

Events that recognise staff and include their wider families are a great way to increase attachment. I remember attending a family day at IBM when I was a young child. My father worked at the company, and it staged an annual event at the large country house where he was based. I was so proud that my father worked for a company that provided such a great day, and told everyone at school, and their parents, about what a cool company Daddy worked for. For my father, it was a chance for him to include us in his work life and help us see where he was when not with us. The investment from the company was minimal, but the feeling that employees were valued enough to be offered such a day was significant.

BSkyB holds an event called Skyfest every year in which it invites all its employees to join in a fun day with their families. More than 25,000 attend annually and enjoy a host of activities. Feedback on the intranet immediately afterwards shows just what an impact the event has on motivation. It's an important occasion that employees feel helps create a stronger bond between them and the organisation. It also creates a bond between their families and the company – an important component for engaging employees.

7. MANAGERS WHO MANAGE RELATIONSHIPS RATHER THAN TAKING A TRANSACTIONAL APPROACH TO PEOPLE MANAGEMENT

Employees will feel a deeper level of attachment to an organisation where their manager understands them and takes time to show an interest in their lives. The move away from transactional styles of management is critical to engaging employees and sustaining business performance – we will explore this in much more depth in Part II. The type of relationship an employee has with their manager highly influences the level of attachment they feel to the organisation, and thus their engagement levels.

8. TREAT PEOPLE AS INDIVIDUALS

Attachment doesn't come when people feel they are simply a payroll number in an organisation. A fundamental human need is to feel valued, and this only happens if we are treated as individuals. Managers play a vital role here, but there are organisation-wide factors that also contribute.

Partners at the John Lewis Partnership have plenty of opportunity to raise questions and concerns and contribute ideas in the business. The Partnership Council is a formal forum for partner involvement, and anyone can feed an issue into this through their local elected representative. There are also other sanctioned outlets, such as writing anonymous letters to newsletters or senior leaders. Partners' Counsellor Patrick Lewis explains:

> Our aim is to provide as many opportunities as possible for partners to be involved and provide feedback. It takes time to listen and converse when issues are raised, but it means we reduce the risk of unknown problems existing under the carpet and only surfacing once they are larger and harder to control. It ensures we have an open culture, and that's crucial because it's in line with who we are. Very often, issues raised may be due to a lack of understanding, and so I talk with the individual about the context and ensure that they have the full story. Interestingly, it's these interactions that create even deeper levels of attachment with people because they remember the time we spend treating them as an individual and because we absolutely want to hear what's on people's minds.

Patrick believes that an incredibly deep attachment often exists with partners after they've experienced a difficulty in the business or in their personal lives. He likens it to a consumer relationship, with the JLP brand being stronger when they've had a problem that has been exceptionally well resolved. Patrick explains:

> Deep attachment comes when a partner sees that we truly live our purpose and care for them as an individual. There are instances where a group of partners may have seen a difficult decision taken or a colleague going through a tough time. How we respond to them can create an even more engaged partner. For example, in an instance where we found a partner had the bailiffs visiting, we provided support and funds to assist. We did this because our purpose is about our people and helping them to be able to give and get the most from their working lives.

As we move higher up the Four-stage Model of Engagement, the role of leaders and managers becomes greater. Many of the levers to create attachment and significance are enabled or facilitated by line managers. Their role in engagement is therefore critical.

8 *Significance*

If understanding is base camp, alignment of personal and organisational significance is the peak of the mountain. The views are incredible, and the satisfaction is richer than at any other level.

Amazingly high employee engagement comes when individuals see a connection between their own sense of purpose and that of the organisation for which they work.

This level of engagement starts with people understanding what gives them meaning and significance in their life and what they stand for. Where individuals see alignment between their contribution at work and what gives them meaning, incredibly powerful performance follows. It's not just extraordinary in terms of outcomes, but also far more sustainable than any other level of engagement. When this happens, people are able to be the best they can possibly be. It's a deep level of engagement – and sadly, rarely seen in organisations today.

During my work as Managing Director at The Energy Project, we'd explore what gives people significance and meaning. I estimate that 99 per cent of the hundreds of senior leaders and managers I met didn't have a clear idea about what gave them significance and meaning. If this is needed before alignment can occur, the potential for higher performance in organisations is truly phenomenal.

> *I see significance in what I do each day as part of this organisation and it aligns with my personal values and what gives me meaning in my life.*

Not only does this give us huge potential to increase engagement in organisations, it's also essential because future generations are going to expect it.

Studies demonstrate beyond doubt that individuals maximise their psychological wellbeing when they are engaged in meaningful work that provides positive emotional experiences. As our working lives extend with growing longevity, people will want – and demand – a greater sense of psychological wellbeing and meaning at work. We're already seeing this with younger generations coming into the workplace. Sarah Henbrey, Organisational Development Director at 3 and former Organisational Development Director at Sony Europe, says: 'Graduates coming into Sony Europe just a year ago had a much higher need to ensure their work aligned with their beliefs.'

As Dame Carol Black emphasised in her 2008 report:

> *for most people, their work is a key determinant of self-worth, family esteem, identify and standing within the community, besides of course material progress and a means of social participation and fulfilment. ... Helping people to gain all of these components is a sure way to higher company performance.*

As Black indicates, for many people it's family that gives them meaning in their lives. Sadly, for the majority of people I have come across, the balance of time and energy spent with family is often low, and in favour of career and work. Over time, this will become a factor of disengagement.

There is a huge body of research that gives more evidence of the link between personal significance, meaning and performance. Much of the work in the field of positive psychology does exactly this.

Researchers Boniwell and Henry identify two broad approaches to the measurement of psychological wellbeing: the 'hedonic' associates wellbeing with the experience of positive feelings (moods and emotions) and factors such as overall life satisfaction; the 'eudaimonic' takes account of the importance of having a purpose (Boniwell and Henry 2007, cited in Macleod and Clarke 2009). Aristotle was the originator of the term 'eudaimonic'. He proposed that true happiness is found by 'doing what is worth doing'. Thus, if people see that their work is meaningful, they are more likely to engage and perform.

As Stuart Fletcher, then President of the International Division at Diageo believes:

> *An emotionally intelligent strategy is about people getting fired up by the thought that the world will somehow be a better place as a result of what they're doing, playing their part in delivering the strategy. If a strategy engages people emotionally, there's an authentic commitment to making it happen.*

With so much evidence backing the importance of alignment of personal and organisational significance, the remaining question is how to achieve this superior level.

How to Increase Levels of Significance for Engagement

The answer lies largely at the level of the individual leader and manager, and will be explored in depth later in this book. However, the organisation as a whole must have the right culture and environment to enable people to make connections between their own meaning and their role at work. More fluid-style organisations will be more naturally equipped to provide such an environment. This doesn't mean that more traditional companies can't also achieve this level of engagement; it's just likely to require more intentional effort and great leadership role modelling.

1. HAVE ALIGNMENT WITH A CLEAR PURPOSE AND VALUES

When discussing emotional commitment, we looked at the importance of an organisational purpose and reason for being. This leads to a higher emotional connection and commitment, where employees understand and buy into the purpose. That starts an individual on the road to being an investor.

To achieve the greater level of engagement borne by significance, employees not only need to buy into a purpose, but also to see how their own purpose and values align with those of the organisation. This develops a much deeper engagement level than achieved with emotional commitment through purpose.

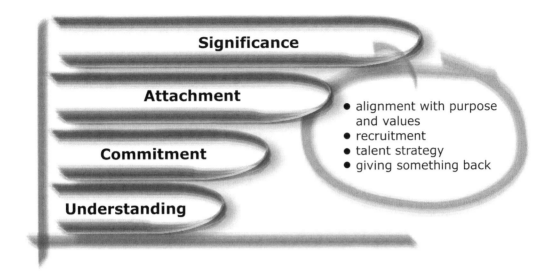

Figure 8.1   Increasing levels of significance

The BBC World Service is an organisation that has a very clear purpose and historically had high levels of engagement among employees, according to former member of the team Naomi Climer:

> *I remember being very clear of our purpose to bring news to help inform and educate people in far-flung places across the world. We'd come into the office sometimes and there would be people chained to the railings making a protest about something happening elsewhere in the world. Inside the building, we had massive diversity and respect for each other. People were hugely engaged because there was an extraordinary uniting force in that building. We had a very clear purpose that was in tune with most of our personal values.*

When it analyses its engagement data, Innocent finds that the items related to 'purpose, vision and values' are always the highest scores. Jo Huddie, Innocent's Learning and Engagement Manager, observed:

> *We know that the higher the scores for these items, the higher the scores for engagement overall, so keeping the values alive through leadership and decision-making is vital to keeping people motivated and performing at their best.*

Regular communication about the company purpose and values is the first place to start, but this also needs to be born out in actions, especially those of the top leadership team. Many teams have decided to develop their own team 'purpose' which connects to, but is different from, the company purpose. This helps people to understand the contribution they are making at a local level and why their role is important.

Andreas Ditter, Managing Director of Sony Pictures Home Entertainment, Germany, says:

Whenever I see values printed on a mug or mouse mat, it fills me with horror. I've seen so many companies where the values are defined clearly but behaviour is actually the complete opposite. Having values is meaningless if they aren't embodied by everyone in the organisation. I've found that trust is the deepest and hardest value to turn into reality if it's shaky to start with. However, it's the one value that can truly change a culture, and thus worth the investment.

At an organisational level, defining and communicating a clear purpose and values helps to create an environment where people can see more alignment between their sense of meaning and that of the organisation. However, it's hard for individuals to make the connections themselves, so managers must step in and help them to do just that. For many people, exploring and understanding their personal purpose is a new experience, and is thus difficult for them to do on their own. This means that managers also need to be skilled to help individuals explore their own purpose in depth and then draw conclusions about alignment. This is most commonly done today through leadership development programmes where managers develop the capability and confidence to be manager as Coach (covered in more depth later, in Part II).

Novartis runs such a leadership development programme for its top talent across the globe, focused on helping individual leaders understand more about who they are, why they exist, and thus their core purpose. Part of this is a two-and-a-half-day mentoring process, where participants use leadership challenges to explore what makes them tick. This gives them a foundation to explore where their own meaning aligns with that of Novartis.

Similarly, in Diageo, people have been supported in establishing how their personal purpose connects with Diageo's purpose of 'Celebrating Life Every Day Everywhere'. This has been done as part of Diageo's Leadership Performance Programme and Diageo's International's Breakthrough Every Day Everywhere Everyone programme, where facilitators help individuals to identify what gives them meaning and significance, and work through how that aligns with their role. Stuart Fletcher, former President of International, believes this has had a big impact on the engagement levels of his people. He explains:

We tracked super engagement scores in Diageo as part of our annual values survey. Our International Region scores five points ahead of the rest of Diageo, and we have more than 40 per cent super engagement. That's a huge amount of discretionary effort, energy and talent that is contributing to a stormingly successful growth rate.

In some areas, it's not necessary to help employees to connect with their purpose, but the trick is for leaders to spot the signs and work with them. 'During my time with Stakis Hotels, I was fascinated by the breakfast waitresses,' remembers Gordon Lyle. Gordon was Human Resources Director at the hotel group, and took it through the merger with Hilton before becoming Human Resources Director for Hilton Hotels in the UK. He found that the typical profile of breakfast waitresses in the Scottish Stakis hotels was that they were mothers with older children that were less dependent. They saw massive significance in their roles because each had a fundamental belief that people couldn't go out into the working day without breakfast. Most had been brought up understanding the value and importance of breakfast, and their caring nature meant that they wanted to ensure the hotel guests didn't leave without the right sustenance for the day. The job was important and engagement levels were extremely high because each breakfast waitress saw significance in their role. They believed that they truly made a difference.

Once it's clear to people what personal purpose looks like, leaders can start to create alignment with the company's purpose. Where leaders spot this connection, it's important that they work with it and find ways to keep it alive and value it.

Starbucks is a great example of an organisation that helps their people to see meaning and significance in what they do. Gordon Lyle was responsible for Human Resources in the UK on 7 July 2005, during the London bombings mentioned in the Introduction. He remembers how the strength of significance was demonstrated that day:

> We found out about the bombings from one of our Regional Managers that called us in a traumatised state after being in the carriage where one of the bombs had exploded. We immediately told all branches to shut their stores, find out where their partners [the Starbucks term for employees] were and ensure they reached home safely. All branch managers were asked to report in once stores were closed and people accounted for. I had my car at our London office and so immediately started driving our regional managers and employees out of the city to their homes. En route we passed Starbucks branches that were open. I remember one of the Regional Managers in the car called the Branch Manager to ask why they had not followed a direct and clear instruction to shut their doors. The Branch Manager was adamant that it wasn't appropriate for them to close. Offices were closing and people needed an option of another meeting place. People were also leaving the city and needed the opportunity to buy refreshments en route. The manager reminded us that our partners were hard-wired to live the values of caring for the community and they saw themselves providing a significant and fundamental role in supporting others through crisis.

It's clear that high engagement levels come when people see a deep connection between the values of the organisation and what's important to them. Gordon remembers visiting a branch in Austria. He asked one of the partners employed there why people like working in Starbucks. She paused and said that it was because she could change something. Gordon probed this further, and found that she felt she had the power to change a cup of coffee if it wasn't right for a customer; she had the ability to change someone's day if they were miserable; she believed she had the opportunity to change the community and make a difference to others. In short, she saw significance in what she did.

In BskyB, Internal Communications Director Nick Green wanted to ensure that employees felt they were working for a TV, company and not just 'Company A or B'. One idea from a group of people in the business was a simple yet powerful way to 'reconnect people with television'. A team was pulled together, and two-and-a-half weeks later hosted the first Friday afternoon session in the staff restaurant. All employees were invited to join and watch TV. Field-based staff were given their own television channel, for employees and their families, that could be watched at home. Each month they see new programmes and premium content earlier than the wider public. It has helped remind staff that they are working as part of a fast-moving television business, and Nick hopes it will continue to boost levels of pride and attachment.

Before being purchased by L'Oreal, The Body Shop was one of the other few examples of an organisation populated by people who had a high emotional connection to their employer and saw significance in what they did. Interestingly, as a result, Emma Berry, former UK Head of Internal Communications, believes that line managers were less critical in engaging people for performance because they already had a high personal desire to perform at their best every day. She explained:

> People at Body Shop had an emotional connection to 'the cause' that Anita Roddick created. They joined Body Shop because their values aligned with hers and the organisation she had created. Employees had a very high emotional connection to the company because they were passionate about the cause.

Most people who joined The Body Shop did so because they loved Anita's ability to stand up and challenge the establishment and status quo. Emma reflected: 'Employee engagement was never an issue in head office or in stores because the purpose and personal alignment was so strong.'

It is also important to consider the values of an organisation when discussing the importance of significance in employee engagement. Many organisations spend outrageous sums on launching values programmes in the hope that employees will change their behaviour and embrace the desired ways of working. Sadly, the majority of values programmes remain an aspirational set of words or a poster on the wall. Those that are successful result in employees truly embracing values and behaving in accordance with them every day. They become 'the way we do things around here'. This tends to happen when there is alignment between personal values and company ones. It also occurs when embedding behaviour changes involves managers, rather than the communication or human resources function alone.

When media company Discovery wanted a different way to express its values that was easy for people to understand and put into practice, it chose to talk about 'growth traits'. These aimed to bring each value to life by expressing the behaviours associated with each of them. Employees were encouraged to think about the growth traits and how they could take action that was in alignment with them. Judy Goldberg, Director of Learning and Development at Discovery Networks International, explained:

> One of our values is creativity, but the growth trait is innovation. This means people thought about what they could do to be innovative. For example, to be part of brainstorm sessions, read about a new trend or competitor. By focusing on the growth trait, we helped people to live the values.

The growth traits were introduced through a series of action learning groups across the globe. Teams had real dialogue about what each value meant for them and their department. Leaders built action plans as a result of the conversations, and managers agreed a minimum of one growth trait objective with each individual as part of their appraisal. Judy said:

> In some cases, a whole team would decide to focus on the same growth trait. In other areas, colleagues would find they had different ones to work towards. I chose expertise for my first year of coming to the UK. I felt I needed to build my expertise in a new environment and geographies to be the best I could be in our international business. In 2011, I chose innovation as my focus because I could see that new technology is changing constantly. I read new books, made new connections, studied articles and worked with new people to help achieve my aims.

In 2012, Discovery planned to have between five and seven performance goals, three to five development goals and one growth trait goal per colleague. Judy believes:

> *The growth traits approach has been a great way to quickly embed our values in a way that people can understand day-to-day. We'll probably start talking more about values again in the future, because people will have the foundation to understand that it's who we are. If we had started by using the values vocabulary alone, I don't believe our culture would have changed in the way that it has.*

There are examples of how to begin articulating and aligning people with company purpose and values more effectively. Chapter 23 will highlight some specific examples.

2. RECRUIT PEOPLE WHO SEE AN ALIGNMENT BETWEEN THEIR VALUES AND PURPOSE AND WHAT YOU STAND FOR AS AN ORGANISATION

When the purpose and values of an organisation are clear, it's important to make these part of the organisational DNA. This means integrating them into the recruitment and selection process. Increasingly, leaders who have high emotional intelligence (EI) are using EI-based recruitment strategies. During interviews, technical competence is explored, but leaders who search out the true values of candidates will test whether there is likely to be alignment between the person, the various roles, the culture and the individual's purpose.

One way to do this is for the recruiter to explain the purpose of the organisation and ask the candidate to explain how they feel this aligns with their own identity.

It's important that this happens at all levels in the hierarchy too, because more and more leaders are choosing roles in companies where they feel there are shared values. Kai Boschmann has held a series of large corporate communication roles. She took her current role because she fundamentally believes that the company values align with her own:

> *I have an opportunity to feel a deeper, significant connection to my work. We protect and save lives and I don't feel there is anything more important than that. With this clear alignment of personal and company purpose and values, I am investing all of myself to make a difference.*

3. INDIVIDUAL TALENT RETENTION AND DEVELOPMENT STRATEGIES

Alignment of what gives an employee meaning and significance is a very individual factor, thus it requires leaders or managers to understand their people. Achieving high engagement levels demands talent strategies tailored to individuals that support and enable the alignment of individual and organisational purpose. Where a manager can offer a development programme that moves an employee closer to alignment, both parties benefit.

4. GIVING SOMETHING BACK

Corporate social responsibility has become increasingly talked about over the last few years. The result has seen employees' expectations rise in terms of their organisations giving something back to society and communities. It's not surprising, therefore, that 'giving something back' is one of the eight factors of engagement that Best Companies measures.

Organisations need to consistently involve employees in defining what contribution is being made to society, and then communicate this widely internally. Where the contribution is based on what gives employees significance, the employer has a double advantage of giving something back while also increasing engagement levels.

Significance is a deep lever to higher employee engagement levels. It's more challenging to achieve than understanding, but the level of investor gained will give higher return than a fair-weather saver.

*   *   *

In summary, all four levels of engagement are needed for a high-performing business. However, different situations may require only understanding or commitment. It's important to consider what is needed before embarking on any action.

Nigel Edwards, a Communication Director with responsibility for Europe and Canada at Pfizer, believes there are three aspects of change that often need to be communicated: structure, process and behaviour. For changes in structure, the communication is more about gaining understanding. Changing processes often involves engaging at an emotional level with people to take action. True behavioural transformation requires all four levels of engagement. With so many businesses needing to compete in a global economy, more and more will need engagement that leads to true transformation, so it won't be enough for most to simply 'tell' employees what's happening and expect them to be engaged.

9 *Measurement*

Before devising an engagement strategy, many organisations need to measure their current ability to engage people successfully. In some companies, an annual engagement survey will exist, so the latest results will give a good measure. If it doesn't, it's worth considering conducting some kind of measurement to understand where the biggest issues are likely to be.

There are a number of ways this can be done, and the trick is to pick the best method for your organisational culture.

External experts are a good choice if you want to benchmark against other similar organisations. Gallup, ICMA Group and Best Companies all have tried and tested questions that measure key factors of engagement. The ability to benchmark against others is particularly useful if you feel the scores are likely to be low, because it gives a robust case against any defensive justifications of the results.

Other options include asking an independent body to run a survey tailored to your needs, or for the internal communication or human resources department to develop a set of questions and run the survey on an intranet or survey tool such as Zoomerang or Survey Monkey – you don't need to spend a fortune to poll your people. The downside here is that employees will often want anonymity if they are to be honest with their feedback, so an internally run approach may not be the most effective.

An annual survey is useful, but in large organisations it's helpful to take the 'pulse' at more regular intervals. An annual survey may take place across the entire company, but pulse surveys can pose a shorter list of key questions and rely on a reduced sample size of the population more frequently. This is often useful in companies where a global survey takes place once a year. Business or country groups can then run regular pulse surveys that are more specific to their needs.

In addition to surveys, it's a good idea to measure with focus groups too. This can give more context for quantitative results from surveys and what is being said. It can also help with prioritising action later.

In great organisations, a blend of formal and informal measurement is happening all the time. Leaders at the John Lewis Partnership have a strong finger on the pulse about how partners are feeling in the organisation. Feedback gets to the top very quickly, and the chairman is constantly aware of the climate across the partnership. The Partnership Council exists to represent the partners, and has the power to pass a vote of no confidence in the chairman if it truly feels he isn't listening and acting on valid issues. This has never happened to date, but does show the importance JLP places on giving all partners a voice. It's probably the most powerful measurement tool in existence to ensure that leaders are in tune and listen to their people.

Innocent places huge importance on measuring engagement levels across the entire business on a regular basis. Each quarter, it asks three questions of all employees to identify any issues that need to be addressed early. Jo Huddie, Learning and Engagement Manager at Innocent, said:

> *We measure employee advocacy, motivation and excitement about the future. This gives us a clear understanding of current levels of engagement, and means we can pinpoint any teams where one area is beginning to drop.*

After each survey, the insights from the results are shared with the leadership team and action is planned. Line managers with eight or more people in their team receive a scorecard of their results so they can immediately see if anything has changed. Managers gather their teams together to talk about the results. Jo explained:

> *We run the survey as a way of driving conversations among teams about engagement and how it can be constantly improved. If this is happening then there shouldn't be any major issues identified in the annual survey.*

With any formal measurement, it's critical to be clear about why you are conducting it. If it's to measure levels of engagement, be extremely clear about what specifically you want to measure, and don't forget to share the results with everyone that participates. I am stunned at how many companies I encounter that either wait months before sharing results or forget to share them at all, and only remember to do so when they start preparing for the next round of surveys.

It's also important not to assume you're 'doing engagement' just because you're measuring it. As Fujio Nishida, President of Sony Europe, once said to me about culture change: 'I don't need to measure it – I can feel it.'

In a similar vein, Andrew Templeman of the Cabinet Office Capability Building Programme framed it in the MacLeod report in this way: 'No one ever got a pig fat by weighing it' (MacLeod and Clarke 2009). So, yes, it's great to measure engagement levels as a way to help you pinpoint action, but you then have to do something to try to improve them.

Manager as Culture Builder

10 *The Importance of the Manager in Culture Building and Engagement*

The manager is the critical link between creating an organisation of savers and investors. Much of the strategy discussed in Part I of this book was about creating understanding and emotional commitment at an organisational level, looking at ways to achieve higher levels of engagement using attachment and significance. This work has a great influence on levels of engagement, but human resources and communication professionals alone – the groups that most often take the lead on organisational engagement – cannot create investors. In most cases, higher employee engagement and performance demands that leaders and managers do more than organisation-wide initiatives can achieve alone.

Managers are the most audible, unavoidable and potentially influential communication feed to employees, and thus have the ability to drive and enhance change, or strangle it at birth. How this group is engaged, equipped and developed is *the* most important consideration for organisations. You cannot by-pass managers – doing so immediately indicates a broken organisation.

The Evidence

According to Best Companies, 'my manager' is the factor with the highest bearing on sustainable levels of employee engagement, and has a significant impact on energy and performance.

A wealth of evidence from elsewhere supports Best Companies' finding. According to Business Link's *Become a More Engaging Manager* report: 'A manager who motivates, challenges and supports team members can inspire them to give their best – improving productivity and performance' (Business Link with the Department for Business, Innovation & Skills 2011).

In 2001, the Institute of Work Psychology at Sheffield University demonstrated that among the manufacturing companies in their study, people management practices were a better predictor of company performance than strategy, technology, research and development (cited in Macleod and Clarke 2009).

In Melcrum's *Developing a Communication Toolkit for Managers* report (Melcrum 2011), Nick Howard, former Retail Communication Director at Lloyds Banking Group, said that improving communication was 'the most important thing' his organisation could ever undertake:

we want to coach managers to become better communicators and ensure that they're equipped with the right tools and support to do that. For example, if they want to hold a team meeting, they should have something tangible that explains the best way of holding and structuring that meeting.

Managers have the most incredible leverage to energise people to execute strategy, interact with customers and spearhead innovation. They are also a great source of accurate and current information about what's going on in the market, customer needs and trends. It's no surprise, then, that this community has such a significant impact on employee engagement and organisational performance.

The sheer number of line managers in most organisations also means they are a key lever for employee engagement. According to Fred Hassan (2011), line managers directly supervise around 80 per cent of the total workforce. They clearly play a major role in influencing the overall engagement and performance level in an organisation.

The Challenge

The MacLeod and Clarke (2009) conclude that the joint and consequential failure of leadership and management is the main cause of poor employee engagement. They cite various pieces of evidence, including a report from Towers Perrin that noted that only 29 per cent of UK employees believed their senior managers were sincerely interested in their wellbeing, only 31 per cent thought their senior managers communicated openly and honestly, only 3 per cent thought their managers treated them as key parts of the organisation, and no fewer than 60 per cent felt their senior managers treated them as just another organisational asset to be managed.

They also referenced the 2008 NHS staff survey, which revealed that only 51 per cent of staff felt they were involved in or consulted on decisions that might affect their work area, team or department, and only 27 per cent thought that senior managers involved staff in important decisions.

Although evidence strongly indicates that line managers are the most important factor in employee engagement, this is clearly not working as well as it needs to in most organisations. The reasons are clear for most managers, and fall across three areas: workload, capability and pressure outside the work environment.

WORKLOAD

Most managers are overloaded. Even magnificent managers who know their job is to enable people to do their best and add most value are struggling with mounting pressures reducing their capacity to do so.

Managers are constantly expected to perform operational tasks, meet their own delivery targets, respond to ever-growing numbers of communications, keep abreast of new developments across the organisation and manage larger numbers of people, in flatter structures, across more locations.

CAPABILITY

In an ideal world, all individuals in management positions would have the ability to actively lead others while also managing themselves and their businesses. However, we don't live in this Utopia, and the average organisation doesn't devote sufficient funds to the extensive management development required to turn all line managers into great leaders. This means that managers are expected to be masters of engagement to build and maintain great cultures without the development needed to enable them to achieve this. Without strong competence, it's energy-draining and time-consuming. Organisations generally cherry-pick the best managers to take part in the development that they offer, but the challenge here is that the gap between talent development and a consistently performing manager is often vast, and demoralising.

PRESSURE OUTSIDE THE WORK ENVIRONMENT

Another factor influencing managers' ability to engage people is the significant pressure on most middle managers outside their work. Roy White, General Manager of Global Sales and Marketing Human Resources at Sony, felt that the pressure is linked to the way we tend to progress our careers:

> Think about the career journey that the average person takes; it usually starts in our twenties in a role with no significant responsibility. We are enjoying the freedom of few ties and living life to the full. We then move into a middle management role at precisely the time when we take on more responsibility at home. We buy a house, have a mortgage to pay, perhaps get married and have a family. At the same time as demands increase on us outside our work, we also have more responsibility and a higher expectation upon us to deliver within work. Add in the building pressure caused by our 'always on' environment enabled by Blackberries and mobile phones, and it's unsurprising that the average middle manager is totally overwhelmed. As a career progresses, a manager may move into more senior roles. Usually this coincides with the time in life where children are grown up, financial security exists and a wider perspective is held on life. There is more time available to reflect and concentrate on engagement. The pressure on middle managers in every company I see is huge: to deliver and do.

11 *The Five Roles for the Manager as Culture Builder*

The manager's role in engagement starts with leaders and managers seeing it as a core part of the management job. I believe that the primary reason we aren't in a world where every manager is adept at managing *and* leading is because organisations don't value people management enough. It's not surprising that managers feel that their role is to deliver operationally first, with people management and engagement a secondary consideration. The preference in most company cultures is to measure progress through key performance indicators and financial targets. This drives what the organisation values, and thus heavily influences management behaviour.

Often, I hear managers describe their people management skills as existing 'in spite' of the organisation. While it is partially within a manager's remit to balance workload with 'people load', the leaders of an organisation have a significant role to play in driving attitudes, behaviours and values that put the employee first.

To see engagement levels soar in organisations, there needs to be a fundamental shift by leaders to see people management as core to the management role. Their operational responsibilities then sit in partnership with that, rather than as the primary focus.

In tandem, line managers also need to embrace change. They need a full understanding of the importance of people management in the manager role, and to see that executives value delivery in this respect. A manager has the power to decide how to make delivery happen – utilising and unlocking the power of the team. Outstanding managers know that making success a reality is pursued most effectively by enabling teams to perform at their best. This is achieved by ensuring a manager has the right talent in the team and then valuing those individuals for delivery, not the hours spent. However, many other factors are necessary in the behaviour, belief system and actions of a manager. The results can be outstanding where this shift happens and leaders fundamentally believe that a manager's role is to engage people and fundamentally influence culture.

Innocent is a good example of an organisation that recognises that a manager's role is centred on engagement, not just tasks. Jo Huddie explained:

> We know that if people have a great manager, they're much more likely to be motivated and engaged at work, so we spend a lot of time developing processes and people to be great managers.

Innocent has a standard that no manager should manage more than five people directly. Every manager's top objective concerns managing people. For anyone with a team of eight or more people, engagement is a measurement right at the top of the list of objectives.

The company specifies that people managers should devote 10 per cent of their time to each direct report. This means up to 50 per cent of the company's managers' role and time should be spent on people management, supporting and coaching others.

The Four Lenses

Managers who want to increase engagement levels within their areas of influence need to recognise that four levels of focus, or lenses, are necessary (see Table 11.1).

Table 11.1   The four lenses for manager engagement

I (me)	You (my colleague)	Us (our team)	All (the organisation)

I

The first lens involves being fully engaged yourself (the 'I'). It's not possible to fully engage others if you aren't fully engaged.

Understanding yourself is crucial if you are to communicate and connect with your people without feeling like you are expending a huge amount of energy. It's easy to abdicate responsibly of your own engagement to your manager or 'the company'. However, the reality is that only one person is truly responsible for it – you. This requires a deep understanding of yourself, your drivers, what makes you passionate, your strengths, values, weaknesses and preferred working styles.

Let's recognise that most leaders and managers have been successful and achieved manager or leader status in an organisation because they have an element of 'self' and drive at their heart. Understanding this psychology helps if it can be advanced so that managers recognise that the best way to achieve their own goals and status is to ensure that they have a high-performing team. A high-performing team will make a manager look good and increase their credibility, reputation and chances of promotion. To achieve a high-performing team, managers need to be exemplary at engaging their people. To excel at this, the manager needs to start by being engaged.

YOU

The second step is to engage your people as individuals (the 'you' – the individual on the other side of the conversation). Each person in your team is an individual, and maximum engagement comes from that person being understood and treated as such.

US

The third level is the wider groups ('us' – your team, along with you). The team that you manage and lead will require engagement techniques to maximise performance and optimise the way they work together.

ALL

There is often a need to engage others outside your own direct sphere of influence. This is the fourth level, which encompasses the entire organisation ('all' – the company, from top to bottom). As a manager, you have a part to play in the overall engagement and performance of the organisation in which you operate. This will happen indirectly through the results of your behaviour with others whom you manage, and by association, their behaviour and interactions. It also needs to happen by intentionally contributing to the bigger picture through sharing best practice and virally extending your brilliance to your wider network.

Organisations would do well to support their managers in understanding these four areas of focus. What is needed is a way to put into practice the various skills, behaviours, attitudes and habits that bring them to life, to understand what is needed and when, and how managers can use the organisation around them to develop their own engagement tools.

The Five Manager as Culture Builder Roles

To be a great engager, and have the capacity to deliver through all four lenses, a manager must master five fundamental roles and able to recognise when each is appropriate and needed. The manager will need to move between them on a daily basis to achieve maximum engagement levels and thus performance in the team.

To give the roles context and to help explain the core activities, I have labelled them as seen in Figure 11.1: the Prophet, the Storyteller, the Strategist, the Coach and the Pilot.

Using the four lenses described earlier, we can build an understanding of what is essential across each of the five roles of manager as Culture Builder.

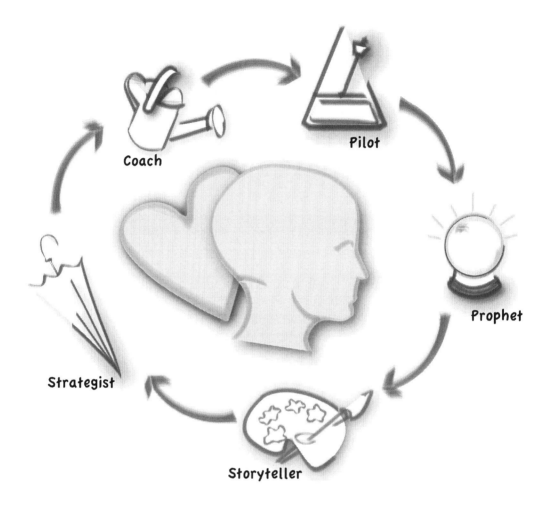

Figure 11.1 The five roles of manager as Culture Builder

THE PROPHET

The Prophet identifies and uses purpose, in self and others, to create alignment. Prophets do this by identifying their purpose and what they stand for, awakening in others the desire to find their own purpose and creating an environment of pride among their teams. The prophet is all about passion, vision and inspiration. They paint a visual picture of the future in a highly emotive way that others can get hold of and want to be part of.

Figure 11.2 The Prophet

Figure 11.3 The Storyteller

THE STORYTELLER

The Storyteller shares context, content, metaphors and examples to engage others. Storytellers understand the story of the organisation, its direction and purpose, or the need for change at global, regional or local levels. This role involves helping individuals to own the story by providing context and clarity to the team. It involves working with people to enable them to understand their role in the story and how they can best use their strengths to contribute. It's a mixture of logic and emotion at work.

THE STRATEGIST

The Strategist's role is a highly logical one, and is needed to identify and build plans for the engagement of others. Great intentions often don't move into a practical phase if there is no clear plan to make them happen. Managers need to develop strong activation strategies to ensure that the desired level of engagement becomes a reality. This means developing and owning the plans, and sharing that ownership with the team. It requires a focus on developing and retaining talented individuals, and involving them in creating higher levels of engagement.

Figure 11.4 The Strategist

Figure 11.5 The Coach

THE COACH

The role of the Coach is centred on getting the best out of people. Managers have a responsibility to facilitate team members on the journey to full engagement, and being a proficient Coach will help them do just this. Managers as Coaches start by finding their own fuel to engage fully and nurture team spirit. They work with others to understand their passions and what 'makes their heart beat'. Ultimately, Coaches turn this into energy and fuel for others so they can be their best in every element of their work.

THE PILOT

The Pilot is a key facet of the manager as Culture Builder – the respected role model. The Pilot is the adult who keeps a hand on the tiller and ensures that an environment exists where everyone is clear about their purpose and brings the best of themselves to work each day. They may regularly hand over the steering responsibility to others within a trusting environment. However, they never take their eye off the end goal. To be a strong Pilot, a manager needs to be trusted and trusting, always mindful of when to be inclusive and when to be authoritative.

Figure 11.6 The Pilot

Each of the five roles summarised in Table 11.2 is needed to convert individuals from savers to investors. Communicators, human resource professionals and senior leaders can very rarely create an organisation full of people who remain investors on their own. Line managers make the difference in producing this shift, then ensuring that people keep investing in themselves and the organisation.

Table 11.2   A summary of the five roles of manager as Culture Builder

	I (me)	You (my colleague)	Us (our team)	All (the organisation)
The Prophet (E) Identifies and uses individual purpose to create engagement	Identify my purpose and what I stand for.	Awaken your purpose.	Create an environment of pride.	Spark wider excitement.
The Storyteller (E/L) Shares context, content, metaphors and examples to engage	Understand and own the story.	Make the story your story.	Provide context and clarity.	Be part of the bigger story.
The Strategist (L) Identifies the approaches and builds the plans to engage	Own the plan (for what's happening).	Develop and retain talent.	Share ownership.	Extend ownership.
The Coach (E/L) Gets the best out of people	Find the fuel to engage.	Work with what makes the heart beat.	Nurture team spirit.	Energise the organisation.
The Pilot (E) A respected role model	Work on and with personal styles.	Trust and value others.	Keep an eye on the end game.	Contribute to the whole.

Note: E = emotional; L = logical.

The Five Roles in Different Contexts

Different situations will require the five roles at varying times. For example, during a period of turbulence, people may be experiencing journeys similar to those shown in Figure 11.7.

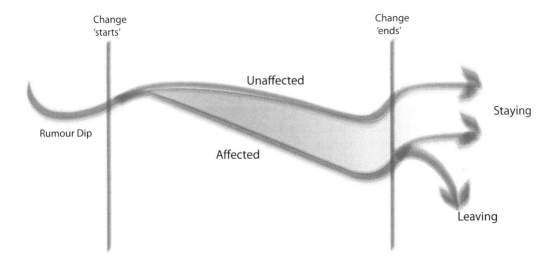

Figure 11.7 The change flow

Often, models looking at this area start at the 'go live' point of communicating the change – failing to recognise that in any sizeable organisation, the majority of individuals will be aware of it long before the actual announcement. News, rumours and failing performance figures circulate quickly – people don't need to feel the rain to know the storm is approaching.

It is also necessary to recognise that two groups quickly emerge: those who are affected, and those who are not. Both suffer a drop in morale, productivity and loyalty, but those affected dip lower. How this change is implemented can have a significant bearing on where this group's engagement goes next.

To support people through this process, managers will need to move across the roles, as illustrated in Figure 11.8.

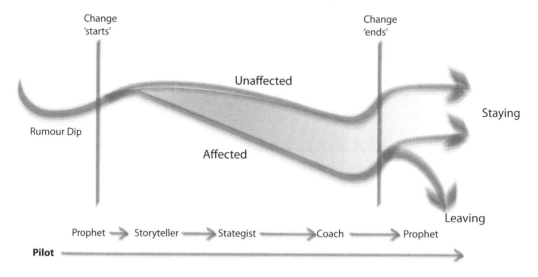

Figure 11.8 Navigating the change flow

During organisational change, the roles have varying degrees of importance as individuals and teams move from seeing the vision to sustaining a new way of working. The adaptation of Kotter's change model in Figures 11.9 and 11.10 show how the different roles are required during each phase.

Moving Forward

If you're already a manager, I'd like to assume that you have a high level of competence in many of the five areas discussed here. That is how you have got to where you are now. However, imagine if you could be even more inspirational and a master in each them. Most leaders and managers would love to be even more inspirational than they are today, particularly because inspiration coupled with the other aptitudes of the five manager as Culture Builder roles can unlock masses of innovation and performance.

For senior leaders, human resources and communication professionals who want to boost engagement levels, helping your managers to become masters in the five roles of a Culture Builder is a must.

The following chapters will give you insight and practical methods to boost performance through your line managers, and show how organisations can build a competitive advantage through engagement. You may notice that the pronouns used in the chapters alternate between gender, but they apply to managers of any gender, of course.

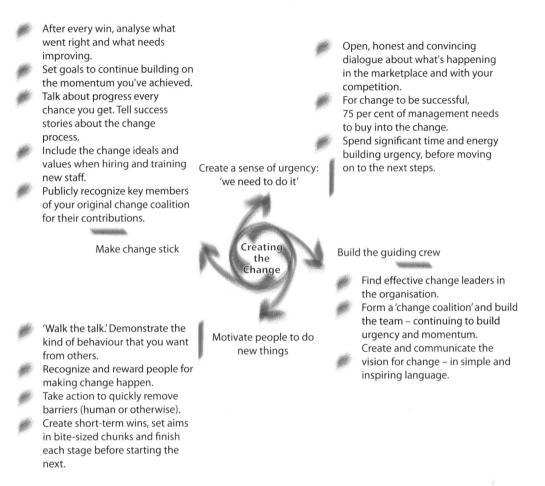

- After every win, analyse what went right and what needs improving.
- Set goals to continue building on the momentum you've achieved.
- Talk about progress every chance you get. Tell success stories about the change process.
- Include the change ideals and values when hiring and training new staff.
- Publicly recognize key members of your original change coalition for their contributions.

Make change stick

Create a sense of urgency: 'we need to do it'

- Open, honest and convincing dialogue about what's happening in the marketplace and with your competition.
- For change to be successful, 75 per cent of management needs to buy into the change.
- Spend significant time and energy building urgency, before moving on to the next steps.

Creating the Change

Build the guiding crew

- Find effective change leaders in the organisation.
- Form a 'change coalition' and build the team – continuing to build urgency and momentum.
- Create and communicate the vision for change – in simple and inspiring language.

Motivate people to do new things

- 'Walk the talk.' Demonstrate the kind of behaviour that you want from others.
- Recognize and reward people for making change happen.
- Take action to quickly remove barriers (human or otherwise).
- Create short-term wins, set aims in bite-sized chunks and finish each stage before starting the next.

Figure 11.9 Change creation

Source: Adapted from Kotter. http://kotterinternational.com/kotterprinciples/changesteps.

Figure 11.10   Navigating the creation cycle

Source: Adapted from Kotter. http://kotterinternational.com/kotterprinciples/changesteps.

12 *The Prophet*

The role of the Prophet is to identify and use individual purpose to create alignment. It involves inspiring others, encouraging them to think for themselves about the future and what it will look like for the individual and team. In the role of Prophet, a manager imagines a bigger, better tomorrow and ignites emotions connected to how it will feel when it's reached. Prophets are inspirational, passionate and visionary.

It's difficult to awaken others' purpose and create an environment of pride if you yourself are not fully engaged and clear of your own purpose and what you stand for. Others will notice that you're simply going through the motions rather than fully believing what you're saying. It's therefore critical that a manager is personally fully engaged before starting to engage others. This is the case for each of the five roles that a manager must play to maximise engagement, but it will show most in the role of Prophet, because it involves using individual purpose to create engagement.

To be an effective Prophet, a manager needs to develop the aptitudes to be:

- visionary
- determined
- inspiring
- persistent
- effervescent
- connected
- infectious

Table 12.1 The Prophet

	I (me)	You (my colleague)	Us (our team)	All (the organisation)
The Prophet (E) Identifies and uses individual purpose to create engagement	– Identify your purpose and what you stand for. – Identify your personal purpose and what you stand for. – Live what you stand for.	– Awaken your purpose. – Create space and a safe environment for others to explore their purpose. – Use aspirational language during one-to-one conversations. – Challenge others to think differently.	– Create an environment of pride. – Plant the vision of the future. – Use visionary language during group dialogue and presentations. – Celebrate moments of pride. – Never let the organisation/team purpose stall or hide.	– Spark wider excitement. – Light a fire of desire among key stakeholders.

From the Perspective of I (Me)

A manager setting out to play the role of Prophet must consider the following:

- Identify your personal purpose and what you stand for.
- Live what you stand for.

IDENTIFY YOUR PERSONAL PURPOSE AND WHAT YOU STAND FOR

The role of Prophet starts at an individual level by identifying one's personal purpose and 'stand'. This is an area that many spend a great deal of time trying to achieve, so it's not a rapid process for most people. There are hundreds of books and self-help tools in existence to help individuals find their purpose and what they stand for. A series of coaching sessions often helps to unpick and identify the core of 'what people are about'.

Personal purpose is a constantly evolving area based on what's happening around you. However, it has a consistent set of factors at the core. The execution may then vary in line with life circumstances, but revolving around these central tenets.

When working with individuals, here are several techniques that I often use as part of the process. Be aware that finding purpose and meaning requires reflection time, and answers don't always appear immediately. This means that much patience is required, and that can take some perseverance! However, having a clear purpose that you deeply understand can make the difference between being a great manager and an average one. It can also make the difference between a lifetime of fulfilled work and one that has you yearning for the end of the working week.

Using Example to Develop Exemplars:

1. Look at the people around you whom you admire.
2. Identify people in your life whom you have admired in the past.
3. Consider specific examples of the things they do or did that make you feel positive towards them.
4. Explore how you are similar and how they map back to you.
5. Unravel each of the specific examples you identify and work up to a more global level. You'll often find insights to the essence of your purpose this way.

For example, Jo reflects about a fellow project manager and how he always seems to find time to spend with other colleagues when they hit blocks with their programmes. Joe often sees that the people the other manager spends time talking with aren't even his direct staff. However, he'll sit down and discuss the issue or challenge they're experiencing. A week earlier, Jo noticed how her fellow project manager had spent time with Tracy after a comment that she 'couldn't see how the project would be delivered on time'. The project manager was under massive pressure himself as his customer had just shortened the delivery time for a piece of work by half. However, he offered to buy Tracy a coffee and talk through the challenge.

Jo noticed that this was a regular practice with him, and something she herself also enjoyed doing whenever she could. She did take similar action with her direct team whenever time allowed, but she didn't spend as much time as she'd like.

Over the weeks that followed, Jo noticed that when she spent time with others, helping them work through their challenges, she felt a huge sense of energy and positivity. This led her to further unravel what she was learning and identify that her purpose had enabling others at its heart.

In this scenario, she started by noticing what was going on nearby and giving herself the time and space to be mindful of the world around her. She gave herself space to reflect. This in itself is something we rarely do in our modern, busy working lives. By unravelling her observations, she concluded:

The specific observation – The project manager spent time with Tracy at a turning point in a project.

The general observation – He has time for others when they need it despite being a manager with extremely heavy workload, running a critical project and not always confining his time to his own team members.

Global unravelling – He is about supporting and enabling people.

In developing an effective global purpose, it is useful to think about three areas:

- **An action** – I support.
- **An outcome** – I enable.
- **A focus** – people.

Other examples are:

- I understand and simplify issues.
- I seek and build harmony.
- I value and share vibrancy.

Another way to explore personal purpose is to draw up a life map.

The Life Map

On a piece of A3 paper, draw two axes to create a life map template. Label the vertical axis 'Fulfilment' or 'Happiness'. Label the horizontal axis 'Time'. You may want to use one piece of paper per decade of your life, or capture your entire life on one sheet.

Capture any examples in your life that spring to mind. Go back as far as you can remember. Plot them on your map so that you start to build a picture of what is at the top and what it at the bottom of your Fulfilment axis. The picture that emerges should help you to gain more insight about what gives you meaning in your life.

The Meaning and Significance Scrapbook

Another useful technique is to keep a scrapbook or noticeboard that contains materials that appeal to you as you go through life. This could contain images, words, headlines, articles that inspire you or catch your attention, quotes or names that you keep and add as you come across them.

Be curious about what they tell you. Identify the trends that emerge, and question yourself about what insight this gives you around meaning, significance and purpose in life.

Being curious is a significant factor that leads people to find out more about their true purpose: curiosity about yourself, curiosity about others, curiosity about happenings when they occur. Try to keep your eyes and other senses open to the environment around you and learn from what it shares at a very practical level.

The Wow Factor Journal

Start by purchasing a small yet attractive notebook. It helps if it has a gorgeous cover that you enjoy looking at or touching. Carry this in your pocket, bag or briefcase, and use it to capture any moments where you feel a 'wow' emotion.

It could be that you hear someone speak at a conference and an example or phrase inspires you. On the train home, capture any moments from the day when you felt particularly high and positive. Some days there may not be anything specific to capture, other days may have more than one example.

The journal will start to build a picture of what gives you emotional satisfaction, but also deeper meaning and purpose. Track the patterns, and be curious about what they tell you.

After using the Wow Factor Journal technique for six months, a senior manager suddenly had a eureka moment where he saw a pattern emerging of what gave him meaning and his purpose in life. He began to see that he found a deep sense of pride at any time when his work had a positive impact on society. He worked in the news industry and wasn't hugely engaged at the time. He noticed from his journal that his core purpose was about having a positive impact on others in the world through specific acts. He realised that he had the opportunity to do this much more effectively by ensuring that news reached people in areas of the world where it could help educate and enrich others. The result was a man who reconnected with his role in a new way and was able to engage others more deeply in their work.

It started by his taking the time to record his 'wow' moments as they happened. At the beginning he had been frustrated that there didn't seem to be many from week to week. However, what he was recording followed a pattern, and once this emerged, the value of the exercise was huge.

LIVE WHAT YOU STAND FOR

Once you understand your purpose, the next step is to live it. This is incredibly energising.

Armed with a better understanding of purpose, managers now need to work through what changes are needed in their roles to live it more fully. This might consist of getting involved in different project areas to best live the purpose, or simply changing the emphasis of the existing roles.

From the Perspective of You (My Colleague)

When fulfilling the Prophet role, a manager can engage others in a series of one-to-one relationships by awakening their staff members' own personal purposes. Igniting this desire and passion to explore their purpose can then be picked up further in the role of Storyteller and Coach to create alignment and action. It's hugely powerful, and is a way of achieving significance for people – the highest level of organisational engagement that we explored in Part I of this book, and the path to building a company of investors, not savers.

For the Prophet, working with other individuals involves the following:

- Create space and a safe environment for others to explore their purpose.
- Use aspirational language during one-to-one conversations.
- Challenge others to think differently.

CREATE SPACE AND A SAFE ENVIRONMENT FOR OTHERS TO EXPLORE THEIR PURPOSE

Creating space and a safe environment for people to explore their purpose is a key starting point if you aim to fully engage others. Exploring and identifying personal purpose is not a quick process for most people, so you need to exercise patience and encourage those you manage. Only if they are given the space and feel they are being encouraged will others take the time to explore this fundamental question.

For a manager, this means not judging your colleague when talking about purpose, and not forcing a view about what it could or should be upon them.

Once a manager has given the space to others to explore their purposes, she can move to the role of Coach to explore this further with the individuals. Therefore, this area is not the strongest action for a manager in a role of Prophet, but it's necessary to provide the context to move to a Coach role and achieve success.

USE ASPIRATIONAL LANGUAGE DURING ONE-TO-ONE CONVERSATIONS

Using aspirational language helps to awaken other individuals' desire to find purpose. If you have taken steps to understand your drivers, what gives you meaning and what you stand for, you're likely to talk and energise others in a new way. Aspirational and inspirational language is contagious, and makes others 'want some of what you have'.

Use clear, compelling, and credible messages when talking one-to-one with others and you will have the opportunity to inspire. Avoid clichés and reusing phrases that obviously came from someone else. Talk about your purpose, how what you are doing gives you a deep sense of meaning, and use your own language when doing so. This means being more aware of balancing emotional language with logic and rational argument. It means dialling up the 'feeling' style of language, using phrases like 'I feel ...', 'I believe ...' and 'How do you feel ...?' rather than language that relies on facts through phrases such as 'We are doing ...' 'The reason we are doing this is ...' and 'I think ...'.

This can feel uncomfortable for people with a preference for rational language. A Myers-Briggs Type F individual will usually be more comfortable using the style of emotional language required. However, this doesn't mean that we all can't be successful in weaving it into our vocabulary. It needs to be used with feeling, though. There's nothing worse than watching someone say 'I feel' when it's obvious that it's painful for them to use such language and they don't actually feel any of what they are 'sharing'.

CHALLENGE OTHERS TO THINK DIFFERENTLY

For some, inspirational language will be enough to awaken their purpose or desire to find purpose. For others, it will take gentler probing or questioning during one-to-one conversations. In the role of Coach, a manager can ask questions to help others find their purpose, but as a Prophet, you are looking to create a desire, so try asking:

- Can you tell me a story about how things could be different?
- Here are the keys to the company – what does the future look like?
- Can you tell me what we're doing wrong – can you tell me how you'd like to make it better?

From the Perspective of Us (Our Team)

The role of the manager as Prophet at a team level is to create an environment of pride where people will understand the vision and purpose of the organisation and team at a top level. The manager then becomes Storyteller, to explain the vision and bring it to life. The Strategist takes it further, putting together and executing the plans to achieve it.

For a manager working with his team as a Prophet, it's worth considering the following:

- Plant the vision of the future.
- Use visionary language during group dialogue and presentations.
- Celebrate moments of pride.
- Never let the organisation's or team's purpose stall or hide.

PLANT THE VISION OF THE FUTURE

The manager as Prophet is responsible for planting the vision and making people highly excited about it no matter what their role or how they contribute to achieve it. Planting the vision is done interpersonally, and not through faceless communication tools. It involves regular dialogue through both formal and informal communication.

USE VISIONARY LANGUAGE DURING GROUP DIALOGUE AND PRESENTATIONS

A great manager drives performance by influencing how people feel. It's feelings that create behaviour, so it's vital for managers to influence the feelings of others in the business. During conversations, team meetings and dialogue, the manager as Prophet must enhance engagement by using visionary language and painting a highly emotive picture about the future.

At a practical level, this means using positive and optimistic language, as shown in Table 12.2.

Table 12.2   Visionary language

	Phrases like	**Rather than**
Talk in certainty	We will ... We can ...	We may ... We should ...
Be assumptive	It is ... We are ...	It could be ... We may be ...
Be strongly optimistic	There will be huge benefits from this.	It could help.
Be forward-looking and sell the dream	When we get there, we will ...	In the past, we have ...

This is also very much about selling certainty – agencies that pitch for work will ensure they use optimistic phrases to ensure that a sense of certainty is achieved. It's far better to be quoted as saying 'We *can* deliver on time' rather than 'We *may* deliver on time.'

A great Prophet is expansive. She can explain the purpose of an organisation in one sentence, and not by just reciting the slogan on the wall. I found Patrick Lewis, Partners' Counsellor at the JLP and grandson of John Spedan Lewis, a fabulous example of someone that was able to do just this. When asked about his organisation, he was able to sum up the purpose in his own words that were clear, consistent and impactful. They weren't the slogan written on the wall that captured the formal purpose of JLP, but they had the same meaning.

Being forward-thinking and selling the dream is particularly important for a manager acting in the role of Prophet. When talking to managers about why this doesn't happen enough in organisations today, it's clear that individuals can sometimes feel uncomfortable selling a dream that they didn't create themselves or don't have 100 per cent control over attaining. However, a great Prophet will sell the team a dream that they do believe in, one that's drawn from the wider story, but tailored appropriately. Having said that, it's fine if the whole dream doesn't come true – in fact, it rarely does. The forward-thinking element of the Prophet creates the dream people want to be part of making happen. The Storyteller then shows how the dream can come true, and communicates the examples of progress along the way.

Prophets don't look backwards, they look forwards. As soon as a manager or leader starts to look backwards, they're either trading on faded glory or raking over the coals of failure – neither of which is useful. Historians don't rally crowds and action; prophets and visionaries do.

Consider Martin Luther King – he had 'a dream'. That was all about the future. The UK Labour party in the 1990s had a simple slogan: 'Things can only get better.'

The Prophet needs to sell a dream that is a stretch, but realistic to the recipients. As an extreme example of this, during early 2011 an American preacher predicted the end of the world. He was so believable that followers all over the globe sold their possessions as the date approached. Come the 'day of reckoning', things passed without event. Following a leave of absence, he returned saying his date had been wrong, but there was a new future date and the world would still end. He still has a strong following because he tempered his optimism with honesty, but continued looking forward, and pushed the vision. You will be relieved to know that his second date has been and gone.

As a more realistic example, when Fujio Nishida entered Sony Europe as President, he found that the business was not performing as well as the corporation wanted. He immediately started to focus people on the excitement of the future by inspiring them with the message of revitalisation. He knew that as a leader, he had a responsibility to be the Prophet and rally people around a forward-thinking aspiration, rather than focusing solely on the reasons why the business was not performing well. He placed huge personal emphasis on ensuring that everyone across the organisation understood that the focus was revitalising for the future. A name was given to the direction – *Fukatsu* – a Japanese word meaning 'revitalisation'. Fujio Nishida used a variety of media on a regular basis to deliver his message that the future was about delivering *Fukatsu*, deploying brightly coloured imagery, emotional visionary video footage and aspirational language. He introduced his rallying cry during a live broadcast across Europe to all employees, then embarked on continuing to be a Prophet through breakfast meetings, town hall meetings and one-to-one conversations across the territory.

Despite keeping momentum with his dream, the goals weren't reached as quickly as the company wanted. Rather than dwelling on the past, he constantly talked about the next step and future growth, launching *Hiyaku* (a Japanese term meaning 'soaring') two years later. His focus was always on the future, and he knew that enough steps were being taken along the journey that people trusted his vision and wanted to follow. He scaled his messages appropriately, often being over-optimistic about soaring growth, because good

Prophets don't look to the past and dwell on it, they look forward – and people pick up enough of this to join in and help make it happen.

Being future-focused and sharing an exciting dream appeals to the need among people to feel they can be successful, no matter what their role.

CELEBRATE MOMENTS OF PRIDE

It's important to recognise and celebrate successes that take the organisation or team closer to the vision or living its purpose. Wherever examples exist of living the purpose, the Prophet can highlight and recognise these with excitement and passion. Use the celebrations as the 'see, I told you so' and evidence that allows you to continually shape a purpose for your team. These are the radioactive isotopes that keep the core of the team hot.

This was achieved particularly well at Mercedes-Benz US International in Alabama. When the first commercial production vehicle rolled off the production line, there was immense pride and ownership among the workforce. The plant was Mercedes-Benz's first in the USA, and was significant for many reasons, including the fact that people who were hired locally did not have automotive production skills or backgrounds in the field. Debra Nelson was the company's Administrator of External Affairs at the time, and saw pride levels rise right from day one:

> There was a defining moment when we celebrated Job 1 – the very first commercial vehicle to roll off the production line. I remember struggling to think of the most appropriate way to mark such a significant occasion, so I asked the team members to come up with a way of demonstrating what they felt would be most appropriate. They came up with ideas to demonstrate their contributions. Their pride was evident. Some of the performances were funny and others were heart-warming. Every employee was invited to autograph the first car as a way to recognise their individual contribution and their role in its delivery. When the car came off the line, it burst through a large sheet of paper to 'I Feel Good', a popular song by music artist James Brown. The atmosphere was electric as the employees celebrated their collective accomplishment.

NEVER LET THE ORGANISATION'S OR TEAM'S PURPOSE STALL OR HIDE

The role of Prophet means keeping the organisational or team purpose central to how people feel and act. An organisation's purpose is its anchor and compass, so it should never be forgotten or lost. The manager who acts as a successful Prophet will always keep purpose at the forefront of his mind and keep his team inspired at regular intervals. It's particularly important to keep the purpose sacrosanct during periods of change and high anxiety. When a business is in crisis, it's even more important that people understand and act with the purpose central to decision-making. However, in a state of panic and survival, it's often then that purpose disappears from sight.

Managers who are great Prophets don't let the purpose slip when it's challenged incorrectly or forgotten. They make it their business to always pull individuals and teams back to the reason for being.

From the Perspective of All (the Organisation)

There are many dimensions to the role of a manager in engaging people to improve business performance. One critical element is recognising the responsibility to engage with people across the business and beyond, so that the manager is able to achieve her full potential and to create the conditions for her teams to thrive. This side-to-side element is often forgotten as energy is channelled into working with direct reports or project teams. However, managers who are skilled at engaging with their wider network will develop relationships and connections that pay huge dividends in the long run.

LIGHT A FIRE OF DESIRE AMONG KEY STAKEHOLDERS

As a Prophet, you can make a difference by painting an emotional vision to encourage key stakeholders to want to be involved. Using the techniques described earlier in this chapter, a manager can inspire and evoke a passion to want to be part of what you need them to be involved with. This works at multiple levels, and is a strong leadership trait.

With an individual stakeholder, a manager may meet one-to-one to share his vision of the future for his team or change project, or to transform the way he operates. The use of aspirational language and planting his vision is key.

At a team or organisational level, a manager can paint an emotional vision of the end point or purpose of what he is trying to achieve so that others want to be part of the journey.

Linked to this is the concept of a manager's team being 'a shining beacon' for the rest of the organisation. High-performing, engaged teams attract attention, so that others then ask 'How do you do that?'

13 *The Storyteller*

The Storyteller is often the role to which most organisations will pay attention when attempting to boost engagement levels. Engagement tends to be the responsibility of the communication or human resources department in many large organisations – hence this focus. The result is a great deal of emphasis on communication competencies and approaches. This is not a bad situation if it applies to the organisation within which you work, because it should mean that resources and development are abundant. If this is the case, there is no excuse for a manager not to be an outstanding Storyteller.

The role of Storyteller as an engagement lever is about sharing context, content, metaphors and examples to engage others. Context and content are the top areas for creating employee understanding and thus setting the foundations to create savers across the organisation. In Melcrum's *Making Managers Better Communicators* study, 65 per cent of respondents said that 'not putting information in the right context' was the managerial behaviour they thought most damaging to communication (Melcrum 2004). The second area was not making time to discuss issues with employees; 55 per cent of respondents considered this to be in the top three factors damaging communication, out of a total of 11 factors.

To be an effective Storyteller, a manager needs to develop the aptitudes to be:

* inclusive
* proactive
* resourceful
* eloquent
* egalitarian
* interpretive

Table 13.1   The Storyteller

	I (me)	You (my colleague)	Us (our team)	All (the organisation)
The Storyteller (E/L) Shares context, content, metaphors and examples to engage	– Understand and own the story. – Become the expert. – Develop the story to include yourself and your purpose.	– Make the story your story. – Enable others to understand their role in the story and how they can contribute. – Enable others to become Storytellers themselves.	– Provide context and clarity. – Colour-in the corporate story. – Sit in the shoes of others. – Share the story using storytelling techniques. – Highlight and celebrate success, milestones and the journey. – Provide context when the journey changes. – Use communication channels and technology that are effective for you. – Take account of cross-cultural nuances. – Check that the story is being understood and internalised.	– Be part of the bigger story. – Share the story and what it means for you. – Share successes – in context.

From the Perspective of I (Me)

Before a manager can engage people through telling the organisational story, he must first fully understand the story and own it. This involves the following:

*   Become the expert.
*   Develop the story to include yourself and your purpose.

BECOME THE EXPERT

Think of instances where a leader or manager has inspired and engaged you in a story about the direction of your organisation. Make a note of what made that a memorable occasion for you and why it left you feeling engaged.

It's likely that one of the factors you have identified is that they were credible and knowledgeable.

As Storyteller, a manager has to be an expert. He has to be credible and knowledgeable. This means knowing more than is written in the newsletter articles or slide decks available on the intranet. In organisations where leaders are outstanding, managers will be given access to the information and dialogue needed to gather a deep understanding about the 'story'. In organisations where this isn't readily available, managers have to take responsibility themselves to find out more. This means setting aside time to proactively find the information, facts and stories that bring messages to life.

In Pfizer, the global Chief Finance Officer at the time of writing is renowned for being an expert on numbers. When he attends town halls, the turnout is huge – he makes the numbers come alive with his certainty, his ability to explain things simply, and how he links it back to what the organisation does.

A good starting point for a manager is to identify formal and informal sources of information. Formal sources could be found through the intranet, manager briefing materials, annual reports, monthly performance presentations and leadership blogs. Informal sources are just as important, and are needed to help bring colour to the story when sharing it with others. Managers who are well-connected and have good networks across their organisation and in their external markets will naturally hear the stories and examples of how direction and change is happening. Those who are new to a company or don't have such a strong network will need to find these informal sources.

Spend time talking to your peers about what they are hearing and communicating to their teams. Ask your manager and senior leaders questions like these when you interact with them that will help build your understanding:

- What will success look like for you when we get to where we need to be?
- How do you think we are doing against our goals right now?
- What are you proud about at the moment?
- What are the priorities for us right now?
- What are the three big things that will make the biggest difference to our success in the next six months?
- How do you feel about our future?
- What changes have you seen happen in the past few months?

It's important to gain an idea about the scale of what is happening, how quickly, and the likely change in direction or what the 'story' could be. Being the expert means then calibrating the story so that you are working with facts and possibilities rather than vague ideas or wild rumour.

DEVELOP THE STORY TO INCLUDE YOURSELF AND YOUR PURPOSE

Telling the story about organisational direction or what is happening or needed is a core part of the line manager's role. It very often starts with a manager taking the facts he has been given and sharing them directly with his team. A good manager will add some narrative about what the facts mean. However, an excellent, engaging manager will start by understanding the story. He will then identify where he plays a part and how his purpose aligns with it. For example, great managers will work through how the organisational purpose and their personal purposes correlate. This not only helps them communicate more engagingly, but also unlocks more energy in the individual because he can see more personal alignment in what he does.

Managers need to make it their business to understand and then develop a story that is comfortable for them to communicate. If the message is a difficult one for you to buy into, try to find out more about the rationale from others. If you don't believe what you are saying, it will show very clearly. This is disengaging for others, and impairs your credibility as a manager.

From the Perspective of You (My Colleague)

Once a manager has understood the story for himself and internalised it, he can take it to others on a one-to-one and team level. In a one-to-one context, the manager has a role to make the organisational or team story belong to each individual. The aim is that the individual feels the story is their story, because the faster others own a message, the quicker they will champion it and take appropriate action. This comes from the following:

- Enable others to understand their role in the story and how they can contribute.
- Help others to become Storytellers themselves.

ENABLE OTHERS TO UNDERSTAND THEIR ROLE IN THE STORY AND HOW THEY CAN CONTRIBUTE

Through one-to-one dialogue, managers can give the space to others to understand the story at a deeper level than they are able to gain from reading materials or attending a town hall event.

After organisational interventions to help build understanding have taken place, arrange one-to-one conversations with members of your team to talk about what they have heard and what they feel it means to them, the team and the future. In some cases, it may be appropriate to talk about whether their individual objectives or focus need to change.

An organisation's vision never lives in purity across the company. It is best viewed as a blurred concept, where individuals create their local, personal versions of it. Leaders, with the support of managers, work to ensure that the 'sharp centre' of the vision is held steady and that the interpretations don't veer too far from this.

HELP OTHERS TO BECOME THE STORYTELLERS THEMSELVES

Asking others to tell the story to colleagues, customers and partners is a great way to ensure they understand, and helps them internalise it themselves. In the same way that your insight and interpretation have made you part of the story, you have the opportunity to involve others. Individuals who feel that they understand and own the direction and the change (the 'story') have higher engagement levels, and will quickly become investors.

To become Storytellers, others need to become expert in the facts and feelings that make up the message. In the same way that you have weaved your purpose into that of the organisation and story, you can help others to achieve this. During your role as Coach, you will have helped others to identify their purpose, so one-to-one dialogue with individuals can fairly quickly help them see alignment between it and the organisation's story. Your role is to ask the right questions that help others knit together their purpose and the story. In some cases, there will be an extremely tight connection; in others, it may be a looser.

Watch for ...

It's easy to conduct a conversation about 'how your purpose and the story fit together' too quickly. If you have already worked this through personally, you will be at a different stage of understanding and alignment than the person with whom you're conversing. The danger is that you will run at speed and leave the other person overwhelmed or confused. One practical technique to help avoid such problems is pausing.

Pause during a conversation, negotiation or dialogue. Refrain from saying anything for at least five seconds. This will seem like a very long time, but try it. Within that time, it's likely the other individual will begin talking. During this time, you'll often unlock new information that will help the dialogue become more successful. It also makes it feel less like you are presenting to them.

Give individuals opportunities to share the story with other colleagues and to repurpose it in their own language for other groups. This will be obvious if your people also have teams to manage. However, if your people don't have direct reporting groups, think of other groups inside or outside the company that would benefit from hearing the story.

From the Perspective of Us (Our Team)

Managers of high-performing teams are extremely competent at providing context and clarity on a regular basis. This involves the following:

- Colour-in the corporate story.
- Stand in the shoes of others.
- Share the story using storytelling techniques.
- Highlight and celebrate success, milestones and the journey.
- Provide context when the journey changes.
- Use communication channels and technology that are effective for you.
- Take account of cross-cultural nuances.
- Check that the story is being understood and internalised.

COLOUR-IN THE STORY

A manager in the role of Storyteller must expand and explain the story to his team. In some cases, this may be a completely new message that you have excited people about when acting as Prophet, possibly minutes earlier. In other cases, you may be expanding on a company-wide message that is much broader in scope than your immediate team.

Whichever is the case, some fundamentals need to be explained to provide context and clarity.

The Context Model

What …
… is our purpose?
… is happening

Why …
… is it important?
… is it happening?
… now?
… us?

How …
… will it happen?
… do we need to take action?

When …
… will it happen?
… will it have an affect on us?

Who …
… is involved?
… is leading?

I …
… believe it means this for me …
… see this linking very clearly with our direction/focus to …
… am excited because …
… feel it links with my passion because …

You …
… have the opportunity to …
… may be affected by …
… have a next step to …

Janet Markwick, Chief Finance Officer at Grey London, believes: 'It's critical that organisations, leaders and managers invest time in people to help them understand the broader business drivers and context.' She's seen many instances where people could see more meaning in what they do if they were able to see the business context and how their work contributed to the whole. In Grey London, Janet worked with teams to increase understanding of their impact on the profit and loss of the agency:

Where people saw how they could contribute more directly to the profit of their business area, they suddenly felt hugely empowered. I saw people taking opportunities to deliver more for their clients and satisfaction of employees and customer increased in the process. Making the full story available and understood is truly important.

Janet realises that where managers are able to provide context and a wider field of vision for their people, the result is higher engagement and increased performance.

The colouring-in of a story is what makes it memorable, using emotive language and paying attention to how you describe key messages.

Wherever possible, you should take the opportunity to make the story yours before you begin telling it. This will make it easier for you to talk about how it feels for you and what excites you about it. The colour will naturally appear and accumulate as you add more depth of information.

Be aware that it's easier to add colour and engage people in change when there is an obvious pressing need, but much harder without. If a business is doing very well, it's more difficult to convince people that there is a need to continue evolving in order to continue doing well. This means that there is an even bigger need to colour-in the detail and answer the questions in the context model explained above.

Adding colour works best when you use a variety of the storytelling techniques described later in this chapter as well as dialogue. When entering into dialogue, remember to be clear about what's fixed and can't be changed, and what isn't fixed and can be changed.

Ensure that people see the relevance of the story for them. Fables can be useful in this sense. The famous stonemason's fable is often used to help people see relevance in storytelling, which can then be explored through dialogue:

> *Three stonemasons are asked: 'What do you do?' The first says, 'I make bricks,' the second stonemason states, 'I'm making this wall,' and the third declares, 'I build cathedrals.'*

A conversation can follow this story to help people to identify what they do, for what outcome, and then place this within the context of your story.

STAND IN THE SHOES OF OTHERS

When formulating your messages to tell the story, it's important to ask yourself 'Where is the team?' or 'Where are others right now?' What is their mindset? Is this the first time that people will have heard about this direction or change? Have you played your part fully as Prophet to inspire them so that they are ready for the detail? What has the potential to excite others about your message? What are the likely issues and concerns others may have when you start to communicate? What might raise hackles as you speak and cause the rest of your story to be lost? Is the story consistent with what has been said before?

Putting yourself in the shoes of others helps to ensure the story is well-pitched and positioned. It will engage people more successfully if it meets people where they are. Toyota has a process within the company known as *Genchi Genbutsu*, which translates as 'go and see'. Any manager, regardless of level within the company, is expected to experience a problem or situation at first hand before deciding on any changes. This can range from visiting dealerships to understand a lack of customer footfall to observing the manufacturing process at one critical point. Only then do they decide on a course of action.

One unit in the Logica business was performing well against its key performance indicators, but analysis suggested it was likely that a dip would occur within two years unless it changed to address some weaknesses. Steve Thorn, Logica's Transformation Director of Global Outsourcing, was faced with the challenge of helping colleagues see the need to change in an environment where they were frequently recognised because the business was doing well. People felt very proud of their business and the success they had created, and they weren't seeing signs of the business declining.

The challenge for Steve and his team was to help people see a burning platform for change yet still keep motivation levels high. He started by putting himself in the same mindset as the people with whom he wanted to engage by asking himself some simple questions about how he would feel if on one hand he was being recognised for a successful business, yet others were telling him it had to change, and now. What would those conversations make him feel like, how would he react, what would make him react better and make him feel that he owned the situation and could bring about the change? As a result, he gained the crucial insight that a story about analyst predictions wouldn't be enough to create a connection and desire to take another look at their business. He needed something more, so he set about gathering robust external data about the market, analyst viewpoints and benchmarking information to build a solid case for change. Using this, he was able to start by painting a clear picture of the likely future, then bring it to life through emotive stories of the potential impact for the business that would be meaningful for the employees.

The result was openness among colleagues to the possibility that a decline might happen. However, full belief wouldn't occur until they started to see clear signs, and that's what Steve and others went looking for – tangible examples within their client base that would build the case and promote an ongoing journey of dialogue with the team. Steve thought about how to engage with colleagues by putting himself in their shoes first. His approach was more successful than if he had jumped into creating a message based on his own needs and insight.

SHARING THE STORY USING STORYTELLING TECHNIQUES

The more compelling a story is, the more engaged and ready to perform a team will be. This is the case in most instances. Compelling stories come from a strong message coupled with powerful delivery. We've all seen conference speakers who clearly have great knowledge of their topic, but appear uninspiring and leave us with little memorable content. At the other extreme, you may remember a manager you've seen who used amazingly complex and compelling images in his PowerPoint slides, but left you feeling unsure of the key message being delivered.

It's critical for a manager to tell the story clearly, with colour, and to be compelling. A variety of storytelling techniques, such as analogies and metaphors, offer very powerful ways to engage people, rather than more rational, left-brain presentations. Metaphors also help people to understand how to solve related problems or challenges more effectively.

Storytelling itself is quite an art, and plenty of in-depth guidance exists as to how to tell a great story. Stories are the way we have handed down knowledge through the ages. Legends help us to connect with information and remember it – critical for human survival in many cases. Consider hieroglyphics from the Egyptians or tribal stories from the Aborigines at Uluru. All use storytelling to continue the process of transferring knowledge across the ages. It's also important to ensure that the ways in which you build the stories allow for change and the inclusion of new elements. History in action is about uncovering, recording and revising as necessary. Don't let your stories become fixed – keep them vibrant with new elements and chapters.

Figure 13.1 shows some quick starting points for managers to help provide the context and clarity needed with teams in organisations.

Figure 13.1 The manager as Storyteller

The Manager as Storyteller

Using empathy involves meeting your audience where they are, and is often an opportunity to tackle potential issues head-on. For example, after you have used visionary language about the future as a Prophet, you could segue into the story by saying: 'I know what you're thinking – "How can this possibly be possible when we have such a big competitor stealing the market?" Well, here's how I would approach this.' Use empathy to build the platform to tell your story.

Metaphors are powerful when used sparingly. I once worked with a senior manager who would use a metaphor or analogy in almost every sentence he spoke. In meetings, people would compete to see how many they could count in the hour spent together. The individual had no idea this was happening, and that his messages were being heavily diluted as a result. A significant area of science has emerged around the use of metaphor in business language, and evidence shows that the type of language used can have a significant impact on the message received and action taken.

According to Thibodeau and Boroditsky (2011), in the 1990s the New York Police Department (NYPD) was involved in a manhunt for a serial rapist. Looking at the case, prominent criminal justice expert George Kelling argued that, had the police used a different set of metaphors to describe the situation, fewer of the 11 attacks would have taken place.

Kelling cited the fact that police forces tend to use metaphorical terms for criminals that cast the perpetrators as predators – ones that 'prey on victims', 'lie in wait' and 'show no mercy'. This means that officers' mindsets will be focused on catching the predator, rather than preventing the spread of the crime. After three attacks, a pattern became clear, and the NYPD could have focused more on community education to prevent further rapes, but it focused its efforts on the attacker instead.

Research has demonstrated that when reading predator-like metaphors to describe a crime, people will suggest law enforcement-based solutions that focus on that individual. However, when the same crime is described using terms that portray it as a disease – say, a virus – the solutions focus more on social responses for prevention.

Using metaphors can therefore be a great way to bring colour to stories and help people to understand, internalise and start to make the story their own, but it's important to be careful about the language you use: describe customers as 'problem children', and solutions will concern punishing their bad behaviour. Describe them as 'genuinely confused', and positive solutions will flood in.

David McClements has run management development programmes in a variety of large organisations. In one, he ran a mandatory management development programme for all managers. It consisted of two modules. He explained:

People often had a hunger to start with Module 2 because it fixed an immediate, and painful, need in their business area. I used a metaphor to explain vividly why we need Module 1 first:

A doctor is walking past a river and sees a man drowning and shouting for help. He quickly dives into the river to save the struggling man. The man thanks him for saving his life, and the doctor moves on. Further down the river, a woman is drowning and shouting for help. The doctor dives in and saves the woman from the river. He continues, and finds another drowning man. Again, he dives in to save the struggling male. This repeats as the man proceeds down the riverside path. A passerby approaches and comments that the doctor looks extremely tired, and asks if he is OK. The doctor says he would be fine if people weren't constantly drowning in the river. The passerby suggests that he stop rescuing people, go onto the bridge upstream and tackle the person on the bridge who is throwing them in.

People talked about the story afterwards, and it captured an immediate understanding about why they were in the room and the importance of starting with the fundamentals that formed Module 1. I simply asked them whether they were the doctor or the guy throwing people in the river each day. People were warm and ready to go once they heard the story. I don't believe they would be quite as bought-in if I rationally explained the reasons why we should start with the content of Module 1.

Here, David is demonstrating the power of metaphor – proven to be highly effective in helping teams to find novel solutions to problems and to uncover the issues without being told what they are. Mythology is often used in this context – for example, the Beowulf story is a powerful tool for helping groups see the true problem, rather than 'the monster in front of them'.

Top Tip

Think about how you can use metaphor and analogy more in your storytelling.

STRUCTURE

A good message structure is critical when giving context and clarity to any audience. This is particularly true where that audience is your team. A story needs a beginning, a middle and an end. It needs emotion and a clear 'what's in it for me' as part of its structure. It needs characters the audience can understand and with whom they can identify. A handy device to use in a variety of communication channels is the PLAN Tool (see Table 13.3).

Table 13.2   The PLAN Tool

P	**Point of the story** – A good story needs to have a topic, a point. Is it a journey, a quest, a coming of age?
L	**Likely impact** – Any story you tell will need to state early what the impact and benefit will be for your audience.
A	**Action and timeline** – What you want the audience to do, and over what time span.
N	**Names of the characters and how they feel** – The character could be yourself and how you feel about the topic.

In practice, this structure can be used day-to-day in email and written and spoken messaging. Good managers follow this model in the first four sentences of emails. The next paragraph then goes into the detail once they have made the connection with their reader. For example:

I'd like to share some news with you about (P) ....

This gives you an immediate chance to get involved by (L) ....

Please take a look at the attached and come back to me by ... with your thoughts (A).

I feel this is the most exciting time in my five years with the company because we'll really have the opportunity to (N) ....

MUSIC

Stories can be told through music and other interpretations in ways that connect with audiences very differently. A whole host of organisations exist that will use orchestras, percussion and dance to help teams embed messages.

The Sony Professional Solutions Group has used a variety of creative approaches to tell its story at kick-off events over the years. I remember that one of the most successful was where the entire audience of approximately two hundred people learnt how to play an instrument over two hours. Groups were given different string instruments and went away to learn how to play a simple piece together as a small team. One group learnt how to play the violin, another how to play the cello. All manner of string instruments were present. The finale was the entire group forming to play their new instruments together, around one coherent piece of music. It had a hugely powerful impact for all those that took part. The story was remembered by all – that the business could create more than they currently imagined if they worked together and challenged each other every day.

Music has a wonderful way of connecting the right and left sides of the brain, bringing logic and intuition together. The result is a more engaging and memorable experience than more traditional ways of telling stories.

THEATRE

Theatre is another way to tell stories that give context, clarity and meaning. Powerful theatre can help people to connect to messages in a deeper and more emotive way. Role-playing and professional theatre are particularly useful in environments where literacy is not high. In the mining communities in Africa, health and safety has been an issue in the past. When addressing this, one large diamond-mining group used theatre to help tell the story of behaviour change that was required to improve the working environment and safety for all involved. People were able to connect and take action as a result in a way that would not have been achieved via written communication.

Often, theatre and metaphor can be linked – a number of companies specialise in using Shakespearean plays to tackle significant issues within teams and organisations. Seeing Richard III's treatment of his brothers played out can give rise to interesting conversations about team dynamics.

IMAGES

Visual images that tell the story are a powerful way to communicate with teams. In Chapter 5, the picture on a jigsaw puzzle lid was mentioned as a way to help people to understand organisational direction. If visuals like this exist at a macro level, a manager can use them to set the context for dialogue with his team.

You could consider asking your team to find images that represent their understanding of the message and what it means to them, or drawing your own set of images that best tell the story from your own perspective.

COMEDY

Comic strips, sketches and skits are often used to help bring messages to life and ensure people really understand them. In some organisations, comedy is confined to after-dinner events. In others, leaders who have the confidence to use it will do so extensively.

Humour connects with individuals in a unique way. I know of advertising agencies that annually attend the Edinburgh Fringe for inspiration, and communication professionals who have taken novel approaches from comedians to use in their work.

HIGHLIGHT AND CELEBRATE SUCCESS, MILESTONES AND THE JOURNEY

In her role as Storyteller, the manager must keep the conversation about progress and success alive. Telling the story about direction or progress is not a one-off requirement in most cases, so the manager needs to keep people in engaged in understanding progress. If time passes without progress to report, it's important for the organisation – and particularly managers – to state that there is no news to share, and why. In too many cases, huge effort goes into launching the story at the beginning of a new initiative, and then silence follows. The organisation, leaders and managers lose credibility simply because they haven't said: 'We are working hard on the original plan, and will continue to do so. We don't have any concrete news to share right now, but expect to have an update by …'.

When success happens or examples of desired behaviours that show values in action are evident, be sure to recognise those moments and explain why they are worthy of a mention.

PROVIDE CONTEXT WHEN THE JOURNEY CHANGES

It's perfectly normal for the journey to change as an organisation progresses towards its vision. Market dynamics often cause the need for a modification to the course that a company needs to navigate. Sometimes, these changes are minor. In other cases, they are significant. Whatever the extreme, it's vital that managers give context when the journey changes, by sharing why and how. If you find that you don't know the reasons or the detail, then make it your business to find out. In some cases, it may be that members of your team are closer to the rationale than you. For example, it may be that one of them is working on the project that has resulted in the change. If this is the case, embrace that individual and ask them to help you provide the context for the wider team.

Often, managers will shy away from explaining why the journey has changed because they feel they will lose credibility among their team or they don't feel furnished with the right level of detail to share with their people. However, a manager who doesn't give context and regular insight to any changes to the journey risks losing momentum and performance.

USE COMMUNICATION CHANNELS AND TECHNOLOGY THAT ARE EFFECTIVE FOR YOU

With a strong and well-prepared story, the manager can engage his people by helping them create meaning about what's going on around them. However, he must also excel in the way he shares the story to fuel performance fully.

There are two main considerations when choosing an effective communication channel for the story:

1. What is my personal preference of communication style?
2. What is the most appropriate communication channel for sharing and conversing around the message(s)?

YOUR PERSONAL PREFERENCE OF COMMUNICATION STYLE

All people managers are responsible for motivating and fuelling their people to perform, and if you're a competent manager, you'll be confident in most options available to you. However, it's likely you will have a preferred style, and if possible, it's worth using that because you will be more confident and comfortable – and thus more likely to be engaging. Playing to your strengths is a good starting point as a manager.

A senior leader in Logica who has a speech impediment has a senior role and a large responsibility to ensure his people perform well and in the areas that align with the company direction. He has recognised that his strength is written communication, so uses this to communicate with people effectively, rather than expending huge effort on spoken formats that suit him less well.

Kirstin Furber is currently Senior Vice President and Head of Human Resources at BBC Worldwide. She remembers a leader from a previous role:

> *Earlier in my career, I worked in a publishing company with an incredibly strong CEO. He was a great leader but wasn't keen on large town hall events or big face-to-face interventions. His personality preference just didn't lend itself to such public events. This didn't mean he wasn't accessible. He'd spend lots of time with people one-to-one and was highly approachable. However, he recognised and played to his strengths. He was one of the few people I've met who was very effective in his use of email to motivate people. He used it in a targeted way and articulated his message to the right people at the right time.*

For shy managers, it may be necessary for them to push beyond their comfort zone and tell the story in ways that aren't their personal preference. If this sounds familiar, consider what would work for you and whether there is development available to stretch you into new communication methods and styles. Remember: a strength over-used will become a weakness.

APPROPRIATE CHANNELS TO TELL THE STORY

A plethora of channels exist to convey your story. Great engagers will consider and use the appropriate communication channel. Different channels will be suitable at varying times, depending on the level of urgency, dialogue and concern it may cause for your team.

There is no substitute for face-to-face dialogue when trying to engage with people, particularly when trying to create a change in behaviour. Technology has a role to play in enabling dialogue, and the latest developments in videoconferencing certainly provide some interesting options for managers operating across large geographical areas. However, they don't replace real-time, real-place, face-to-face interaction. The practical solution is to use face-to-face as much as possible, and supplement this with technologies – but it is vital to use them well.

The 5I Model in Figure 13.2 is a good place to start when considering the most appropriate channel to use. Each organisation is different, so start by drawing up your own version that contains all the options available to you. This will then provide a useful reference to use when considering the type of communication required for the story.

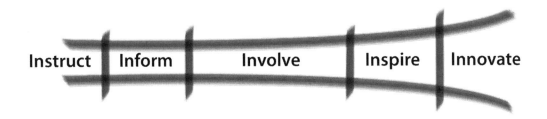

Figure 13.2 The 5I Model

At the base level, there may be occasions when an instruction is needed to ensure that legislation compliance occurs in line with the company story. In these cases, the level of context and dialogue is likely to be lower than in cases where imagining and inspiring to create and innovate are needed. In these situations, the appropriate types of channels are more one-way communication devices rather than engaging methods that allow for conversing, motivation and generating buy-in.

As the aim of sharing the story moves towards a desire to inspire others and create imaginative action, more interactive communication channels can be called upon that are likely to go beyond simple communication to achieve engagement. This is similar to the Four-stage Model of Engagement described in Chapter 4, where the level of time and effort required from managers and leaders is higher depending on the richness of outcome desired. This means that the type of method used to engage people in the story to inspire and create innovative action is likely to take more time and energy than an instruction sent by email at the base level.

The base two levels of 'instruct' and 'inform' should be part of a manager's role, even at a basic competency, and are not truly a part of the Storyteller role in engagement. The Storyteller component of being a manager is to create context and clarity more broadly once the Prophet has used the appropriate means to plant the vision. Thus, the appropriate channels are audio conferencing, team huddles for impromptu dialogue, team meetings with an agenda that facilitates significant dialogue, team lunches, roundtables and managing by walking about, where informal updates and dialogue about what the story means to smaller groups can take place. It's good practice to forward newsletters or bulletins to a team with some commentary about 'what it means for us' and a request to consider the content in advance of discussion if it has the potential to influence daily work or focus.

For managers with teams spread across multiple sites, regular updates to the story are often more challenging, and are conveyed via email rather than face-to-face. This tends to make them more rational than emotionally charged. While working across time zones and languages does cause difficulties, a manager who truly engages his team will make time to hold regular telephone or videoconference dialogues with small groups and individuals. With the cost of travel increasing, it's often hard for managers to justify regular trips to disparate teams. However, the need for real-time face-to-face dialogue has never been more pressing than in a world where engagement makes the difference between average and soaring business performance.

TAKE ACCOUNT OF CROSS-CULTURAL NUANCES

Increasingly, managers have teams that are spread across different geographical regions or company cultures. A manager in headquarters may be responsible for managing teams in multiple locations where the cultures are very different. In other organisations where joint ventures are common, a manager may be managing teams that have multiple reporting lines and different organisational cultures.

Such cultural differences can create challenges for managers if they aren't accustomed to working with the nuances of culture or where there are time pressures that mean day-to-day management is largely done remotely. In the role of Storyteller, managers need to consider the different cultural make-up of their teams and how to best frame and communicate their messages. If English isn't the first language for some of your team, choose the words you use appropriately. Bear in mind that simple language will be more likely to build understanding than complexity, but be careful to strike the right balance and avoid insulting others by using language that's too simple and may appear dumbed-down. A great skill for the Storyteller to develop is to take the complex and make it simple.

CHECK THAT THE STORY IS BEING UNDERSTOOD AND INTERNALISED

An engaging manager will regularly check that the message is being understood and internalised. He will do this both formally and informally. After larger communication events a powerful but simple method is to ask individuals and teams 'What did you understand from today ...?' During dialogues, ask:

- What excites you about what you have heard?
- What questions does it raise for you?
- What considerations or actions does it raise for us?
- How would you describe what you have heard to your family?

It's also important to be sensitive to different cultural behaviours when thinking about whether messages have been understood. It's difficult in some cases to know whether your team is fully engaged or simply paying lip service. For example, I worked with one client where teams were based in the UK and India. The UK teams identified a huge source of frustration where the Indian team members would frequently say 'yes' when asked if they could meet deadlines. They *wanted* to achieve them, and so were optimistic even when they knew that the reality was that it was unlikely to happen. The UK team members wanted more realism and honesty because they were losing trust in their colleagues. Understanding more about cultural heritage and drivers helped both teams to identify how to work together more effectively, taking into account cultural nuance – in this case, the preference not to say 'no' in the particular Indian culture.

From the Perspective of All (the Organisation)

The manager as Storyteller can contribute to the wider engagement levels in an organisation and use stories to engage specific stakeholders by doing the following:

- Share the story and what it means for you.
- Share successes – in context.

SHARE THE STORY AND WHAT IT MEANS FOR YOU

Managers can contribute to the wider organisation by using the same techniques as on the 'us' and 'you' levels referred to earlier. For example, if leading a change, the manager may need to colour-in the story for other key stakeholders beyond the immediate team.

Consider how you can tell the story to each of your stakeholders in the wider organisation.

With matrix reporting lines, similar techniques can be used and tailored to the needs of the group. During late 2011, Sony Professional Solutions Europe continued communicating its new transformation strategy to its Change Leadership Group. During two days off-site, the forty people were taken through each element of its strategy in an experiential and thought-provoking way. The leadership team members told their stories about how they wanted to feel when the transformation goals were reached. The big picture shown in Figure 5.4 was used to represent the journey they were on, and members of the entire group were involved in discussions, creative sessions and asked to consider action they would take if they had ownership after a management buy-out.

The group was tasked with leading the change. A first step was to tell the story to their teams and engage them in the direction needed. Val Elliott and John Cooper are leaders in the Service Division, and arranged a two-day session with the managers directly reporting to them. The group included country leaders from across Europe who needed to take the story and engage their people in it. Those country leaders were critical to making the desired change happen. Val Elliott, Head of Commercial Engineering at Sony Europe, explained:

> We recognised that we needed to share ownership with our management team and let them own the story. We knew we wouldn't change behaviour if we simply went with them to their teams and ran a session telling them what they should do, so we asked the managers how they wanted to take the journey to their teams and how we could best support them. The country leader in each area decided they wanted to take responsibility for engaging their people and that they would use John and Val to take European-wide questions on the day. Some of the individuals had never done this type of work before. We were asking them to take ownership of complex and difficult messages. But they really stepped up and forced themselves to understand everything we wanted to communicate. They created their own stories and really owned them.

The feedback to Val and John after the events was that the experience of owning, telling and keeping the story alive had stretched individuals and helped them to develop. Their teams responded extremely well, and are now working as part of a transformational change in the organisation.

SHARE SUCCESSES – IN CONTEXT

When managing stakeholders across the wider organisation, a manager will find he is more successful if he is trusted and has a track record of delivery. This means living the components of trust; humility, consistency and honesty across all areas of the organisation. It also means sharing stories of success and the learning from failure.

Innovation is a buzzword of this decade, but many experts say that organisations need to improve at valuing failure. In the majority of environments, people don't want to be known for failing because it carries negative connotations. However, leaps forward are often made as a result of trying something new and being curious about why it didn't work quite the way intended. Accepting failure is a humbling experience – 'humbling' literally means 'back to earth', and can be seen as a positive step from which to re-start.

Thomas Edison was renowned for embracing failure – he saw every one as narrowing down the possibilities for success. In creating the light bulb, Edison tried 6,000 different types of vegetable growth before hitting on success.

In the role of Storyteller, managers need to share stories of their success and their insights from failure. Sharing stories does not mean bragging about success and being 'big me/little you'. The way you share the story has to be embracing and with a stated intention.

This means sharing insight through traditional channels in the organisation wherever possible – for example, through newsletters, intranet features, company meetings, and recognition and award schemes. It also means telling stories in a one-to-one setting with key stakeholders – for example, emailing an individual to say: 'I thought you'd be interested to know that we've just crossed a key milestone that's going to make it easier for your team to do …'.

As a Storyteller, you are responsible for helping others see the story as *their* story. This helps them see the company as *their* company. If you do this successfully, it will be your role to encourage others to share their news of success, rather than your being the person who authors the article or is recognised in the annual kick-off meeting. Your role is to ensure that stories are shared with the right intention. This might be sharing a story to influence the way stakeholders feel about you, your team or your project. It might be to show proof-points of success to demonstrate that the journey is continuing. Or it could be more about sharing best practice knowledge to increase the likelihood of wider success in the organisation. Being clear about your intention in sharing stories will increase your chances of positioning them correctly without the risk of being perceived as bragging.

14 *The Strategist*

The Strategist part of a manager's role in engagement for performance concerns building the plans to engage their people. Inspiring others, telling the organisational story, coaching for performance and guiding individuals are all critical for high engagement. However, a significant element of planning and strategy is also required to ensure the passion and energy has direction, boundaries and targets.

To be a successful Strategist, a manager needs to develop the following aptitudes:

- an eye for detail
- big-picture thinking
- execution
- alignment of people and outcomes
- practicality
- acting in measured ways

Table 14.1 The Strategist

	I (me)	You (my colleague)	Us (our team)	All (the organisation)
The Strategist (L) Identifies the approaches and builds the plans to engage	– Own the plan (for what's happening). – Build your plan to maintain engagement levels. – Take responsibility for your own career plan.	– Develop and retain talent. – Identify talent and build a strategy to manage those individuals. – Build talent-retention strategies. – Delegate to give others opportunities. – Give high-performance talent access and freedom. – Create compelling objectives and development plans for all. – Develop appropriate working patterns for individuals to be most productive. – Welcome and integrate new members of the team. – Recruit with emotional intelligence and the culture/values at heart.	– Share ownership. – Keep the team focused. – Build a crew to navigate to the future.	– Extend ownership. – Plan wider stakeholder management.

From the Perspective of I (Me)

The starting point for a manager as Strategist is from her own perspective, by owning the plan for what is needed to achieve strong engagement. Ownership is vital; poor engagers assume that it's the organisation's or someone else's responsibility to ensure people are fully engaged and fuelled to perform. For a manager, this means:

- Build your plan to maintain engagement levels.
- Take responsibility for your own career plan.

BUILD YOUR PLAN TO MAINTAIN ENGAGEMENT LEVELS

We observed earlier that a manager will find it difficult to engage others successfully if she's not engaged herself. A manager who doesn't feel fully engaged needs to start by building a plan to increase her own engagement levels. Much of this involves taking the components of other roles, such as the Prophet (being clear on personal purpose and how your work aligns with it), the Storyteller (finding out more about direction), the Coach (having the fuel to engage yourself and others) and the Pilot (working with/on personal style), and formulating a plan to play each role to the full.

The creation and/or execution of the plan may involve discussions with your own manager, other leaders, external coaches and mentors. This often feels like a luxury for individual managers who are under huge pressure to deliver. However, having a personal engagement strategy will mean that you're more likely to take action to keep your levels of performance high. Without it, it's left to chance and good intentions.

Organisations that take this very seriously will ensure that manager support includes elements to build an engagement strategy in their personal objectives, keeping them focused on their own engagement levels, as well as those of their teams.

TAKE RESPONSIBILITY FOR YOUR OWN CAREER PLAN

In Part I of this book, we discussed the importance of career and development as factors leading to high engagement levels and organisational performance. Having a clear career plan can be extremely motivating, but not having a career plan can be even more demotivating.

In large organisations, it's easy to expect your manager or human resources department to sort out a career plan for individuals. However, the reality is that it's each person's own responsibility to develop their own career plan and then seek support to make it happen. For a manager, it's important to remember: 'I am in control of my own destiny.'

This doesn't mean that a manager must go off and sit in a separate room to create her career plan. She may spend time talking to her own line manager, other senior leaders or consulting the Wow Factor Journal we drew up when talking about the Prophet in Chapter 12. Each of these may give input to a career plan and direction.

In many organisations, people say that they don't receive enough help from their bosses to develop career plans. This is sadly the case in many companies where engagement levels could be better. However, when a manager requests help and is very specific about what she needs, it's often surprising how much support becomes available. Many bosses haven't had great career development coaching themselves and aren't clear how they can help others. For a manager to gain support, she needs to be specific in her requests so that she helps her manager to help her:

1. Ask for time to talk about your career development plan – say how much time you would like, where and when. Ask if they are happy to do this if you send a meeting request and an idea of the areas you'd like to talk about.
2. Think about some questions and give them to your manager in advance – 'What do you see as potential opportunities for me in the future?' 'Where do you feel I have a particularly strong contribution to make?' 'Where could the company best utilise my skills and competencies?' 'Where do you feel there might be opportunities to grow?'

'Who do you know within or outside the organisation who might be able to help me think about my longer-term career development?'

3. Explain that you'd also like to talk about succession planning for your role so that you are developing the right people for the future.

If you have a clear idea about what your career path could look like, it's worth considering how you can explore potential options further using your network. For example, an executive assistant who would like to advance to Chief Operating Officer (COO) can look at her own network and those of board members from her organisation to find individuals and request time over a coffee to talk about their roles as COO. What do they like about it, what challenges do they face regularly, how did they progress through their career to reach COO, what skills and experience has been crucial for them, or do they wish they had developed earlier? As human beings, we love to talk about ourselves, so it's often easier than we think to secure time to talk with others who can help us define our future career path.

With any career development planning, managers do well to remember that they are also responsible for finding and nurturing their successor. A great career plan may never become a reality if an outstanding successor isn't ready to take over and let you have the space to move on.

Simon Ashby believes that it's the role of a manager to make it easy to pluck her out and put her another great role: 'It's important for every line manager to have a successor so that if they are considered for another role, the company isn't anxious about that area of the business being without strong management.' Consider yourself: do you have a successor, and is this seen within your organisation as a positive factor in enabling you to move to your next desired role? If not, what action do you need to take to identify and develop one and highlight what this means for you?

From the Perspective of You (My Colleague)

In the role of Strategist, a manager must develop and retain his key talent. As we've covered earlier, career development and seeing a future with the organisation is a clear factor in engagement. People who see a future and career with their company are likely to be investors rather than savers. It's therefore important for a manager to spend time and energy in one-to-one exchanges with his people to talk about them, their needs, their performance and their future.

Working with 'you' is the biggest component of the role of manager as Strategist, and includes the following:

- Identify talent and build talent-retention strategies.
- Delegate to give others opportunities.
- Give high-performance talent access and freedom.
- Create compelling objectives and development plans for all.
- Develop appropriate working patterns for individuals to be most productive.
- Welcome and integrate new members of the team.
- Recruit with emotional intelligence and the culture/values at heart.

IDENTIFY TALENT AND BUILD TALENT-RETENTION STRATEGIES

Many organisations lead talent management strategy work from a central leadership and development team, so it may be that managers are asked to feed into a bigger, more formal process. This is valuable if it's done well because it means you can identify people you believe are key talent for the organisation, and then be sure the investment is available to grow and retain them. However, even where large-scale talent development programmes exist, it's still the line manager's responsibility to ensure they retain them day-to-day. Retention is influenced by many of the factors outlined in the following pages.

Managers working in organisations where the talent strategy is not centralised or is left as the line managers' responsibility will need to take more ownership to identify talent and plan development and retention strategies. There are many ways this can be done, and one process is discussed in Part III.

Identify strategic talent

A manager will often be asked to identify those individuals who have the most capacity and capability to grow further; to step up at least two levels within the organisation at some point in the future and who are strategically important for the company to retain. It's worth considering hard skills, but also attitude and emotional intelligence at this point. This is unlikely to be a large proportion of people. In a small team, there may be only one or two people. It may even be that you don't have anyone you feel is strategic talent in your team when comparing them with individuals in other areas. The organisation's talent identification process will give you a guide about the criteria. Often there are different levels, such as senior leaders, middle leaders and potential leaders of the future. Be sure not to ignore your emerging talent. They may be more junior at the moment, but you may spot great potential in individuals that is worth harnessing, both for the benefit of the organisation and to increase their engagement levels.

Identify operational talent

Strategic talent aren't the only people it's important to develop and retain. There will also be people within the organisation who are operationally important to the business and excel at their roles. These are the people who 'keep the lights on' each day and without whom the organisation wouldn't succeed. Operational talent also need to be developed and retained, but they may need different approaches compared to the more fluid strategic talent, as they often don't want to move up the hierarchy. Other retention strategies such as flexible working (which we will discuss later) may be more appropriate for these individuals.

It's rare for a centralised talent strategy to include operational talent. The focus is usually on developing the leaders of the future. Therefore, line managers need to take on the responsibility of identifying operational talent, and putting together development plans and retention strategies accordingly.

It's important to note at this point that if a member of staff isn't strategic or operational talent, this doesn't mean that the organisation won't want to develop and retain them. All employees need development plans to help boost levels of engagement, but strategic talent will have more extensive ones with access to other senior people.

The managers' first aim is to ensure that any strategic and operational talent are investors, not simply savers. However, they also need to identify how they can develop and retain those other members of their team who are important to effective delivery of the goals.

There are broadly three types of development plans that influence engagement levels, and thus performance:

1. career development plans that identify what is required by individuals from their organisation or manager to move forward;
2. career development plans that identify what is required by individuals and the organisation to expand or enrich current roles or positions;
3. development and fulfilment plans for those individuals who are happy to stay in their current roles but want to stay engaged.

Strategic talent require the first type of career development plan. Many organisations will have formal processes for holding such conversations with team members. If your organisation doesn't have something that works for you, you might like to explore my tried and tested approach illustrated in Figure 14.1.

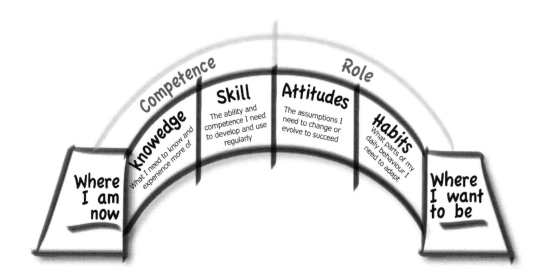

Figure 14.1 The Talent Bridge
Source: Copyright Northern Flight UK Ltd and reproduced with kind permission.

Start on the left-hand side of the model and think about where you are today. What are your strengths, what are you known for in the business, and how would you articulate your role, responsibilities and outcomes?

Next, think about the other side of the bridge. Where do you want to be when you take your next big leap in your career? What does it look like? Use a similar framework to the 'today' thinking, in terms of role, strengths and outcomes.

To reach the other side of the bridge, consider what knowledge, skills, attitudes and habits you need to develop, enhance or change:

- **Knowledge** – the new things you will have to learn, understand and interpret into useable information;
- **Skills** – what you will need to become good at, including practical aspects such as financial acumen, people management, delegation and so on;
- **Attitudes** – what opinions, attitudes and assumptions you will need to change, about yourself, about others, and about what is possible;
- **Habits** – the new processes and behaviours you will need to practise until they become unconscious actions for you.

As you work through this exploration, note the needs you identify. These should not be solutions, such as 'I need coaching.' Aim to articulate what you are looking to build, such as 'I need to see different functions of the business working in more detail,' or 'I have to be better at managing my own energy and passion.'

With those needs in mind, work through specific actions that you need to take, and capture them. These could be training, experience, coaching, development or learning elements.

Talent-retention is necessary not just because individuals' experience is lost when they leave the organisation, but also the networks and knowledge they hold. If one person leaves, it's not just that 'cog' in the machine that goes, it's like losing a part of the machine that includes the connecting wires and fuel. Thus, a manager must ensure she focuses on retention strategies for good workers and always keeps them engaged.

Effective talent-retention strategies that are part of the engagement process take and use knowledge about an individual's purpose and drivers. That means that you'll need to draw on your insight from your role as the Coach about what makes the heart beat to identify possible ways to retain individuals. This takes time and recognition that the action required to retain each employee is likely to be different. What works as a retention strategy for one person may not be appropriate for another. For example, for a person that has a high desire to make more of an impact in the community, a retention lever might involve giving them the chance to participate in a specific programme during company time once a month.

Kirstin Furber is currently researching the role of women in future workplaces and speaks at conferences around the world. She's uncovered that, increasingly, young women aren't ambitious for the top job in the boardroom:

> I'm finding that women talk more about wanting to do interesting work but also have a balance with other interests in their lives too. This doesn't mean their contribution will be less but it will require a different style of management to keep them engaged in the future.

This could be viewed as a double-edged sword – on the one hand, organisations lose the motivation of career progression to get the best out of colleagues, but on the other, it diminishes the background thought for many of: 'How would doing this further my career?'

In other cases, you may find that a team has similar needs and drivers. In these cases, you may be able to work with the wider organisation to give your people access to other programmes that will help to retain them. For example, at the MGM Resorts International's Circus Circus property in Las Vegas, leaders recognised that the children of many employees were about to enter college education. The property's Diversity Council created the Junior Executive Training programme (JET) to help the children learn life skills: how to interview for jobs, and how to apply for scholarships. At the conclusion of the nine-month programme, the parents were invited to a graduation ceremony. Debra Nelson, Vice President of Diversity at MGM Resorts explained: 'The pride in the room was incredible. We were investing in our potential workforce of tomorrow and creating pride among our employees today.' By understanding what was important to its employees, the company was able to develop a more loyal and engaged workforce.

At Innocent, performance management and career development are both treated incredibly seriously. Jo Huddie explained:

> Development chats happen with managers outside of their operational day-to-day, one-to-one meetings. We ask every manager to hold regular development conversations with their people to talk about their learning and career direction. This is not directly linked to our review process. We believe that there needs to be a separate development chat so that it's not clouded by a more tactical objectives conversation. We support managers by training how to hold these dialogues effectively.

With great talent, it's natural to have a desire to hold onto them. Watch for that tendency – the danger is that you may stifle and lose them, and so will the organisation. Be willing to set great talent free elsewhere in the company.

DELEGATE TO GIVE OTHERS OPPORTUNITIES

Delegation is a must for managers if they are to grow their people and ensure high performance. Managers who don't delegate are not only managing an impossibly large workload, but also run the risk of restricting opportunities for those they manage to broaden their skills and thus be more valuable to the organisation.

Look at how you can give your people more space to thrive and grow. Delegate and give people the opportunity to learn and experience new work. Give people the freedom to carry out their work in the way that best suits them without being micromanaged. We all have different working style preferences, and great managers give their people the freedom to work in the way that means they can deliver most effectively. This might mean providing a quiet corner of the office for some, or allowing time to work at home or off-site for others. Be the Pilot (covered in Chapter 16) and find ways to trust individuals. Be the Coach (covered in Chapter 15) and identify with your people how they work best and prefer working. Contract between yourselves that you are happy to be flexible to allow for individual working styles, but that objectives will obviously need to be delivered.

Liz Wiseman and Greg McKeown (2010) talk about two different types of leaders: multipliers and diminishers. Multipliers engage their people by involving them, challenging them and giving them confidence to address seemingly insurmountable problems. They help their teams see blocks as puzzles to solve, rather than expending negative energy moaning about the problems ahead.

A diminisher creates an environment that suppresses people's thinking and is much more command and control-oriented.

Be a manager who is a multiplier, not a diminisher. Managers who engage their people successfully are more likely to encourage and breed innovation. It's innovation that will often result in competitive advantage and a more inspiring place to work.

If a manager is a multiplier, she is much more likely to achieve high performance through the creation of an increased number of investors. If a manager is a diminisher, savers will be what he has – at best.

Becoming a multiplier rather than diminisher will result if a manager is successfully moving between each of the five roles of manager as Culture Builder and engager. The type of positive language used as a Pilot will help others to see challenges, rather than problems. The Coach will help individuals to find solutions to issues, rather than giving them the answer.

GIVE HIGH-PERFORMANCE TALENT ACCESS AND FREEDOM

High-performing people will need different growth and retention strategies from others. These are people who have the potential to be extremely engaged and deliver great results for the business. However, they are also usually more demanding, and may have higher levels of competence than you, their manager. Embracing this is vital, and is discussed further in Chapter 15 on the manager's role as Coach. However, it's also important that as a Strategist, you give high-performance individuals access to senior staff and the freedom to run projects without being micromanaged. High performers expect more freedom and will be motivated by the chance to work across hierarchy. You have a choice between embracing this and keeping engagement levels high, or suppressing it and watching great talent move on.

CREATE COMPELLING OBJECTIVES AND DEVELOPMENT PLANS FOR ALL

As a Strategist, a manager needs to create compelling objectives linked to business goals so that employees see exactly how their work and performance contribute directly to the overall story, strategy and values in action. Great managers will share the story and then discuss on a one-to-one level with each employee how they feel they can best contribute in their role. They will then agree objectives that are specific, measurable, achievable, realistic and timely. They will also include personal objectives that are in tune with what gives an individual meaning and significance.

Once objectives are set, it's vital that managers meet regularly with their people to talk about progress and whether objectives need to change in line with the journey altering. They also need to have development discussions so that each individual has the best opportunity to meet and exceed their objectives.

High-performing individuals have a high degree of certainty about their direction and what is required of them. Their managers, through development, mentoring and coaching opportunities, actively support them.

ENCOURAGE APPROPRIATE WORKING PATTERNS FOR INDIVIDUALS TO BE MOST PRODUCTIVE

Once you have understood what makes an individual's heart beat, you will have a clearer idea about how working patterns can be used to enable maximum productivity.

Treating each person in your team as an individual will allow you to consider strategies to retain people, such as flexible working for those with families. Roy White, General Manager of Global Sales and Marketing Human Resources at Sony, is a strong believer that great people can be retained and perform incredibly well if they are allowed flexibility. He is an advocate of part-time working, home working and sabbaticals as ways to retain key talent – in particular women. Roy says that he would rather have amazing talent delivering on a four-day-week basis than average performance across five days. He's also seen that there are much higher engagement and loyalty levels from those individuals who are given flexible working opportunities because they appreciate that the result is a more balanced life. They are therefore able to give more to their work.

Top Tip

Find the levers that engage employees and maximise their strengths. Understand each of your team members; their strengths and what makes them feel valued. If you manage someone who has a family and struggles to spend quality time with them, give extra time off for a sports day or concert as a way of recognising their contribution and retaining them.

Some managers shy away from treating each person as an individual and giving some people more freedom than others. They worry that it will cause inequality and questions concerning fairness. The solution is simply to spend the time communicating with each member one-to-one so that each individual understands that you are empowering them to work at their best and each of them has different needs. The golden rule is to be explicit, and not to try to make excuses or come to secret agreements.

WELCOME AND INTEGRATE NEW MEMBERS OF THE TEAM

When new team members arrive, a manager has a small window of opportunity to ensure that they are integrated effectively and positively. If this doesn't happen, productivity is lost and engagement levels rapidly drop.

There are some simple actions that make a big difference to any new team member who is joining you:

- Send a welcome pack in advance of their joining – include a handwritten letter saying how excited you are that they are joining your team and that you look forward to seeing them on their first day.
- Involve them in any team social activities before joining, so that the individual has had a chance to meet others socially.
- Implement a buddy system in your team, where one person is assigned to look after the new team member for the first month. This helps the new recruit to integrate and get up to speed quickly. The relationship often lasts well beyond the first month, and

buddies will remain in contact, giving each other support, until much later in their careers.

- Book time in your diary to personally introduce the new person to key people in the business and your team on their first day. Follow the example outlined on page 163, where Steve Thorn at Logica doesn't just introduce colleagues by name, but also explains why they are critical to the business.
- Ensure that new team members are booked on formal induction programmes to help them understand the purpose, direction and culture. Book a couple of hours with them during their first week so that you can tell them your story. Ask a colleague in the team to spend time sharing their story (as mentioned in the discussion of the Storyteller role in Chapter 13) to help them internalise and own the story themselves.
- Set performance objectives within the first sixty days of arrival. Ideally, you will set objectives within the first few weeks so that it's clear where attention and focus should be placed. However, in some cases it's better to wait a few weeks before finalising them, because your new recruit may have fresh ideas that will add more value to their role and your team.

RECRUIT WITH EMOTIONAL INTELLIGENCE AND THE CULTURE/VALUES AT HEART

The manager as Strategist will devote appropriate levels of energy to the recruitment process for new members of her team. She understands that when interviewing and reviewing possible candidates, she is looking for more than sheer competency. She will also want to ensure that new recruits and have the right emotional intelligence to fit within her team and that their working style, personality preference and values will allow them to perform their best within the organisation.

Ensuring the right cultural fit is critical. Without it, individuals will end up being disengaged and perform poorly.

To explore values and cultural fit during initial interviews, try asking the following:

- What working environment would enable you to work at your best?
- What prevents your performing at your best?
- Describe your ideal working day – what would it involve, and what would you prefer to avoid?
- What do you look for in a business and culture?
- What do you value about your working life at your current employer – what have you particularly enjoyed, and what elements of its culture have disappointed you or are not a good match for you?

From the Perspective of Us (our Team)

At a team level, the role of Strategist involves ensuring shared ownership for delivering objectives, plans and goals. It means that the manager as Culture Builder and engager has a responsibility to:

- Keep the team focused.
- Build a crew to navigate to the future.

KEEP THE TEAM FOCUSED

The power of focus is often hugely underestimated in organisations. Lack of focus means that teams risk directing energy into areas that aren't a priority to deliver the goals set. Even highly engaged teams can be unproductive if they aren't focused; because their energy, motivation and passion aren't being channelled appropriately to deliver incredible results.

In his role as Strategist, the manager must keep his team focused, harnessing the passion that exists to reach organisational goals. The importance of this cannot be underestimated. A manager can get everything else right and have an extremely engaged and high-performing team, but if that performance creates loose cannons rather than focused team members, the good work will be wasted.

Keeping teams focused means constantly enquiring how members are doing and who is owning which element of the team's responsibilities. It means always having a clear purpose for team meetings, even if that purpose is free-flowing discussion.

Focus comes from driving teams to prioritise the highest-value work, rather than the quick fixes that will give instant gratification. A manager can maintain this focus by having a regular agenda item at team meetings to discuss current projects and milestones and facilitate dialogue about which areas will give highest value to the organisation. A manager best focuses his team by getting them to share ownership of prioritisation of high-value activities, not by telling them what to focus on. After regularly questioning which areas the team is working on/could be working on that would give most long-term value to the company, individuals will start to naturally ask themselves that question, and the team will become better at taking ownership and staying focused.

In their book *The Power of Full Engagement*, Jim Loehr and Tony Schwartz (2003) talk about the technique of 90-minute sprints of focus. Our body works in rhythms, and if we can tune into these, we can be much more productive. In my work with The Energy Project, I helped many teams become more focused by using this principle. The Energy Project also teaches people to remove distractions so they are able to be more focused. Being in control of email and turning it off when you need to concentrate on a task is another technique widely used by people who have experienced the work of Schwartz and his team.

Examples of techniques to drive focus that have been used successfully by teams with which I've worked include the following:

- Meetings should be no longer than 90 minutes – or 90 minutes and then a decent break.

- Remove distractions from meetings by shutting down email and banning laptops and mobile communication devices.
- Manage pace, ensuring meetings are not monotonous.

Managers also need to make teams accountable for their success and to provide an environment where it is safe to challenge and support each other.

Stuart Fletcher, former President International at Diageo, invited his coaches to each leadership team meeting to ensure that he had observation-based coaching input and that he and his colleagues were stretched and challenged and remained focused on breakthrough strategy delivery. Coaches participated rather than facilitated, and brought new concepts; coaching in the moment. Their presence and contribution helped to grow the capabilities of individuals, keeping them focused and accountable. Stuart feels that this was an extraordinary partnership, and one that was critical to success. He was still the driver and owner of the meetings and set direction, but he was open to the fact that great leaders don't necessarily have all the answers.

BUILD A CREW TO NAVIGATE TO THE FUTURE

Engaged teams have a clear sense of purpose, goals and understanding of how they contribute to the big picture. They work as teams to share ownership of delivering success, and are clear about their strengths and roles to work at their best.

During situations of change, managers must be even more certain that they have a strong crew that knows how to navigate to the future, keep focused and draw on each other's strengths. One practical way to drive such behaviour is to ensure that all members of the team understand the team's objective during change, alongside having individual objectives relating to being effective team players and taking ownership.

From the Perspective of All (the Organisation)

As Strategist, a manager must plan how she will engage other stakeholders beyond her own team. She can also consider approaches to ensure that she makes a wider contribution to increasing the numbers of investors in the entire organisation.

PLAN WIDER STAKEHOLDER MANAGEMENT

Planning wider stakeholder management is important. If you are leading a change programme or initiative on behalf of the organisation, it's even more crucial that you see yourself as responsible for engaging key stakeholders throughout the work. Lack of engagement is a common reason for change programmes failing despite a clear business case being in existence.

According to Ipsos MORI, only 24 per cent of private sector employees believe that change is managed well in their organisations (in the public sector, the proportion is 15 per cent) (cited in MacLeod and Clarke 2009). Therefore, if you are managing a change, it's your responsibility to be in the 24 per cent and play a part in improving that statistic.

Think about a time when you've been affected by change. You'll remember those occasions when you were engaged and felt involved and positive. You'll also remember the times when you were left to flounder and be anxious about what it meant for you. Which environment would you rather create for people?

As a Strategist, it's important to identify who needs to be engaged during change, and why. You can then work through how you will engage people, when, and with what desired outcome. The Stakeholder Mapping Tool in Figure 14.2 can help in this process and assist a manager in planning action.

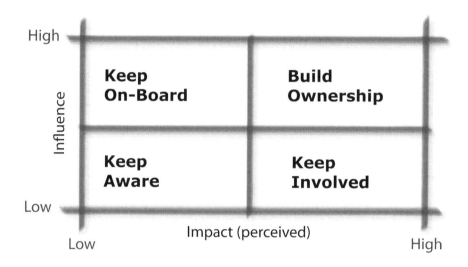

Figure 14.2 The Stakeholder Mapping Tool

1. Identify all key stakeholders who have an interest or who you want to take action to achieve the goals of the programme. This action may be more reactive than proactive, such as 'not to block or stand in the way of success'. Other stakeholders may be more critical in terms of delivering specifics.
2. Once identified, plot the stakeholders onto the stakeholder influence/impact matrix in Figure 14.2. Identify the position for each stakeholder on the matrix now, and where you want them to be in the future.
3. Next, identify how you will engage each stakeholder or stakeholder group – how you can be the Prophet, Storyteller, Strategist, Coach and Pilot to create stakeholder understanding, emotional commitment, and help them see a connection between your project and what gives them meaning. Start with the high-influence/high-impact group. These stakeholders require the most time and energy, but bizarrely, are usually the ones given the least focus. 'The organisation' is often given the most focus (low influence/low impact) because formal communication channels can be utilised with less effort. Work through your plan to engage each person in each quadrant.

For any stakeholders in the high-influence and/or high-impact quadrant, a degree of emotional connection is critical if they are to sustain their interest and take the action you require. The methods for achieving that engagement will vary depending on the individual. For example, if a stakeholder group will need to fundamentally change the way it does things, it will need to be taken on the journey to see how it will benefit and helped to feel consulted and involved in designing the solution. In cases where change is deep and personal, there can be ways to engage some stakeholders by helping them to see that the new world will give them more alignment with what gives them meaning and significance. If it's a stakeholder who needs to give his endorsement to the programme, regular contact and updates that show the benefits in a creative way may be enough.

Once the plan is in place, the Strategist can move to the other four roles of manager as Culture Builder to execute it.

CHAPTER 15 *The Coach*

The role of Coach to engage others centres on getting the best out of people and facilitating team member engagement on the journey to success. It's a very deep and meaningful role, and can unlock overwhelming performance if done well. Coaching can be tackled in a variety of ways – from the simple gutfeel approach to the formal qualification route. For someone who wants to make a career of coaching, the latter is an absolutely necessity. However, for the average manager, the approaches in this chapter will help you take leaps forward in your role as manager as Coach, to a degree that you will have effective approaches in coaching for engagement.

In this chapter, I use the label 'Coach' as a general term for a specific collection of activities that support engagement. To be an excellent Coach, a manager needs to develop the aptitudes to be:

- supportive
- energising
- extrovert (being the energy in the room)
- challenging
- enabling
- creating unity (bringing the team together)

Table 15.1 The Coach

	I (me)	You (my colleague)	Us (our team)	All (the organisation)
The Coach (E/L) Gets the best out of people	– Find the fuel to engage. – Value yourself for growing others. – Understand and work with your strengths. – Make Monday morning the high point of your week. – Take recovery time to improve performance.	– Work with what makes the heart beat. – Use coaching techniques. – Identify what gives individuals meaning and significance. – Identify the personal purposes of your people and create alignment. – Help others to reframe their roles. – Make Monday morning the high point of the week. – Hold appraisals to ensure a high-performance team.	– Nurture team spirit. – Value relationship-building time. – Run social events that are appropriate for the team. – Energise others. – Nurture team spirit among virtual and disparate teams.	– Energise the organisation. – Work with what makes stakeholder hearts beat. – Share when you see an opportunity to help others. – Feed back how colleagues feel.

From the Perspective of I (Me)

As with each of the roles for a manager as Culture Builder, an individual can only be a great Coach if they are fully engaged themselves.

At a personal level, this means a manager must find the fuel to engage people before embarking on coaching-style conversations. Great Coaches have positive energy and leave the other person feeling empowered and fuelled. Poor Coaches sap energy and leave the other person feeling that the glass is half empty. To be fully fuelled in your role as Coach, ensure that you:

- Value yourself for growing others.
- Understand and work with your strengths.
- Make Monday morning the high point of your week.
- Take recovery time to improve performance.

VALUE YOURSELF FOR GROWING OTHERS

As referred to earlier, the starting point for any manager who wants to engage his people is a mindset change to believe that 'my role is about enabling others'. It's as extreme as seeing your role as leader, manager and engager first; implementer of tasks, second.

Sarah Henbrey, Organisational Development Director at 3 and former Organisational Development Director at Sony Europe believes:

A fundamental mindset change is required by middle and line managers; from managing the task to managing the individual. The world has changed. One person can't possibly have all the answers any more so managers need to stop worrying about whether they will lose face if they don't know the answer and instead ask a question.

The challenge here is that this involves managers valuing themselves for enabling others and helping them succeed, rather than for being seen to be worthy of their role in the hierarchy and for having all the knowledge. Essentially, it means managers finding a different way to value themselves and being clear about their identity.

A practical way to help make the shift and keep yourself from deviating is to devise a performance objective that you discuss with your own manager. Make yourself accountable for valuing and growing others. You can do this is by taking on the five roles of the manager as Culture Builder and seeing those as a priority in your working life.

The Manager as Culture Builder Journal

There are a range of different levers that can be pulled to engage people at an organisational level along with the five core roles that a manager must play exceptionally to be a great engager. Our challenge as human beings is that we often forget the obvious or don't use it to our advantage. To keep you focused on the journey, buy a notebook and carry it with you in your bag, pocket or laptop case.

At the end of each day (or beginning of the following day if that's your preference), capture the instances where you took an action associated with one of the five roles of manager as Culture Builder. Note down the action, the impact and how you feel about it.

Keep doing this, and see what emerges. It should help you to see how you devote more time and energy to engagement activity when you see it as the core of your role. It will also happen more naturally if it's at the forefront of your mind because you're checking in with yourself regularly.

We all like to see how far we've developed and how much we've achieved in life, so the Manager as Culture Builder Journal is also a fabulous tool to help you celebrate your success and chart your development. You can use it for self-reflection, but it's also a handy resource to use in preparation for performance reviews and job interviews.

Valuing yourself for growing others may also require a more fundamental mindset or behaviour change.

Stuart Fletcher, former President International, Diageo had a clear personal commitment to make his region's performance fantastic as he started to put his breakthrough strategy in place during 2005. But he quickly recognised that his stand needed to shift to become more about his own breakthrough as a leader, rather than focusing purely on business performance. He explained: 'I knew that, to lead a fantastic business to deliver our strategy, I needed to actively focus on areas that would cause me to lead in the most powerful way.' One area he put his heart and soul into was demonstrating that he cared about others and wanted to enable them to deliver:

My personal stand became: I care so much, I don't care. This was shorthand for the fact I deeply cared about individuals and teams and their performance and I wanted people to be the best they could be but I was inhibited by what people thought about me. Worrying about what people felt about me was getting in the way. So I focused upon taking me out of the equation and being less worried about me, and more about them. In other words I care so much I don't care (what you think of me). The result was that my relationships deepened, my ability to contribute to people increased significantly and together we did amazing things and delivered the performance we needed.

UNDERSTAND AND WORK WITH YOUR STRENGTHS

When talking about the Prophet, we explored the importance of identifying purpose and meaning for oneself. It's also a source of fuel to be clear about strengths and how to best work with them before embarking on too many coaching conversations. Going through this process helps you to think about yourself, but it also prepares you well to go through similar activities with your team members.

There are many formal tools available to help you gain an in-depth view of your strengths and how they manifest themselves.

Alternatively, put aside some time to walk through the park or go for a run and reflect on the questions below.

The My Strengths Tool

- Where am I, and what kind of work am I doing when I'm at my best?
- What kind of work am I doing when I feel most fulfilled and really 'humming'?
- What qualities am I using when I excel?
- What kind of work environment am I at my best within?
- What is my preferred working style? – On my own? With others?
- Do I perform best while advising others or making decisions?
- Am I a detail person or a big-picture type?

Capture your insights and use these to identify your strengths.

Identifying your strengths is the first stage to help fuel yourself and enable you to get the best out of others. You can also consider sharing the same process with your team members and suggesting they complete the same exercise, then share their insights with you during one of your first coaching conversations.

The second area of action is to decide how you can use this knowledge and change the ways you work so that you have more opportunity to play to your strengths and therefore be the best you can be. There may also be development opportunities that you have identified as a result of this exercise that are worth including in your future planning.

MAKE MONDAY MORNING THE HIGH POINT OF YOUR WEEK

The phrase 'Thank God it's Friday' (TGIF) is commonly used in many cultures. It represents our desire to get to the end of the working week and celebrate time out for ourselves. Very often, this is the time when we do what matters most to us in our lives. For some professions, the working week stops on a Friday. For others, it could be a different day, but the sentiment is the same.

For most line managers, it's not as easy to be energised and positive on Mondays as it is on other days. Studies show that Tuesday is the most productive day of the working week. People spend Monday getting back into the spirit of work and refocusing after downtime at the weekend. By Tuesday, they are back at the top of their game. By Friday, they are either exhausted or turning their attention to downtime again.

Imagine if Monday was actually a high point in your week – if you were saying 'TGIM', and not because your home life was so exhausting that coming to work was a rest!

Spend some time considering how you can make it more of a high point. Very often, the secret is in a mindset change that can occur after better alignment is recognised between what gives you meaning in your life and finding ways to achieve that through your daily role. Another practical way to make Monday more of a high point is to schedule meetings and activities that you will enjoy and that allow you to be at your best by drawing on your strengths. Who are the people that energise you most? How can you find ways to spend time with them on a Monday?

Once you have found a way to feel better about Mondays, you can move on to help your people do the same. The result is higher engagement levels and a potential increase in performance at the start of the week.

TAKE RECOVERY TIME TO IMPROVE PERFORMANCE

The need for recovery as human beings is well documented. Great athletes and performers understand the role of recovery in sustaining high performance, as do fabulous leaders.

To be fully fuelled to hold coaching conversations, a manager needs to be in the right frame of mind. He needs to have taken a break from whatever he was doing in a previous meeting, and clear his mind. Coaching involves being in the moment and completely attuned to the other person. This can't happen if a manager is flying from one meeting to another or has a mind that's full and darting around all over the place.

Taking a break before any kind of coaching conversation is absolutely critical, both for you and the individual with whom you are conversing.

From the Perspective of You (My Colleague)

Now fully fuelled as a manager, it's time to work with individuals to find out, and work with, what makes their hearts beat. This part of being a manager as Culture Builder is deep, meaningful and can be exceptionally rewarding. It's about working with drivers of passion. The manager who can identify these drivers in his team and then work out how he can use them to drive individual performance will be promoted very quickly. It's likely he'll also be remembered by the individuals he managed. He'll be mentioned when people ask of others, 'Can you think of a great manager you have worked with during you career?'

As with the Strategist, the main component of the role of Coach is within the context of working one-to-one with others. It involves the following:

- Use coaching techniques.
- Identify what gives individuals meaning and significance.
- Identify the personal purposes of your people and create alignment.
- Help others to reframe their roles.
- Make Monday morning the high point of the week.
- Hold appraisals to ensure a high-performance team.

USE COACHING TECHNIQUES

A coaching conversation has a different structure from a more traditional dialogue between two people. It tends to be more challenging, but with use of positive and inquiring language. The phrase 'ask, don't tell' is commonly used by people when describing the characteristics of a coaching conversation.

Before embarking on coaching-style conversations with individuals, it's useful to have been on the receiving end too. Managers who are good Coaches will often have had their own coach or a leader who was also excellent at holding coaching-style conversations.

Traditional management development doesn't focus upon developing managers' coaching skills, so it's often difficult for them to switch into a coaching style of managing people. It's also hard to understand what a coaching-style conversation looks like if you haven't experienced it yourself. If coaching is new to you, ask for a business coach as part of your career development programme. This will help you to perform even better, and also give you a better understanding about how to unlock more from your people. If the investment isn't available for external coaching, find someone who's a good leader in the organisation and ask if they will coach you for several sessions to get you started. Once you've experienced a coaching relationship, you'll see the possibilities and want to undergo the training to help you embed this way of working as part of your everyday behaviour.

When experiencing coaching-based conversations, you'll notice a number of powerful techniques in action.

Great coaches prepare for their conversations. They allocate plenty of time for the session, consider the location that's most appropriate (for example, off-site rather than in the office), the most effective time of day for the other person, and ask themselves 'Why is this coaching conversation important for me?' before they begin. In short, they get into the right space physically and emotionally.

John Whitmore's GROW model (Whitmore 2005) is used extensively in leadership development programmes across the world. This is an incredibly effective approach because it's easy for managers to remember. However, although a simple acronym helps to make it memorable, it's the power of the inquiries used at each stage that make for great coaching experiences.

One of the most important factors of coaching-style experiences is the ability of a manager to demonstrate active listening. This means really being attuned to the other person and not letting the mind wander.

Be interested: use positive body language rather than sitting with folded arms. Mirror the body language of the other person and be genuinely interested in what they're saying. Maintain plenty of eye contact, but don't stare, as this will put the other party off.

Clarify your understanding of content. Use the power of asking questions and making inquiries to clarify your understanding. Summarise what you have heard, without judgement, to be sure you are interpreting correctly and to demonstrate active listening. Be sure not to cut across people – let them make their point, and above all, don't finish sentences for them.

When they first begin, most people don't find that coaching comes naturally. It's easy to experience an emotional hijack when in a coaching role where the other individual doesn't react in the way you feel they should. Letting yourself enter a negative space doesn't help you or the other person in the long run, so it's vital that you notice it and deal with it before you take action that causes disengagement rather than engagement.

Notice the hijack beginning – a feeling that is in any way negative. Often, we can spot a hijack if we feel a fight or flight emotion – for example, beginning to feel frustrated and angry (fight), or a desire to withdraw or feel disappointed (flight) in reaction to what the other person is saying or doing.

Take a deep breath and imagine hitting the 'pause' button inside you; re-take control of the situation.

Get your optimistic voice to take over and ask yourself what's good about what is happening.

Use your calm voice to ask a question to help buy time and diffuse your emotions.

Your aim as Coach is to be in control, but never to dominate. My belief is that most managers need to strengthen their ability to coach and enable rather than tell and instruct. However, there is an important balance to be struck between the two to achieve the right levels of listening and empowering versus abdicating responsibility. A CEO who listens too much may eventually be asked by his fellow board members to show more leadership. A manager who simply guides and isn't seen to have an opinion will lose credibility. Worse still would be a manager who appointed a high-potential team to run an initiative or change programme and then sat back and let them struggle. Therefore, a balance is necessary, and that relies on the manager sensing when it's most appropriate to guide and coach, and when to take the reins and move into a more authoritative leadership role.

IDENTIFY WHAT GIVES INDIVIDUALS MEANING AND SIGNIFICANCE

Humans are meaning-making and meaning-seeking beings. We try to create meaning in everything we do. It's not surprising, therefore, that to fully engage others we need to help them work out what gives them meaning and significance in their lives. We have to guide them to identify their own purpose.

The need for managers to do this themselves was discussed in Chapter 12 when we explored the role of Prophet. It's in a coaching capacity that managers need to progress the desire by individuals to find their purpose and then work together to create alignment with their role and the organisation. When large numbers of people have such an alignment, the organisation will find that its engagement levels are much higher. More is possible, and a body of investors exists to take the company forward.

Through coaching sessions, a manager can use the same tools with others as he has used himself to identify purpose, meaning and significance. Once this has been done, conversations about how individual purpose aligns to company purpose, direction and values can take place. For some individuals, the connection will be easy for them to spot. For others, it will take a series of questions to help them explore where the dots can be joined up. The reframing exercise explained below is one tool that can help to bring this about.

HELP OTHERS TO REFRAME THEIR ROLES

It's often easy for individuals to see the glass as half empty if they aren't fully engaged in their work. It's also difficult sometimes for people to see how their job plays to their passions and what they care about. Managers in their role as Coach can often help individuals by helping them reframe their job and to see it differently.

As with the other exercises set out in this book, it's a good idea to take yourself through the process of reframing before coaching others through the same approach.

You have the power to reframe your job and to make it feel more meaningful and aligned to your passions in life. The result can be re-energising and motivating, helping you eradicate that Monday morning feeling. This involves redefining your job to incorporate your passions, strengths and values more fully and putting you more in control of your day-to-day work and emotions.

It starts with seeing your job as made up of a series of building blocks that you can reconfigure to create more engaging and fulfilling experiences at work each day (see over, 'The Reframing Tool').

The Reframing Tool

1. Identify the building blocks that make up your job – what are all the components? Try to be as detailed as possible
2. Think about, and capture on paper, your motives, passions and what gives you meaning in life.
3. Go back to the building blocks you have identified and look at how each one gives you an opportunity to use your passion and what gives you meaning in life.
4. Consider what other tasks, responsibilities or relationships you could take on or build to better align with your passions, without changing jobs completely.
5. Pinpoint with whom you need to have a dialogue to make this possible.

The result for you will be a happier and more satisfying job, and thus an ability to manage others even more effectively. You will have role-modelled how to take control and create alignment with your passion. It's a process you can share with your team, either one-to-one through coaching or by giving them the exercise to complete privately. The critical component is that you support any changes they request as a result of the exercise where possible. This means that individuals will feel that they have been given the opportunity to shape their role and take ownership for it, but that their manager is also supporting their success. Actively enabling changes to the job that are requested shows a joint interest in helping the individual to excel.

Working through the reframing process via a coaching approach gives a manager deeper insight to his people. For many managers, it's also a very rewarding process because you're helping someone to see a deeper and more meaningful connection with their job and thus be much happier in their lives. If successful, you'll have made a deep and lasting impact on someone else's life.

In some cases, a manager may find a team member who identifies that his purpose and values are not congruent with the organisation. In this case, an open conversation may be required about whether there are better places for that employee to move and flourish. In such instances, it's vital that a manager treads carefully and with respect. It may be that the individual can find a very effective way of working with the differences by accepting them.

MAKE MONDAY MORNING THE HIGH POINT OF THE WEEK

In the area of 'I (Me)' as Coach, we explored the importance of making Monday morning a high point of your week as a manager. It's important, too, that each individual around you feels the same. Emotions and feelings are very contagious, and a team filled with people who feel positive towards Mondays will almost certainly outperform one that isn't.

Use the approaches in the earlier section in this chapter to help each individual make Monday morning the high point of their week.

HOLD APPRAISALS TO ENSURE A HIGH-PERFORMANCE TEAM

In the role as Coach, a manager must hold good-quality performance reviews and appraisals to focus and motivate his people. Individuals need clear objectives that are linked to the direction and desired behaviours of the organisation. People need to have regular opportunities for open and honest feedback, rather than waiting for an annual appraisal meeting.

A Watson Wyatt survey published in 2009 called *Continuous Engagement: The Key to Unlocking the Value of Your People During Tough Times* reported:

> *our data shows that engaged employees have frequent work related discussions with their immediate manager in comparison to their colleagues with medium to low engagement levels. 43 per cent of high engaged employees receive feedback at least once a week compared to only 18 per cent of employees with low engagement.*

I recommend that managers meet with their people one-to-one at least every two months. For some individuals, monthly or even weekly meetings may be more appropriate. However, for top talent, every two months is often the right balance to ensure that they feel they are free to act rather than that they're being micromanaged.

Very often an organisation will have a formal performance management process that all managers are required to follow. Good managers as engagers work within these frameworks, but always ensure that appraisals are conducted in a coaching style. This means asking the other person how they feel about their performance and gathering feedback from colleagues before jumping in with your own judgement.

Appraisals are different from career development conversations. It's a good idea to keep the two dialogues separate. Performance management is primarily about the requirements of the organisation or manager from the individual. A career development conversation, as discussed as part of the Strategist role, is more about what the individual needs from the manager and organisation.

From the Perspective of Us (Our Team)

At a team level, the manager as Coach can boost engagement levels by nurturing team spirit. This could be in a formal team or a project team, where the people working within it do not have a direct reporting line to you.

The factors to work with are as follows:

- Value relationship-building time.
- Run social events that are appropriate for the team.
- Energise others.
- Nurture team spirit among virtual and disparate teams.

VALUE AND DEMONSTRATE RELATIONSHIP-BUILDING TIME

A manager who displays great coaching behaviour recognises the importance of giving team members time to get to know each other and build relationships. In busy work environments, it's very tempting for interactions across teams to be transactional-based rather than relationship-enhancing.

As a manager, you have the opportunity to encourage relationship-building time. However, just giving people the space and saying the right words is not enough. Managers also need to show they value this relationship-building time by participating in it themselves.

Think about how much time you take each day to discuss non-work-related areas in conversations with colleagues. Do you do this enough so that you can honestly say that they feel you know them and care about them as individuals?

Consider actively encouraging team members to spend time talking over coffee. Join them occasionally to show you are comfortable with this valuable time that team members are spending together.

When Sarah Henbrey headed the Organisational Development team at Sony Europe, she worked with the leadership talent pool, both scoping and delivering programmes for the leaders of the future. She remembers a workshop that focused on individual values and purposes, and that people were astonished by the results of spending time talking to their team members about non-task-related issues:

> We saw our talent pool having conversations with their team members in new ways, primarily spending time talking to them about their lives rather than just tasks. The individuals hadn't seen the connection between those types of conversations and unlocking new performance among people. They were surprised at what their team members could achieve when they were managed this way. Individuals who came on our programme talked of their delight at seeing such quick results as a consequence of conversations that were about building relationships rather than being transactional to get the work done.

It's harder to build relationships when managing teams across sites or geographical areas. This means that more effort is needed when spending time face-to-face. It also means that social conversations need to take place during telephone meetings or virtual interactions. It is important to rely less on email and more on telephone conversations in this respect.

One word of caution: building relationships is important, but be careful not to go overboard. A manager who becomes best friends with his staff will find it harder to be effective during difficult conversations about areas such as redundancies or restructuring. The result can be uncomfortable and unclear conversations between manager and close friend colleagues that leave both feeling unsatisfied and unfairly treated.

RUN SOCIAL EVENTS THAT ARE APPROPRIATE FOR THE TEAM

Social events are often arranged by team members to build team spirit and cohesiveness. As a manager, it's important that you attend social events that the team has organised, even if they don't suit your personal preferences. It's also worth considering the individual preferences of your team members and encouraging others to arrange social events that appeal to all. For some teams, a Thursday night curry may be a welcome event in the diary. However, a team member with a partner who has a regular commitment on Thursday evenings may be riddled with guilt that he should be at home caring for the children but doesn't want to let his team members down. Vary the activities, and be sure to take account of personal situations and preferences.

ENERGISE OTHERS

Energy is contagious, and a fully fuelled manager will have a better chance of engaging her people than a partially fuelled one. The role of a manager as Culture Builder includes energising others. A team with the ability to feel good about what they do, to see significance in it and to deliver in alignment is a group of investors, not savers. They are more likely to sit at the top of the organisational engagement model discussed in Part I of this book.

Managers can energise others by using many of the techniques covered earlier in this part of the book. It's good to remember that positive energy is often created by using an 'ask, don't tell' approach in team situations as well as individual ones, so a manager who has regular dialogue with his team members will create more energy than one who prefers team briefings. Dialogue is much more inclusive, and allows others to share their points of view. However, it also requires more time, and in a time-poor work environment, even well-intentioned managers struggle not to move into 'direction' mode. A practical tool that has helped many managers maintain dialogue against this challenge is the Question Funnel, illustrated in Figure 15.1.

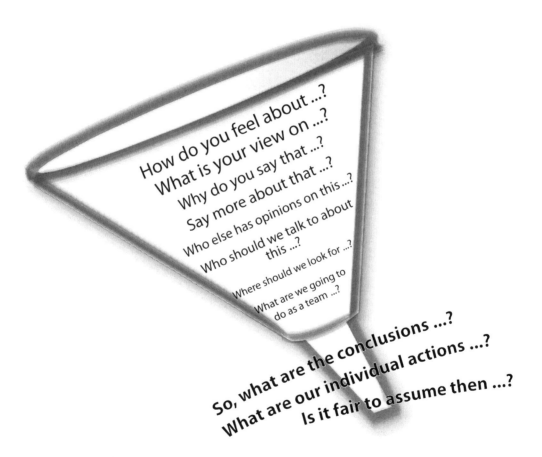

How do you feel about ...?
What is your view on ...?
Why do you say that ...?
Say more about that ...?
Who else has opinions on this ...?
Who should we talk to about this ...?
Where should we look for ...?
What are we going to do as a team ...?

So, what are the conclusions ...?
What are our individual actions ...?
Is it fair to assume then ...?

Figure 15.1 The Question Funnel

NURTURING TEAM SPIRIT AMONG VIRTUAL AND DISPARATE TEAMS

With the increasing number of virtual teams in existence across organisations, managers face the additional challenge of how to nurture team spirit across cultures and geographical areas. There are no easy answers. A team whose members are situated in the same building has much more opportunity to talk, socialise and enjoy water-cooler moments. Creating those same moments across boundaries requires intentionality from the manager and team members alike.

Facilitating the building of relationships is the heart of nurturing team spirit across virtual and disparate teams. Every team will go through stages of formation as it comes together, which can be summarised as:

* **Hello** – understanding the basics of each person, forming first connections.
* **Queries** – people start to have more robust conversations about what the aim of the team is, what's expected of them, and why.
* **Control** – lines of power are drawn, people take on the roles that suit them in terms of control, drive and delivery.
* **Team** – it all comes together, with individuals working well together, delivery happening and smooth processes emerging.
* **Celebration** – the team members recognise what they have built, own it, and show great pride in being effective. The whole becomes greater than the sum of the parts.

The team members obviously need to understand their common purpose and what strengths each member has to realise it. Giving people opportunities to meet face-to-face regularly is important, as is setting aside agenda time for individuals to get to know each other, and these are fundamental to moving people through the stages above. Too many conferences or meetings have packed agendas and often don't even include enough time to eat lunch and take a comfort break. As a manager, build in plenty of downtime and break time to allow people to talk. Use energisers to help virtual teams get to know each other quickly and break down barriers. Use questions like those in the question funnel tool to encourage dialogue and viewpoints to be shared.

Think, too, about the knowledge you have about the passion and 'what makes each heart beat', then use this to introduce colleagues to each other whom you feel will have shared interests and passions.

Debra Nelson, a former Manager of Diversity at Mercedes-Benz USA, believes that having a company culture of shared values and vision are the keys to maximising performance and motivation where teams cross cultures and locations. She believes that job rotations, job shadowing, mentoring programmes and employee volunteerism initiatives are ways to build team spirit and enhance productivity and morale.

When Mercedes-Benz was preparing to open its first manufacturing plant in the USA, newly hired team members were sent to work and live in Germany for one year to learn about the culture of the corporation, its production processes and their colleagues. The individuals who had this opportunity came back and shared their knowledge and experiences to help foster the best possible cross-cultural working relationships.

Year-long programmes aren't always going to be appropriate within teams, but day-long or month-long rotations can give a very fast return. The return on investment of such activities is difficult to measure, but those managers who encourage them say that they would do so again and again.

From the Perspective of All (the Organisation)

By taking action to be part of something bigger, the Coach can help build and change culture in the following ways:

- Work with what makes stakeholder hearts beat.
- Share when you see an opportunity to help others.
- Feed back how colleagues feel.

WORK WITH WHAT MAKES STAKEHOLDER HEARTS BEAT

As a Coach, a manager finds out what makes his people's hearts beat. He also understands what makes the hearts of other key stakeholders and the organisation as a whole beat. At a practical level, it may not be possible to have regular coaching conversations with your senior leaders or other people in your stakeholder network, but by building relationships with them, it should be simple to identify some of the drivers, passions and what they care about.

Engagement comes when you spend time with people one-to-one to understand them, their strengths and unique capabilities. Only when a manager does this can they truly draw the best out of people. This applies to their own team or wider virtual teams.

Top Tip

During conversations with stakeholders, ask 'What does success look like for you at the end of this journey?'

The response will give you huge insight about the hot buttons of your stakeholder and help you to position your messages (as Storyteller), develop appropriate approaches (as Strategist) and create win/win opportunities as a Coach.

The manager as Coach works with stakeholders' needs and passions to find opportunities for mutual benefit. This starts by proactively understanding other business unit drivers and issues so that you can work together to find solutions, pooling resources and strengths to deliver even greater results. These solutions may even dovetail with other areas of your strategy as an engager, such as offering a member of your team to work on a particular project. This could be part of their development plan, and thus increase their propensity to be an investor. At the same time, it boosts your relationship with another key stakeholder because you have given them something to help them succeed.

In her role as Head of Diversity at Mercedes-Benz USA, Debra Nelson sponsored unique training methods to help leaders understand the company's diversity vision and how to incorporate it within their work. She assumed that attendees would buy into the direction and would embrace specific approaches as a result. She remembers the day when her supervisor told her there was actually inertia towards the diversity vision rather than buy-in. She was shocked, but immediately tried to find ways to move forward. She realised that people weren't necessarily resistant to diversity, but weren't sure what it meant for them, or in some cases, were uncertain how to implement the new direction.

She sought to create an environment that encouraged people to invest in the diversity vision in their own ways and in their own time. She found ways to bring leaders into the approach, helping them to succeed and grow. The leaders were then better able to develop their own business strategies to support diversity. She did this by meeting one-on-one with each of them and by taking the time to understand their motivations, drivers, challenges and opportunities. She was then better equipped to help them understand how embracing diversity would support their respective business objectives. Debra said:

The secret was spending time with each person. While getting to know them as individuals, I also identified ways to help them win. It took time, however the result was executives who better understood the business rationale for diversity.

Top Tip

At monthly team meetings, invite a person from another area of the organisation to attend. Rather than asking them to prepare a presentation, have a dialogue about what work they are involved in, how it impacts or is impacted by our work in this team, and how you can help each other to deliver even more successfully. Encourage your team to think of questions in advance that will help them to develop their knowledge. Task everyone in the team to ensure that they learn something or give something significant during the dialogue.

SHARE WHEN YOU SEE AN OPPORTUNITY TO HELP OTHERS

As a Coach, you can add extra value to the wider organisation when you find other teams that are working to achieve similar aims or could benefit from using the approaches modelled by you or your team. A manager who shares knowledge and collaborates is able to engage others at a higher level than one who operates in total isolation.

Managers can also create long-term engagement with stakeholders by offering to mentor or coach a member of their team, where appropriate. This benefits the wider organisation by moving savers to become investors through higher engagement levels. It also boosts your own level of experience as a Coach. Multiple benefits are achieved when the stakeholder you aimed to engage visibly appreciates this action.

FEED BACK HOW COLLEAGUES FEEL

Managers have a part to play in providing feedback about how their people and other colleagues feel about what's going on in the organisation at any given time. They can share insights about the reactions to general activities and specific issues, which is useful for senior leadership and the wider good of the organisation.

In many organisations, there will be formal ways to provide this feedback. It's also the manager's responsibility to find informal methods to share useful insights directly with senior leaders or project managers. When sharing such information, remember to state your intentions clearly so that you avoid appearing critical or negative.

16 *The Pilot*

The goal of the Pilot is to be a respected role model. As a manager, it's important to be an 'adult', rather than too parental or childlike in style. The Pilot is the measured, calm component of being a manager. Pilots have their hand on the tiller and gently guide to ensure the destination is reached without incident. They are trusted by those around them, and trusting of others. Pilots value others, and just like the pilot guiding a ship out of port, sometimes they will take control. On other occasions they will use their experience and knowledge to guide other competent individuals.

The Pilot has the ability to authoritative. This doesn't mean being pompous or using jargon in speech. It means displaying confidence and showing they know what they are talking about. When times get tough, it is the Pilot who speaks calmly and gives assurance that 'we will get through' – galvanising teams into action.

The role of the Pilot needs a selection of aptitudes, including being:

- persistent
- collegiate
- adult
- authoritative
- temperate (not extreme)
- in control
- trusting
- trustworthy
- appreciative

Table 16.1 The Pilot

	I (me)	You (my colleague)	Us (our team)	All (the organisation)
The Pilot (E) A respected role model	– Work on and with your personal style. – Be self-aware. – Be visible. – Use appropriate body language. – Request feedback. – Role-model at all levels.	– Trust and value others. – Treat people as individuals. – Build trust. – Grow self-esteem and confidence in others. – Value others. – Challenge individuals if they display inappropriate behaviour.	– Keep an eye on the end game. – Champion inclusive dialogue and language. – Use an appropriate tone when conversing. – Deliver what's required.	– Contribute to the whole. – Take control of stakeholder relationships to ensure success. – Socialise and gain buy-in to plans/direction.

From the Perspective of I (Me)

Before reading on, take a pen and reflect for a moment on the following:

> Think of a boss or manager you really loved working with – the best boss you've ever had. Why do you rate him/her so highly? Make a note of the reasons why. How engaged did you feel in the business when working with that individual? How much did you perform at your best versus simply achieve a handful of objectives?

The characteristics you've noted that make that person great probably centre around a set of core qualities: great managers discover what is unique about an individual, and then both value them for it and capitalise on it. They find a way to excel themselves and ensure that you excel. They act as adults, and rarely display childlike or irrational behaviour. They provide a sense of 'it's OK' and make you feel empowered to achieve.

Most people have worked for a great manager during their life. Most of us know what it's like to be inspired and have a high desire to perform at our best. Be honest – how many of the people you manage right now feel that buzz that you have just remembered and reflected upon? Even if you believe that they do have a similar feeling, it can disappear if not worked at and sustained, so how can you replicate what you've experienced from your own great managers? How can you ensure that you engage all of your people so that they excel and perform at their very best?

A good manager as Culture Builder will spend time observing, socialising with and interacting with his people. He'll watch reactions to events, listen and take mental notes to gather a deeper understanding of their strengths and style. He values others, and expresses his appreciation regularly.

> Ask yourself – what was the best day you've had in the last two years at work? Why?

As with each of the other manager as Culture Builder roles, managers need to start by looking in the mirror and challenging themselves to work on, and with, their personal style. The Pilot role of keeping a firm hand on the tiller means using personal preferences and being aware of blind spots. Only armed with this knowledge can they work with it to ensure an environment rich in trust, with high engagement, and where team members use their expertise to deliver.

At an individual level, the role of Pilot requires the following attributes:

- Be self-aware.
- Be visible.
- Use appropriate body language.
- Request feedback.
- Role-model at all levels.

BE SELF-AWARE

It's useful to have a high degree of self-awareness to perform each of the five manager as Culture Builder roles well. However, it's particularly important for Pilots if they're to be respected role models at all levels in the organisation. Everyone has areas of preference in personal style, and many of us also have blind spots. Becoming more aware of these means that a manager can work with them, rather than being unaware of their existence. Without knowledge that the blind spots exist, it's common for individuals to find themselves tripping up in their relationships with others without really understanding why.

Once you've understood more about your own personal preferences and become more self-aware, you may want to consider taking others in your team through the same process. It's exceptionally useful for top talent when devising career development plans.

BE VISIBLE

Great leaders ensure that they are visible among those they lead. This is essential if you're to be an effective Pilot. Visibility isn't just a question of having a desk on the same floor as your team, although this is a good start, as we will discover in Chapter 23 when talking about Simon Ashby's leadership style at Sony Europe. It's being available to others to talk about what's on their mind, giving advice and guidance. It's about demonstrating that you care about what people are doing because you are regularly showing an interest by attending update meetings, showing up on time and asking people 'How are you doing?' at the coffee machine.

For a manager who has a team spread across locations, it's important to be visible at those sites. Plan time in your diary for visits, and while you're there, find ways to see as many people as possible. Schedule a team lunch or arrange to meet for coffee with specific individuals. Techniques that we have talked about earlier in this book, such as management by walking about, all help to raise and maintain a good level of visibility.

USE APPROPRIATE BODY LANGUAGE

Body language is critical to role-modelling a good emotional connection with people. It's important for managers because negative or closed body language sends a strong message about how much you value the other person. Individuals who don't feel valued won't be engaged. They're also unlikely to trust their manager. These two factors influence engagement and performance levels significantly.

Body language that is open and warm is much more likely to create a connection than closed or defensive signals, such as crossed arms and lack of eye contact.

We judge ourselves by our intentions, yet we judge others by their behaviour. The same applies to other people, so it's critical that our body language and behaviour properly display our intentions.

Much has been written about the science of body language and its impact. Most managers will have seen the statistics about the power of non-verbal communication and how it accounts for around 55 per cent of the impact of what we communicate. The question is: how many are aware of their body language and its direct impact?

It's therefore important for the Pilot to use body language and non-verbal cues actively and appropriately with others, whether with individuals or in team scenarios. In some cultures, you may need to dial up certain non-verbal gestures. In others, it may be more appropriate to dial down. For example, I make a point to increase the range and enormity of arm gestures and tone when on conference platforms in the USA compared to the UK, where too much can be offputting for an audience.

In practice, this will depend on the individual. For example, a manager who tends to think deeply may withdraw during a conversation to consider what is being said – requiring them to give more non-verbal affirmative cues (such as nodding or sitting forward) to ensure that the other person feels they are engaged. The challenge will be that an 'organisational language' may exist that often dictates how people act, with shared phrases and gestures. Avoiding these is a big step towards using far more inclusive and novel communication approaches.

Remember that appropriate body language also helps you to feel more confident. If you smile as you speak, you'll feel better about what you're saying. If you frown when you speak, you're more likely to feel anxious. In relational terms, the first person to smile has control over the interaction, as does the person who extends the hand to shake.

The Golden Rules of Body Language

- Hold an open and good posture.
- Refrain from multi-tasking when conversing.
- Avoid crossed arms.

- Maintain eye contact.
- Face the person with whom you are talking.
- Sit forward, but give others enough personal space.
- Be the first, not the last, to interact.

REQUEST FEEDBACK

A Pilot who is self-aware also asks for feedback on a regular basis, because engaging managers want to know 'How can I work more for you so that you can be successful?' They then use that feedback to tailor their approaches, giving their style and interactions constant 'nudges' to remain in keeping with the group dynamic, to best engage individuals and to feel part of the group themselves.

Top Tip

Early during an appraisal, ask your team member two questions:

1. What do you appreciate about me?
2. What would you like to see more of from me to help you succeed in future?

Asking for feedback during appraisals can help to develop a feeling of shared ownership for employee success. This is powerful, but it's critical to ensure that it's a quick conversation with a commitment from you, as a manager, at the end of it. Too much feedback in this scenario will take the emphasis away from the other person and make them feel disempowered and that the appraisal actually turned into 'a meeting about you'.

Top Tip

During one-to-one conversations with your team members, ask them to score the relationship they have with you on a scale from 1 to 10: 10 is 'huge love between us', while 1 is 'little shared ground and respect'.

Once you have the answer, stay positive and inquire: 'What would take us closer to 10?'

This opens a very different conversation about performance, and is empowering for those on the receiving end – though it can feel a little uncomfortable the first time you do it.

Feedback doesn't just come from team members. Managers can learn a huge amount from asking customers, partners or colleagues and other managers for feedback about their style and how they make them feel when interacting with them. If there is an opportunity through development processes to undertake 360-degree feedback, take it. The insight for you as a manager aiming to play all five roles to engage others will be invaluable.

ROLE-MODEL AT ALL LEVELS

The manager as Pilot is the adult in the organisation. She is solid, dependable and trusted. During times of difficulty and challenge, she is like the airline pilot who speaks to passengers during turbulence and declares, 'Ladies and gentlemen, boys and girls, as you will have noticed we're experiencing a few bumps on our journey at the moment. Nothing to worry about, just going over a few cobbles …' – and you believe her wholeheartedly.

The Pilot is a role model. She displays the appropriate behaviours and follow-through so that others trust and believe her. If a manager loses control or panics during a crisis, those around her will lose confidence and join in the panic.

For a Pilot to be a great role model, she must remember to use engaging behaviour at all times.

In some instances, managers shy away from role-modelling behaviours, because they don't see them in their own leaders. If senior leaders aren't role-modelling, don't use that as an excuse: role-model upwards. If your own leaders aren't displaying engaging behaviour, it doesn't mean that you can't. In fact, many senior leaders will notice managers who role-model engaging behaviour and quickly start to pay positive attention to them – it's hard to discipline people for being good.

From the Perspective of You (My Colleague)

Using the role of Pilot to be a truly engaging manager involves a range of activities when working one-to-one with team members. At its heart, the Pilot's role involves stabilising, reassuring and strengthening others. The following attributes are critical to success in this:

- Treat people as individuals.
- Build trust.
- Grow self-esteem and confidence in others.
- Value others.
- Challenge individuals if they display inappropriate behaviour.

TREAT PEOPLE AS INDIVIDUALS

There's a danger that we see using engagement to build cultures as a daunting science, but let's remember that at its heart, engagement comes from treating people as individuals. Higher attachment to an organisation is achieved where people feel that their own needs are being met and valued, rather than simply having their needs met as part of a team.

From your work as Coach, you'll understand more about what makes individuals' the hearts beat, their passions and purpose. This will give you the insight you need to treat people as individuals and engage them using different, appropriate approaches.

It's obvious to managers that different personalities require different engagement approaches. However, by having more insight into the drivers of team members rather than just their personality types, you'll be able to create individuals who are real investors rather than just regular savers. The big outlay for you, as a manager, is to invest your time in thinking about what each person needs to be fully engaged.

For example, engaging high-potential talent requires different approaches to other employee types. My experience is that high-potential people value freedom of access to senior management and have a hunger to be empowered. They need you, their manager, and other leaders to give them advice and support, but in an open context. They also crave opportunities to be creative and show their potential. There's also less of a need to communicate with high-potential individuals because if they have access to the right people, they will be the ones sharing the latest knowledge with you, their manager. This can leave a line manager feeling vulnerable or threatened. However, those that succeed are the ones who embrace this and work with their talent, rather than trying to suppress it.

BUILD TRUST

A high level of trust between a manager and colleague is absolutely crucial to engagement. If employees don't trust their organisation or their managers, their levels of effort and investment will be minimal. If trust is destroyed or does not exist, individuals won't even be savers, let alone investors.

It's very difficult to rebuild trust if it breaks down, so managers must devote sufficient time and effort to building it, maintaining it and nurturing it at every level. Trust comes from four fundamentals, as shown in Figure 16.1.

Investment in relationships has been referred to when discussing the other roles of manager as Culture Builder. It's a thread that runs through all of the roles and underscores the need to devote quality time to engagement. Giving some insight into yourself as a manager, your drivers and passions, will help others feel closer to you and build a foundation for trust. It can be uncomfortable for some managers to expose themselves in this way, but the results are often much more positive than they may imagine.

It's highly important that senior leaders and managers are open about their lives and personalities. Kirstin Furber, Senior Vice President and Head of Human Resources at BBC Worldwide, says:

> I find that when I'm open with my team about how I am feeling, I get much more out of them. My experience is that leaders who are open about what they did at the weekend or what's important to them in life are much more likely to sustain engagement and trust levels with their people.

A great deal of theory concerning emotional intelligence suggests that people who make themselves 'knowable' in this way are seen as more authentic by their colleagues.

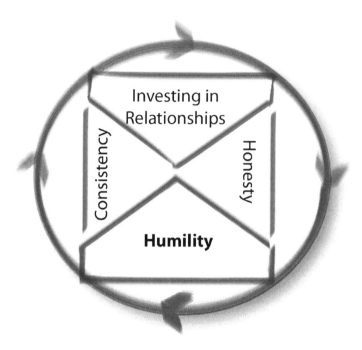

Figure 16.1 The make-up of trust
Source: Copyright Northern Flight UK Ltd and reproduced with kind permission.

I once worked with a CEO who had a family crisis the night before a quarterly business update. His wife had been rushed into hospital for treatment. The condition wasn't life-threatening but it was serious, and she was in a great deal of pain. She had also left her husband to care for their two children. I knew the sketchy details of the situation, but when I arrived at the update, I had several conversations with managers before we began that were clearly highlighting frustration at the news of the CEO's absence. I very quickly realised that the trust and respect they had for him was rapidly reducing by the minute. The cause of their negative feelings was a lack of knowledge about why he wasn't present. Nobody had told the managers who were supposed to be sharing the stage with the CEO *why* he wasn't going to be able to attend. As soon as they were informed why he wasn't in the building, the managers actively changed their posture, facial expressions and tone. The attitude changed to making sure that they pulled together to close the gap at the business update. It was remarkable to watch how something so simple could make a difference between rapid disengagement and speedy re-engagement.

Humility involves putting aside your status and pride to say and do the right thing. As mentioned earlier, it's a word that refers to being grounded – people who are humble will stand on solid ground, making it difficult to throw them off balance.

Consistency is a matter of sticking to it. Trust is not born from making great promises or telling people what we assume they want to hear. It comes from being consistent in our words, beliefs and attitudes. Above all, in the role of Pilot, a manager needs to be consistent in her behaviour.

Top Tip

When a personal crisis hits you, convey it appropriately – don't hide it.

People are hard-wired to be curious about those around them. Denying this need leaves space that is often filled with wild conjecture. This is not a soul-baring exercise, it's a context-setting approach that removes doubt, prevents rumours and makes people feel included in your thoughts.

Matching what you say with what you do is fundamental for any manager who wants to engage others. Leaders are always in the spotlight. It's the same for anyone who manages people. Team members watch every behaviour and judge whether it matches what has been said. There's not just one person watching, but many in the organisation and beyond. For managers, every day is like walking onto the stage and feeling the lights beaming down on them, the eyes of the crowd and the need to deliver a performance equal to or better than the previous day's. It sounds tough, but it can be a highly motivating situation if seen as a challenge, and can drive individuals to be better managers.

Being honest is a huge lever for trust. A manager who lies or is perceived to be deceitful will struggle to engage others. Being honest may sometimes involve admitting 'I don't know.' That's perfectly acceptable every now and then, because a manager can't always have all the answers, and it feeds directly into the humility element of trust.

Building Trust In Practice

After receiving feedback – either one-to-one or through more formal methods such as employee surveys – make sure that action is taken and that you thank people for their input. Take on board the negative feedback as well as the positive.

Be prepared to admit if you got something wrong, then follow through and deliver action based on what you've been told. This might not always be a matter of changing direction or your behaviour. It could be that simply stating why something has to be the case or why you've behaved in a particular way is what's required.

In organisations where there is a high level of trust, it's more likely that engagement levels and thus performance will be higher. Trust comes from people seeing each other do the right thing, from the leadership and throughout the organisation. It's promoted by visibility and spending time face-to-face. Trust is much harder to gain if people have limited connection with each other, for example in a field sales force where individuals work from home and spend little time with leaders, managers and colleagues.

Building trust also requires recognition of what management style is needed for the culture and context of the time. Andreas Ditter, Managing Director of Sony Pictures Home Entertainment, said:

> *The leadership and management style I need to adopt is very different in my current business to when I led the Audio team in Sony. Different times require different styles. Where people are ready to be empowered and feel confident to take some control, a manager can give a high degree of trust and be trusted in return. In other cases, a manager can have a good intention to trust colleagues by empowering them but people actually require more hands-on mentoring and support. The skill is to know how much trust to give. It's also important to be consistent once you have stuck to that decision, otherwise there is a risk people will stop believing in you.*

Trust cannot flourish in environments where there is a lack of understanding and no emotional commitment. It disappears when people feel they don't understand what is happening and question what is going on. Once lost, it takes a huge effort to build it back up again.

This is particularly important during periods of major change. At times like these, make people feel secure. Individuals will remain more emotionally engaged when they have a relationship with their managers and feel certain they will be honest with them. This may be difficult to achieve in cases where jobs are at risk or uncertainty is inevitable. However, it's worth looking for ways to provide as much security and certainty as possible. Some of the best practice examples in Chapter 23 illustrate ways to achieve this. Other practical approaches are to keep talking with people at regular intervals about the change. Even if no news has developed, it's important to convey the message 'We don't have any more news, but will update you as soon as we do.'

GROW SELF-ESTEEM AND CONFIDENCE IN OTHERS

A good manager as Coach will unlock potential in her people, and thus contribute to a growth in self-esteem and confidence within them. The Pilot has a role to build upon that work beyond the Coach's role.

Individuals are capable of more if their self-esteem and confidence is high, so a Pilot should help others to constantly look for ways to find richer futures for themselves as a result of being more confident and growing in capability.

Gordon Watt believes this was central to his success as an effective leader and manager during his time at Galileo. He made it his job to grow the self-esteem and confidence of others to enable them to perform to the best of their abilities. He looked for opportunities to trust people with new projects that would push them out of their comfort zones, but where he felt they had the capability to succeed:

I'd often find people had the potential for far more than they realised, if they were given the opportunity. The result was a more confident person who valued themself even more than they did before.

He would regularly fill vacancies by encouraging people to step up a role. By displaying confidence in them himself, he grew their confidence.

VALUE OTHERS

Valuing others is a key part of the Pilot role. Every human being has a fundamental need to be valued. If ever we feel undervalued or ignored, it affects us deeply and can cause extreme reactions of withdrawal or aggression.

Feeling that we have value goes part way to building a sense of purpose in life. Without a purpose, it's very difficult to find motivation. It's certainly hard to be engaged in anything if we don't feel valued by those around us.

Consider a time in your career when you've been at your best and felt valued. Now think of a period in your life when you haven't been valued. Immediately, you'll feel an emotional reaction to your memory of the two. To be a great and engaging manager, it's essential to show that you value others. Don't assume others know that you value them, and what for. In the craziness of working life, managers have to be very explicit.

In my work, I regularly observe how many individuals spend significant time in their average day sat in a state of high negative emotional energy. At the heart of what pushes someone into this state is a sense that his or her value is under threat. If we feel our value is being questioned, we are emotionally hijacked and become frustrated, angry, defensive and shut down. Our reactions to the other person are rarely productive, and a spiral of negative occurrences often follows.

If you behave in a way that hijacks others, you'll find a disengaged, defensive team that make poor decisions, has little trust and delivers poor performance and whose members hardly even class as savers. Conversely, if you behave in a way that values others, you'll unlock amazing engagement and performance levels. People will do things you never imagined possible if they feel valued.

One positive way to show that you value others is to regularly practice the art of appreciation. This will be a natural behaviour to some people, and completely alien to others. Be aware that it may feel very uncomfortable if it's not something you're used to doing, but stick with it. I remember one CEO with whom I worked telling me that regularly appreciating people by saying 'Well done' was one of the hardest practices he'd ever had to undertake in his career. He found it personally difficult, but he persevered, and three months later in our coaching sessions, he reflected how appreciating others had become such a natural and important part of his leadership style. I've come across others who always have pre-printed cards at hand to write notes of appreciation as soon as required.

Work by Towers Watson prior to 2008 showed that appreciation from line managers affects engagement scores directly. In 2008, it supplemented its research base on employee engagement by conducting a global recognition study for O.C. Tanner. That research reinforced an important conclusion from its earlier Global Workforce Study: relationships between employees and their direct supervisors play a key role in the system of factors that drives engagement. Towers Watson found that a manager delivering recognition of employee performance boosted engagement 'the way a turbocharger cranks up a sports car's horsepower' (cited in MacLeod and Clarke 2009).

Top Tip

Purchase a card or source some good quality letter-writing paper. Think about someone in your life whom you really appreciate, then write a card or letter to tell them so. Be as specific as you possibly can about why you appreciate them.

It's easy to say 'Thank you' or 'Well done,' but they're wasted words if the recipient doesn't feel there is much understanding of the work that goes on behind the scenes. If you're saying thank you for a job well done, explain why you believe it was such a good job and what the impact on others has been. The more specific you are, the more impact your appreciation will have on engagement levels.

Think of the last time you received a note or card of appreciation. How did it make you feel? How engaged did you feel at that moment?

For Gordon Watt, former Vice President of Systems Development at Galileo, an early experience of appreciation shaped his management style for the rest of his career:

> *My time at Galileo had a huge impact on my future leadership style and how I prioritised engagement. In my organisation design role during the merger between Covia and Galileo, I worked away from home a huge amount of the time and had left a young family behind. At the end of the merger, the then CEO John Zeeman delivered a handwritten letter that was addressed to my wife and myself. He delivered it personally and said he wanted to make sure it reached me. The letter expressed his appreciation for my work during the merger and to my wife for managing a young family at home to give me the space to deliver for the organisation. With the letter was a £5,000 cheque as a token of that appreciation. The doubly incredible thing about this incident was that John was leaving as a result of the merger – he didn't have a future in the company – but he'd taken the time to keep me engaged throughout the period of change and to thank me at the end. That taught me a great deal and shaped the fact that I put managing people and engaging them at the centre of my purpose from then on.*

Later in Gordon's career, he regularly used the power of appreciation as a way to value others and engage them. When he saw that an individual had done something great from a weekly progress report, he'd find them and congratulate them personally. Gordon recalls:

> *I would say 'Well done,' but also inquire what had helped them make it happen. I was interested, but also wanted to show that it wasn't just a pat on the back: I really understood the gravity of what had been delivered.*

As a manager, it's imperative to appreciate people on a one-to-one level as well as publicly or with fellow team members. It's good to celebrate success in internal publications, put individuals forward for awards and say 'Well done' during team meetings. This helps to formally recognise the value people bring. However, try to be specific in these instances too. Doing this also strengthens the individual's engagement with the organisation – seeing recognition coming centrally alongside the praise from the manager.

As part of a board workshop, Sarah Henbrey, Organisational Development Director at 3, asked attendees to share what they appreciated about each other and what they'd like to see more of from each other. Although this was conducted in a team setting, the feedback was individual-to-individual. This can be an extremely engaging type of conversation to hold, and encourages a spirit of honesty and ongoing development of engaging behaviour.

Managers in the John Lewis Partnership have to manage well, not only as a point of best practice, but because all of their staff are also owners of the business. This is an interesting twist on valuing others. Stop and think for a moment: how would you manage your people differently if they were the owners of your business? What can you learn from that insight?

CHALLENGE INDIVIDUALS IF THEY DISPLAY INAPPROPRIATE BEHAVIOUR

Part of the role of a Pilot is to challenge others if they're displaying behaviour that is at odds with the direction, values or norms of the organisation.

From the Perspective of Us (Our Team)

At a team level, the Pilot can influence engagement in a variety of ways, including these:

- Champion inclusive dialogue and language.
- Use an appropriate tone when conversing.
- Deliver what's required.

CHAMPION INCLUSIVE DIALOGUE AND LANGUAGE

The need for inclusive dialogue was highlighted when talking about the manager as Coach. However, it's also an important tool for a Pilot.

A strong Pilot will champion regular dialogue among teams, whether that involves chairing dialogue-based team sessions or encouraging others to hold them. It's an important part of engagement – the Pilot needs to keep an eye on the end game and provide guidance with maturity and authority. This is the role a Pilot plays during dialogue.

Pilots use inclusive language, ask the team for other views, and won't interrupt others. They practice active listening and use language centred in 'we' not 'I'. They'll provoke debate positively in team discussions to help stimulate more insight or to ensure that all viewpoints are considered. Unlike managers adopting the role of Coach, Pilots may do more telling than asking, because they'll be guiding and advising. It's therefore vital that a manager knows when to be a Coach and when to be a Pilot.

USE AN APPROPRIATE TONE WHEN CONVERSING

Tone of voice is the way in which we write and speak, what we say and how we say it. What you say is dictated by your principles, experiences and aspirations; how you say it is driven by your personality. Possessing good self-awareness will immediately ensure that you spot your strengths and areas to watch in terms of tone of voice. For a manager as Pilot, it's important to pay attention to that knowledge, as appropriate tone has a major impact on engagement levels and your ability to keep the team focused on what's important.

A Pilot must act with authenticity, so if a tone of voice is forced or falsified to try to achieve a particular effect, it will often fail miserably – team members will notice the obvious effort. Never forget that we are all highly adept at recognising emotion and intent, to the point that inauthenticity will stand out a mile. As a demonstration of this, the next time you're in the car, make an effort to focus on the act of driving (as we do when a law enforcement officer drives past us) – it all falls apart and your driving becomes irregular. When we force something normally conducted without conscious thought, it comes out badly.

It's important to think about what you're trying to achieve when using tone of voice. If you're trying to instil a sense of urgency, you'll use a different tone compared to when you need to reassure a team.

A calm voice is a strong trait of an effective Pilot. Imagine yourself on an airline during extreme weather or when an engine fails. Comfort and confidence comes from a pilot who explains what is happening in a calm tone. Pilots don't need panic or uncertainty among their team if those people are to be engaged and perform at their best. They need focused, measured and mature behaviour. Tone of voice plays a big part in creating that environment.

A successful Pilot will use a range of tone, but the following will feature regularly:

- strength
- exuberance
- confidence
- good use of volume
- pace

DELIVER WHAT'S REQUIRED

Keeping a hand on the tiller – either in real time or through others – is the core requirement for a Pilot. A manager as Pilot will gently steer everyone in the right direction and put people back on track if they begin to deviate.

This requires the Pilot to keep a weather eye on the destination for the team so that she can keep talking with them objectively about where they are now and what needs to happen next to progress.

This creates expectations on both sides – the Pilot has to consistently deliver to ensure that credibility and support is maintained. Managers who don't deliver on promises or reassurances will lose all elements of engagement, as the 'brokerage' collapses and people feel used and cheated.

Equally, the Pilot will hold others accountable, and ensure that team members equally deliver on their promises, or seek explanations as to why elements have been missed, sharing this appropriately with the rest of the team to ensure that fairness is observed.

From the Perspective of All (the Organisation)

The manager as Pilot is authoritative and trusted. She is able to navigate the wider organisation to achieve personal and team success. She can also make a significant contribution to the engagement of the entire organisation by doing the following:

- Take control of stakeholder relationships to ensure success.
- Socialise and gain buy-in to plans/direction.

TAKE CONTROL OF STAKEHOLDER RELATIONSHIPS TO ENSURE SUCCESS

In the role of manager as Pilot, you have a responsibility to take control of wider stakeholder relationships that you have identified as important to your personal success and that of your team.

Don't rely on others to manage these relationships. If they're important to you, you'll want to ensure that they're managed appropriately.

Using the Pilot attributes, you can influence others by being perceived as solid, in control, adult and trusted. Managers with strong Pilot competence find it much easier to manage multiple-stakeholder relationships at complex levels because they're immediately respected and trusted.

SOCIALISE AND GAIN BUY-IN TO PLANS/DIRECTION

A competent Pilot will engage with key stakeholders across the organisation by socialising and consulting before proposing a new plan or direction. Talking to others about your ideas, thoughts and plans helps others to take ownership and provide input. Those involved heavily in scoping a new plan or direction will invest more heavily in its long-term success. This means that when the implementation phase of your plan is reached, you'll already have engagement from the stakeholders who are important to success. They're much more likely to take the action needed as a result.

Through your work as Strategist, you'll have identified the key stakeholders who need to be fully engaged for success, and to what level. Consider involving those individuals or teams that you need to move and keep in the 'high-power/high-impact' quadrant by painting an overview picture of your plans early in the process. It's even better if you can involve them at the beginning by explaining the challenge you're working to progress and asking for their initial thoughts and ideas as input.

PART III

Leader as Culture Builder

17 *Supercharging the Five Roles of Manager as Culture Builder for Senior Leaders*

Senior leaders who truly lead and engage are unforgettable. They inspire and help their people to excel in everything they do.

Almost all senior leaders have teams, and thus are also managers. If you are a leader who has turned directly to this part of the book, I suggest you start by reading Part II.

The five roles of manager as Culture Builder are just as pertinent for a senior leader who is looking to build an engaged organisation as they are for a manager.

In addition, senior leaders should consider their impact on engagement by looking at each role through a broader leadership lens. The biggest impact is at an organisational level, where senior leaders have a huge influence on engagement levels. However, there are also some specifics that senior leaders need to think about at the individual, team and colleague level. These are explored in this chapter.

The Prophet

From the perspective of I (me), there are considerations at multiple levels. To be an effective Prophet, a senior leader has to advance his understanding of personal purpose and identify what he stands for as a leader in the business. For example, Stuart Fletcher had a clear stand in Diageo to be 'fantastic'. During conversations at the beginning of the planning for his Breakthrough Thinking Intensive programme, 'fantastic' was the word he kept using when talking about his vision and desire for the future. He therefore took this on to be his stand: fantastic performance, fantastic leadership, fantastic teams. He worked on a 'stand cascade' that articulated what 'fantastic' looked like in each area – for example, entering new markets and delivering fantastic profit. He talked about taking advantage of fantastic growth opportunities and making a fantastic impact. There was no doubt about Stuart's stand for the business and himself. He wanted to do a fantastic job. That stand evolved once he put his breakthrough strategy in place during 2005. Even as it evolved, people were left in no doubt about Stuart's passion and purpose.

Employees need to understand what a leader stands for – to be sure that he has an inner compass that will guide his decisions and behaviour. A senior leader who has this clarity is likely to be more consistent as a communicator and engager than one that does not.

A senior leader who directly manages senior people has a role to inspire them and to ascertain what they also stand for as leaders.

Naomi Climer, Vice President at Sony Europe, worked at the BBC with Tony Hall (now CEO of the Royal Opera House in London) earlier in her career. She remembers him having a strong vision in the BBC, and considers him a great example of a Prophet. However, she believes he has become even more of a Prophet in his current role:

> Tony is passionate about bringing opera to the masses. He's already done the unthinkable by bringing £5 opera to us all. However, it really feels he has a connection to his purpose and communicates great clarity of vision.

On a recent visit to Tony, Naomi was deeply impressed to see that he greeted every employee by name, from the doorman to ballerinas.

Great Prophets are highly inspirational, and this role is often underplayed by many leaders and managers. During my interviews for this book, I asked for examples of leaders who displayed the inspirational traits of a Prophet. David Patton, CEO at Grey EMEA, was mentioned as someone who is a highly inspirational leader for many. Colleagues describe him as a visionary. He inspires by being clear about what he wants the business to achieve from different perspectives. Janet Markwick, Chief Finance Officer at Grey London, reports: 'He is also great at believing in me and having confidence in my abilities. That has always engaged me and let me contribute more than I imagine is possible.'

From the perspective of us (our team), the role of senior leader as Prophet involves creating an environment of pride. This means being able to celebrate success and value failure among teams. It's easy to forget to do this for senior teams because at a senior level, we expect people to be engaged naturally. However, every individual needs help to engage in the organisation and be a true investor. If executive board members don't feel proud themselves, they will set the tone for the rest of the organisation.

The Storyteller

The senior leadership role as a Storyteller adds another dimension. The organisation will expect senior leaders to be even better Storytellers than their other managers, so there is an even bigger requirement for them to live up to this expectation if they are to truly engage employees.

As a manager, you need to understand and own the organisational story. As a senior leader, you also have to create it. At a team level, a senior leader needs to do more than provide context and clarity for her team. She also needs to involve others in co-creating. This might mean bringing other team members together to explore how they best tell the story and having a clear thread that is consistent when told by any leader.

Senior leadership groups then need to come together regularly to explore the story and build or adapt it.

Debra Nelson, Vice President of Diversity at MGM Resorts, believes that having a clear vision and mission were key to the development of a highly engaged workforce at Mercedes-Benz's first manufacturing facility in the USA. She was responsible for helping establish the facility in 1994, and credits success to the entire team. For everyone on the team, including the leadership, buy-in and executing towards the same mission –

'Nothing but the best for our customers – let's do our best together' – was at the core of how they operated. Debra remembers:

> At the very beginning, the leadership team recognised that there was a need to create a common language and a way of operating since so many of our executives came from different automotive companies and cultures. The decision was made to create a language and way of doing business that we all could share and embrace as our own. This helped ensure ownership from the beginning. The words were kept as simple and meaningful as possible so that everyone could understand what they meant. We had a very customer-centric culture where every worker understood that their productivity impacted the work of their colleagues at each stage of the production process. They saw each other as customers, as well as the end users. Our mantra, 'nothing but the best for our customers – let's do our best together', was communicated at multiple levels and was a central part of the belief system of those working with us.

The mission was a consistent message that was integrated into everything people delivered. The leadership team bought together the entire workforce on a regular basis so that colleagues could celebrate the growth of the company. While sharing information, these team meetings also explored how employees were executing the mission.

In 2008, Logica created a six-chapter Logica Story. The six elements share the story of Logica's goals, direction and strategy. Once created, it was distributed to all 40,000 employees, in their local languages, within nine weeks. Each business update signposts directly to one of the six panels of the Logica story so that people have a clear line of sight from the message they hear through to the strategy. Managers are expected to host dialogue about progress towards the goals outlined in the story, and a series of innovative suggestions about productivity and effectiveness have come directly from such discussions. Within the Logica People Survey, employees are asked whether they've had the chance to engage with the Logica story. In areas where scores are low, leaders immediately talk to the managers responsible and suggest ways to ensure that their people see the connection between their role and the bigger picture.

Logica has found that it can't substitute face-to-face sessions with technology, but it does use it where it's not practical to regularly gather global groups together. Teams have found higher levels of understanding when applications such as Live Meeting are used alongside video and teleconferencing. However, true effectiveness comes from the way meetings are structured and followed up. The top 250 leaders in Logica regularly meet via videoconferencing for an update about strategy and performance, gathering in 20 local hubs across the world to participate in a three-hour session. A significant effort is put into preparing the right content and anticipating the types of questions that may be asked. It starts with a global plenary, then breaks into local team discussions at each hub. The whole group reconvenes and each team feeds back its discussions and conclusions in a plenary session before the next steps are identified and action owners assigned. The structure is highly involving, and allows each group to digest the information shared and interpret what it means for them. Each leader is much better equipped to share outcomes and information with their teams than if they had spent three hours listening to one-way presentations.

The Strategist

Senior leaders are critical to designing plans to engage employees. This includes working with individual managers to build talent strategy for their business areas, and helping to identify the key roles and what high-potential talent is most appropriate to fill them. It also means encouraging and supporting your people by moving employees if they aren't good people managers. Poor engagers are poisonous and infectious at a senior level. If managers remain in post despite being consistent poor engagers, it sends a negative signal to the rest of the organisation. It's an essential leadership role to remove such individuals.

Senior leaders have an additional responsibility to share ownership effectively by developing strategies as a leadership team.

Diageo sees leadership behaviours as a significant lever to achieve its desired goals, and has a leadership standard that was devised by a subset of the executive team with input from leaders across the globe. It's published internally, and each leader is measured against these six factors:

1. Be authentic.
2. Create possibilities.
3. Bring purpose to life.
4. Create the conditions for people to succeed.
5. Consistently deliver great performance.
6. Grow yourself.

The Coach

For a manager to engage people effectively, he must find the fuel to engage others. He will also encourage greater engagement by understanding the deep drivers of his people and working with them.

For a senior leader, it's also important to build harmony within his team so that all individuals are pulling in the same direction. This means demonstrating a consistent approach to the organisation and developing a shared language. A coaching style of leadership takes more time than a more dictatorial approach, so a great Coach will also create time to engage people. Debra Nelson, Vice President of Diversity at MGM Resorts, framed it very well during an interview with her for this book: 'There is an urgency to perform, but as leaders we have to learn patience.'

Janet Markwick, Chief Finance Officer at Grey London, is known for her ability to coach others informally in her business. She often helps managers when they are faced with performance challenges by asking 'Have you spoken to the individual about the issue?' and 'How do you think that person might feel?' She has found that these two questions unlock a different way of perceiving and tackling problems. 'Coaching isn't something that's written in the job description of most CFOs,' she reflects, 'but I believe it's a fundamental part of my role as a leader.'

The Pilot

The role of manager as Pilot is all about solid, adult and trusted behaviour. Pilots are consistent and anchored. As a senior leader, it's critical that you understand the impact of your personal style on others. Most employees tend to look to those in more senior roles for leadership by example, and will be ready to judge the match between saying and doing.

As a senior leader, value your own engagement style. Be aware of how best to use it to create employees who are investors. The way you behave as a leader will determine the level of trust others have in you.

One of the most important factors for senior leaders to demonstrate and build in the organisational culture is trust. Managers need to trust their senior leaders, and senior leaders need to trust their managers and empower them appropriately in all ways if they are to give them the best possible chance to turbo-charge their people. High levels of trust are needed at every stage within the organisation if it is to operate at its best. Managers need to feel trusted, and thus will be more likely to trust their people.

Trust between employees and management makes it possible to do business in an environment packed full of rules and regulations. Organisations where people at every level trust the people at every other tier work more effectively. When trust is low, efficiency breaks down and costs go up as people invest time and effort in defensive behaviour to protect themselves.

As Pilots, senior leaders will go beyond their management roles and devolve responsibility by trusting others. As Coaches, they will guide others to be successful within that trusted environment. In doing so, they create ownership, and thus engagement within their management groups.

Leaders need to be deliberate in increasing their efforts as Pilots during times of huge uncertainty or crisis, when people look to them to check whether they have a firm hand on the tiller. Retreating is not an option, even when circumstances dictate that you turn your attention elsewhere. This is the time when people need to see you.

In 2010, airspace in many areas of western Europe was closed because of air safety concerns created by a volcanic ash cloud. Naomi Climer, Senior Vice President of Professional Services Business at Sony, and numerous team members were in Las Vegas at the time, attending a major trade show. The ash had closed airports, and it quickly became clear that it wasn't going to be easy to return home to Europe. Naomi heard that most hotels were already fully booked. She could see the anxiety of many members of staff, so she dialled up her role as a Pilot.

Naomi personally called a number of hotels and secured rooms for all her employees. She booked a suite for use as an office so that the group had a central meeting place to come to each day. She explained that people could drop in and out as they pleased and there was no pressure to show up and demonstrate that work was taking place. Naomi booked a show for everyone to attend and arranged other activities such as a cycling trip at Death Valley.

She asked her personal assistant to call all employees who had already left Las Vegas and were due to fly home from other airports. Her personal assistant asked whether each individual needed anything. One person required medical help but wasn't sure whether insurance would cover it. Naomi's assistant was able to resolve this issue and give permission for the individual to seek the help he needed. Naomi remembers:

I realised I had to do something – taking charge was not my preferred style, but circumstances forced me to do things differently. I learnt a lot and I could feel that this was what was needed at the time.

Leaders in their role as Pilots must know when to encourage managers and teams to open up their field of vision and when to keep them focused on one point. Think about when you last went for a walk in a forest. What did you notice? Did you see the destination in front of you, or the process to reach your destination? Or did you see the total environment around you and the different fauna and flora nearby? Managers are often focused on the target or destination ahead, and forget that they have the ability to look more widely and see what's around them – discovering more and occasionally finding new routes to explore.

Stretch your arms out in front of you, palms facing you. Wiggle your fingers. This is your field of vision.

Now take your arms and stretch them out either side of you so that you have 180 degrees of vision in the air. Turn your head and look around you. What do you see?

How much do you really use your abilities to see what is going on around you and consider the impact you have, and the implications of the environment on your team.

As a leader, you can give managers the courage to widen their field of vision and understand that it's appropriate to be aware of some of areas on the periphery, but not to focus on them all the time. The narrow periphery is the vision of a hunter. The wider field of vision is the social, exploratory approach.

Senior leaders as Pilots also have to role-model by demonstrating the importance of people management and engagement in multiple ways. David McClements, Managing Director of Whitewater Training and Consultancy International and former Organisational Development Director at BBC Worldwide, has worked with leaders of all levels throughout his career. He constantly challenges leaders by asking them to think about what they are paid for. He explains:

There are two key things that leaders are here to do: think and manage their teams. They aren't paid to run around with their hair on fire at a leadership level. However, it's easy to lose that perspective in business, so getting people to focus on their primary role is important.

David himself has changed his management style as a result of posing this question to leaders:

I ask myself regularly, what is it that my team can't do? I then focus my efforts on the areas where I can add the most value. In team meetings I ask my people to share an update on progress but I also ask them to give me a things-to-do list too. This usually involves connecting with board members or gaining buy-in to a new initiative. I've learnt that this gives my great talent the space to learn and grow. It also means I can add value where it's actually needed: by providing vision, support and enabling their projects to be a success.

For managers as Pilots, it's important to demonstrate how much they value individuals. The art of appreciation can be practised by leaders across multiple tiers, but at a practical level, leaders who get to know their people make a big difference in promoting emotional, engaging feelings about the business.

Steve Thorn is an exceptional leader. I asked him where he'd been inspired during his career and who had played a part in influencing his leadership style. He told me that his first employer was the Royal Navy. On his first day aboard the ship after only weeks of training, a young and nervous Steve was greeted by the captain. Within hours, that captain took him on a tour and introduced him to all 226 crew on board. He introduced Steve to each individual using their name, and commented on their role and how they played a critical part in keeping the ship at sea. Each person had a personal introduction no matter what their rank – from senior officers through to the laundry team. Steve remembers the experience vividly, and how proud each person looked as he was introduced. Years later, as Global Transformation Director at Logica, Steve has a deep understanding of the importance of valuing each individual with whom he works. When he attends a new programme meeting, he goes around the room and greets each individual. He uses their name, and comments on the role they play and its importance to the programme: 'I believe you do xxx role and you therefore do xxx for the programme.' He spends a few minutes the night before a meeting consulting the Logica White Pages directory online to ensure that he knows the faces, names and what each person does. Before the meeting, he will spend five minutes with the programme manager to check that the attendee list hasn't changed. To Steve, this isn't a best practice or unusual – it's simply the way he works. As many will realise, it *is* unusual in most organisations. For a small amount of investment of time, a project manager can achieve an immediate connection with the group and gain huge respect. That's the basis for effective teams, and thus performance.

18 *The Senior Leader as Prophet*

In the role of Prophet, senior leaders have an additional organisational role to play in the broader sense of conveying the company's purpose and direction to staff at multiple levels. As managers, Prophets provide aspirational examples for their staff. At senior leadership levels, it's vital to use this role to engage employees by doing the following:

- Provide extraordinary visionary language that inspires at all levels.
- Understand that the organisation will filter messages.

Provide Extraordinary Visionary Language that Inspires at All Levels

This involves using every opportunity to talk with different communities within the company about the vision, using highly aspirational language. It's important that senior leaders talk constantly about the purpose of the organisation and inspire people in everything they do. The core of each message about the purpose should be consistent, but the Prophet may change emphasis depending on the types of people within the organisation being engaged. Just like the manager as Culture Builder, the leader never forgets the purpose, and keeps it at his core.

Understand that the Organisation Will Filter Messages

An effective Prophet understands that visionary messages will be filtered as they work through the organisation. As a child, you may remember playing the game 'Chinese whispers'. The Prophet's message will undergo similar distortion as it works through the various layers of the hierarchy – this isn't a criticism of the organisation, more a fact of life when one message travels through many. There are two considerations for senior leaders as Prophets.

The first is that they must directly reach as many employees as possible with the vision. This reduces the risk of dilution and helps to ensure that front-line staff hear, and are inspired by, the message.

The second is to ensure repetition, repetition and repetition. You may express the vision differently each time, but it's important to repeat it over and over to break through the filters at all levels.

Debra Nelson, Vice President of Diversity at MGM Resorts, calls it the 'waterfall effect that has to flow from the leadership level through every management layer and beyond'. With conscious intent, the leader must ensure that the waterfall doesn't become blocked along the way, she says.

19 *The Senior Leader as Storyteller*

Senior leaders in organisations have a vital part to play in ensuring that everyone understands and shares the direction of the business. High levels of engagement come when people feel like they own the company. To do this, they must feel like they are part of the story about where the organisation is heading, and how it is doing so.

Senior leaders need to be articulate and clear in conveying the story about organisational direction. They also need to involve people so that they feel shared ownership and thus are more likely to be investors. Specifically, for senior leaders this involves the following:

- Involve the organisation to create the story.
- Brief managers.
- Tell the story often and differently.
- Help others to value uncertainty.
- Represent the company story externally.

Involve the Organisation to Create the Story

A senior leader can use a variety of methods to involve others in the organisation to co-create the story about direction and stepping-stones. In her role as Prophet, she will have excited people about the top-level company purpose and ignited a desire among individuals to understand more about what the purpose and direction mean to them.

Co-creating the story takes more time and energy than simply defining the story and telling others about it. Inviting the wider organisation to participate and shape the detail takes more investment and patience from senior leaders. The return on investment, though, is huge, because if teams feel they have been involved and have a deeper level of understanding as a result, they will be able to implement programmes more rapidly.

Involving people helps them to gain the level of understanding required to take action. High levels of performance result when people are all pulling in the same direction.

Involving the organisation in creating the story means sharing the overall purpose, then providing a framework and environment to allow people to explore it themselves and offer input about how they feel they can contribute as departments, groups and individuals. The CEO can start by giving a clear picture of his desired destination for the organisation. Other senior leaders can then join in by expressing how they see the future. Teams across the organisation can then be invited to think about what the journey to get there involves.

As a leader, it's your responsibility to be involved in involving others. This can be done in a variety of ways, including focus groups, large-scale conferences and workshops. Fujio Nishida, President of Sony Europe, did exactly this when defining the purpose of the organisation at the start of a culture change to place creativity more firmly at the centre of its business values. He invited senior leaders to a workshop to discuss and define the purpose and values. The result was a feeling of shared ownership and the capability to introduce and socialise this with their teams. Full details can be found in Chapter 23.

Brief Managers

It is senior leadership's responsibility to ensure that managers are briefed about the stories in the organisation, and explicitly how they will support the need to engage colleagues. Therefore, leaders need to involve managers and brief them about the top-level direction as well as day-to-day achievements and progress. If leaders are not proactive in ensuring that the managers who report to them and other managers throughout the hierarchy are aware of developments, priorities and direction, problems of alignment and disengagement quickly arise.

Good managers always want to be on the front foot. They want to have the information they need so that they can do a good job and appear in control. Managers require this of leaders, so senior leadership members need to deliver.

On the third day of his annual leadership conference in 2008, Stuart Fletcher, former President International of Diageo, asked for all operations, including warehouses and manufacturing and customer service centres, to be shut down for 30 minutes so that staff could participate via conference call. Seventy-five telephone lines were used to connect 6,500 employees across the world to hear Stuart express his heartfelt appreciation about what had been achieved to date and how essential each individual would continue to be in the future. Before the call, managers were given the key messages so they could schedule team sessions after the event to explore what they had heard in more depth. Some places held events immediately; others waited until the next business day to hold team meetings. The feedback was so personally moving for Stuart that he has continued this approach ever since. In 2010, 8,500 people participated in the call.

Burger King International welcomed a new President, Nish Kankiwala, in 2003. He quickly developed a new strategy, and was keen to help people understand and engage with it effectively. Kai Boschmann former Senior Communication Director at Burger King International, explained:

Nish understands the importance of internal communication and engagement. We wanted to find an inspirational way of getting key messages across to our people and that started with engaging our managers.

At the annual management conference, Kai created an experience aligned to each of the organisation's five strategic pillars. Kai explained:

Nish would talk about having an aspiration for Burger King having the first quick service restaurant on the moon, so one of the presentation rooms at the event was made to look like a moon landscape by bringing a load of sand into a hotel suite. People were asked to put on an astronaut costume before entering.

The group also talked about it being a challenge to find 'talent among the jungle', so another room was decorated to resemble a jungle, including reproducing a thunderstorm and rain. People wore safari suits as they entered. Kai reported;

The experiential element opened the senses and made the messages stick for managers. This fun and memorable way of telling the story made it much easier for people to understand and engage with. It also meant they had more confidence to go back and share the story with their people vividly.

The task of briefing managers doesn't take a huge amount of time. What it offers in return for leaders is an organisation that is more capable of understanding different stories and taking action as a result. It's also a likely contributor to high performance, as reported by Melcrum in it's *Developing a Communication Toolkit for Managers* report (Melcrum 2011), which highlights research from HSBC and the UffindellWest consultancy in 2008 that looked at the challenges of building dialogue between managers and employees, and found that organisations that were high performers in this area:

*   make communication a formal part of the line manager's role and give each line manager effective communication training;
*   send briefing materials direct to front-line managers that are tailored to the local context;
*   audit the process to ensure that it's happening;
*   use technology to enable faster, more professional solutions;
*   have a supportive leadership team.

Tell the Story Often and Differently

The Storyteller role involves imparting context, and this applies at both a leadership and management level. Senior leaders have an additional responsibility to provide context across the organisation. 'Why' and 'What it means for you' are the core components of the leadership narrative for engagement. To understand it at a deep level, employees need to hear the story on more than one occasion. They need to hear the story often, and in ways that appeal to their individual engagement styles. The leader must tell the story at least seven times over a period of six months to be sure that people even have a chance of understanding it. She must also tailor the story to the audience.

This means that when a senior leader goes to a location to share the top-level story, she needs to take time to understand the types of people she is talking with – their roles and issues. Leaders who are great Storytellers and engagers are able to pitch the story at the correct level by making it meaningful for their audience. This means using anecdotes and metaphors that will resonate with the audience. It entails using real examples that show that the leader understands them and their challenges.

The stories need to be consistent and told by senior leaders to as many people as possible in every interaction. In some cases, it may be best to hold a formal story-telling session, such as an all-staff broadcast or conference. In other cases, a senior leader can sit with a group in the staff restaurant at lunchtime and take the opportunity to tell the story in a very different way by explaining some of the challenges she has been dealing with that morning.

At the Bellagio Resort in Las Vegas, leaders understand the importance of making desired behaviour practical so that employees can understand what's expected of them. The team is obsessed with delivering excellent customer service, and the President recently made a video that illustrated specifically how employees could demonstrate respect for individuals at the resort. He gave practical examples of going beyond saying 'May I help you?' and expressing a genuine interest in guests' stay. He wanted to show how simple it was to live the values, but in a highly practical and engaging way.

It's essential that leaders share the story with managers across the organisation too. If managers understand the purpose and direction of their organisation, they are much more likely to be able to take it on board and become Storytellers to engage their own people. It's also important for leaders to share with managers because a clear purpose acts as a compass for the organisation and enables managers to feel comfortable with the levels of empowerment they're given. A clear purpose and strategy provides a framework within which decisions can be taken. This means that managers can work with their teams to be efficient, effective and innovative because they have a check and balance for themselves.

Ensuring understanding of the organisation's purpose is the first stage in engaging people and making managers' jobs easier in terms of sustaining engagement. It's the first part of the strategic narrative that the MacLeod report identifies as a core component needed for effective engagement (MacLeod and Clarke 2009).

Help Others to Value Uncertainty

Large organisations tend to engage their people in terms of purpose, vision and values or specifics connected to change. Smaller organisations are often more focused on engaging people to be more agile, confident about uncertainty and happier with the chaotic world that businesses operate within. For people working in a small or medium-sized organisations, it's often easier for them to see and become affected by the market conditions around them. For many in large companies, they are further away from the rapidly changing dynamics outside.

A senior leader in a small or medium-sized company therefore has a significant role to play in helping people see that they can manage what they can control and stop worrying about what they can't. Acknowledging that it's perfectly all right to feel uncertain as a result of market dynamics is part of the context-setting role of the CEO and other senior leaders.

If people feel more at ease with uncertainty, they are less likely to become unnecessarily anxious. However, there is risk that they will underestimate the severity of issues in some cases. This means that senior leaders have to very quickly be explicit about any crisis that could hit the business, and not assume that employees will be able to work out the degree of severity of any impact for themselves. There's a fine balance here between motivating and scaring people – the latter is a short-term unsustainable fix that will make future change harder.

Represent the Company Story Externally

A strong employer brand is important because it helps to ensure that future employees have the correct values, fit within the organisation's culture, and that the organisation attracts the best talent. This means that leaders as Storytellers must be involved in representing the company story externally in all their outward-facing actions.

Company brand image, reputation and what it stands for also play a significant role in the degree to which employees are engaged at work. Internal engagement can be boosted hugely if the company is seen as somewhere people want to come and work. Senior leaders need to remember to represent the company purpose and values in every interaction with external people. They also need to place enough emphasis on an employer brand strategy and devote time to working with human resources to understand how they can play a key role in delivering it.

Where outsiders have a clear understanding of an organisation's brand values and then seek employment with it, their levels of engagement are likely to be higher than where they don't actively select the company based on shared values. According to former Human Resources Director Gordon Lyle, Starbucks has found that a significant number of consumers become partners. As consumers, individuals may understand the Starbucks brand values (as we discussed in Part I) because they see them being lived in the branches they visit. Next time you visit a Starbucks, see what you notice: a community board on the wall with details of local contributions and community activity; pictures and photographs of communities where coffee originates that have been helped through sales; a service ethos among staff. The toilet facilities are often clean and available – another mark of the commitment to customers and community. As consumers, many people identify with what Starbucks stands for, and thus have a high desire to join the company. Shared values and a feeling that their work will make a difference is a major reason why great talent will join Starbucks rather than one of its competitors. Once someone becomes an employee, they already have a high degree of engagement. There's a good understanding about where the company is going, its purpose, vision and guiding principles. An emotional connection exists before the individual even becomes an employee, and partners often see significance in what they do.

Employer brand work is hugely important in helping to ensure that candidates join the organisation because they see a connection between the values of the company and their own beliefs.

CHAPTER 20 *The Senior Leader as Strategist*

As a manager, your role as Strategist is to engage others. As a senior leader, you need to be more involved in defining the leadership engagement strategy and your organisation's design at a macro level. This means being actively involved with key talent at different levels of the organisation so that you can nurture them and ensure that plans are in place to grow your leaders of the future. Specifically, as a senior leader, you need to:

- Ensure your organisation's design is appropriate.
- Spend time with key talent and be involved in departmental talent strategies.
- Ensure that processes are fit for purpose.
- Measure management success in engaging others to perform.

Ensure Your Organisation's Design is Appropriate

An appropriate organisational structure and design is a must. Clear roles and responsibilities help people to take accountability and avoid duplication of effort. It's the senior leader's role to be involved by giving input to the organisational design needed for success. This is particularly important if the business is in a changing environment and needs to reposition itself for the future. For example, the executive leadership team at UKTV recognised the need to change from being a business that predominately showed television 'repeats', to one that entertained audiences through newly acquired and commissioned programmes. They saw the requirement to grow fans of brands rather than channels. Although this strategy kept UKTV in the television business, it also needed a new organisational design and capabilities. The leadership team actively gave input to the design they felt was needed. An overarching structure was developed and then given to the managers across the business to define in more depth. This was a way to engage managers but also allowed them to create the design needed for the business that they believed would best make UKTV successful in its ambition.

Spend Time with Key Talent and be Involved in Departmental Talent Strategies

It's a leadership responsibility to ensure that the right talent is placed in the most appropriate roles to enable them to bring the best of themselves to everything they do. If great talent is in key positions, they are likely to engage people naturally. Simon Ashby,

General Manager at Sony, believes that the primary way to engage people for improved and sustained business performance is through an effective talent management strategy. He says that this starts at a leadership level:

> *If great talent are in the right places, they know what has led to their success and therefore they will engage their people so much better than the average manager. This creates a multiplier effect, because people in that team see a great role model and start to demonstrate those behaviours themselves. The result is a higher performing organisation over time.*

It's important for leaders to keep focused on development and retention strategies for key talent because they have such a significant influence directly on business success and also indirectly through the way they engage people to perform at their best. This is important, not only because it's a way of retaining talent in itself, but it's also a way of giving hope to others that the company values people that perform at a high level and continue their own professional development.

Leaders have a direct responsibility to spend time with key talent as part of any retention strategy. Where talent pools are identified, leaders should attend development programmes and consider breakfast sessions, work shadow opportunities and sponsoring a member of the talent pool.

Novartis runs a Leadership Discovery Programme for emerging high potential talent. The Head of Europe runs a 13 billion dollar business yet is a passionate believer in building talent. So much so that he is highly involved with the selection of all talent development programmes, particularly the one for more junior talent pools. He attends the whole programme and ensures his entire leadership team is present for the end-of-programme dinner. People going through the programme feel a huge connection to him as a result of their time together and he is able to get to know each of them personally. Through building relationships with his leaders of the future, he is building trust and role modelling the exact type of behaviours he expects from them. Line managers are invited to attend at various points throughout the programme so that they can see the journey their people have started upon and be best equipped to support them to continue it. By inviting line managers to the talent development programme, Novartis aims to ensure that managers see the value that is placed upon providing a climate that allows people to perform at their best; to learn and grow. Line managers feel included in the development process and feel more ownership for the successful development of their people. It's a simple quick win that hits many of the areas of leader as Culture Builder.

During 2010–2011, Sony Europe undertook a restructure of its back office operations across the continent. It was one of the most significant programmes the company had ever embarked upon, involving huge complexity at a business and people level. Simon Ashby, then VP Sony Europe, led the highly successful programme. He was absolutely clear from the beginning that if the programme was going to be successful, it needed to draw in the best possible talent from around the business. When recruiting for the programme manager, Simon enlisted the help of an external recruitment agency and encouraged people from within the organisation to apply. 'The result was even more successful than I had anticipated' remembers Simon. 'I'd seen this as a great opportunity to make visible the aspirations and desires of some great people in our company. I also saw it as a way of key people receiving feedback that would help them develop their careers further. We'd also get a great candidate. This all happened, but in addition we also chose an internal candidate that surprised some people because it wasn't a person well known throughout the business. This gave others the signal that there was a chance for anyone with the right skills and attitude to flourish'.

During my research I heard of a global company with a leadership development programme open for applications from any individuals within the organisation. It's a high profile example of signifying the importance of investing in people within the organisation and that anyone can progress to higher levels if they have the right attitude, capability and capacity. The programme acts as a totem for people in the business. It shows that anyone in the organisation has the opportunity to be successful and that is a strong message to employees.

At a more practical level, within Innocent, every manager has a one-page document that captures their main responsibilities and objectives. This is no more than one page and sits on the intranet so everyone can see.

Ensure that Processes are Fit for Purpose

The organisation needs to have the right processes for people to be able to perform at their best. Leadership has a responsibility to ensure that processes help rather than hinder performance. Leaders will have their own areas of responsibility within the operation. Process improvement is often an area of ongoing focus in many organisations. However, it is rarely seen as having an influence on employee engagement. Yet if processes stifle performance or innovation, it's disengaging for people. Leaders therefore need to be aware that more operational areas have an impact on engagement and performance if they are not operating at their best.

Measure Management Success in Engaging Others to Perform

Leaders have a role in checking that all managers are engaging with their people and that they are setting a suitable climate to encourage others to engage and perform. It's critical that they do this, and don't just leave it to their communication professionals.

In some businesses, managers are measured through annual engagement survey scores. This gives leaders a clear and quantitative way to gauge how good managers are at engaging their employees. Great senior leaders will include specific targets in managers' performance objectives that can be measured by company surveys. This is an excellent way to signal the importance of engagement to middle and line managers. It's useful if this is supplemented by conversations between senior leaders and managers about how they are engaging teams or individuals, and with what outcomes. This helps engagement to become part of the organisational culture rather than simply a key performance indicator.

At Diageo, in the International Division, line managers are measured on their ability to release the potential of their people. They have been given the tools to do the job, and are now measured accordingly. The key point here is that managers have been given the tools to do a great job of realising the potential of their people. It's not enough simply to measure; as a Coach, Pilot and Storyteller, a leader has to share the tools for the job.

The Novartis performance management process measures people on 'how they do' as well as 'what they achieve'. Managers set performance goals with their people to ensure that values are reflected through behaviour in addition to the 'harder' business measures. Managers are also incentivised and appraised on the behaviours they display and how they bring the values of the organisation to life. Managers are expected to develop talent, and are judged on their ability to achieve this.

Managers in the John Lewis Partnership have a different sense of their roles than in some other organisations, so it's not just leaders who measure their ability to engage others. Partners' Counsellor Patrick Lewis explains:

> We see it as an upside-down pyramid. As a manager, you're employed by your people, so it's important that you understand what our purpose, direction and any change means for them. It's critical that our managers are the best they can be, because partners judge their ability to contribute to the business on a daily basis. We have elected partners in our stores, so in a typical site of 200 partners, five or six of them will be feeding any issues to their leaders and up to the Partnership Council. This means that any manager who fails to engage partners is quickly identified and action is taken by a leader.

21 *The Senior Leader as Coach*

The role of senior leaders goes beyond that of manager as Coach that we discussed earlier. Senior leaders are responsible for creating a culture where they and line managers hold coaching-style conversations that unlock the potential of individuals, both in formal development terms and more tactically in day-to-day dialogue about what action is needed in the organisation. Specifically, for senior leaders this involves doing the following:

- Proactively create a culture of development.
- Coach managers who do not report directly to you.
- Support investment in people development.
- Give line managers more space.
- Support managers using ongoing dialogue.
- Let people share their ideas directly with senior leaders.

Proactively Create a Culture of Development

Senior leaders can help everyone to flourish by creating a culture of development. This means demonstrating that you value the development of people by investing in it, talking about it and believing that it's worthwhile to devote time, effort and money into advancing the capabilities of employees. 'My personal growth' is one of the eight factors that Best Companies says influences engagement. The organisation and managers have a role in ensuring that individuals feel that their personal growth is being considered, but senior leaders must also behave in a way that shows that development is valued.

Practically, this means protecting training budgets, encouraging those who report directly to you to attend conferences and advance their own potential, and involving executives in talking openly about the development they are experiencing through networking, formal education and sharing best practice.

MGM Grand uses development programmes as a lever to increase employee engagement. Extensive leadership training is available for all levels of employees as part of its development plans, and a culture of development is actively encouraged.

Coach Managers Who do Not Report Directly to You

Senior leaders can make a huge difference to engagement levels by coaching employees who don't directly report to them in the hierarchy. Engagement levels rocket and capability rises among the individuals being coached or mentored.

Leaders need to invest and role-model coaching-style conversations and management styles. This will be more abundant in organisations that proactively create a culture of development. Sarah Henbrey, Organisational Development Director at 3, says:

> So many times I've heard employees go to managers and ask 'What should I do?' The manager responds by telling the person what to do. It's done with good intentions, but giving the answer causes an ongoing issue of lack of empowerment among teams and individuals. More can be unlocked and made possible among most individuals if they are managed via a coaching-style relationship. Given that most managers haven't had the skills development to lead or manage this way, it's vital that senior leaders role-model coaching behaviour and invest in coaching skills for managers.

Stuart Fletcher, former President International at Diageo, dedicated at least 10 per cent of his time each year to directly engaging with management and staff throughout all levels of the business. He met with them in formal town hall sessions in each country, but also held one-to-one 'skip-level' meetings, coaching sessions and mentoring conversations with individual managers across the world. He did this face-to-face when visiting the countries, and also via telephone. He saw it as a core part of his responsibility to engage the organisation and to be a role model for other leaders and managers. Stuart knows that it's a leadership imperative to engage with leaders at all levels in the business, and believes wholeheartedly that it has contributed to the phenomenal growth in the Diageo's International Region over the past six years. Stuart was responsible for a large number of people across Diageo, so if he could find 10 per cent of his time to dedicate to developing others, it's difficult to argue that you couldn't do something similar.

Senior leaders can demonstrate a coaching style in larger forums in addition to one-to-one situations. In large town hall events designed to increase levels of understanding, communication tends to be fairly one-way. A question and answer session may be introduced after speaker presentations. Consider turning this into a large coaching-style environment by asking the audience members questions and opening a dialogue. This promotes greater understanding and encourages people to think more deeply about what's being said. Asking questions has the potential to convert employees from savers to investors because a deeper level of reflection is required. A similar approach can be used in small employee group gatherings or breakfast sessions.

In addition to acting as a Coach, there are times when more insight is useful to help yourself or the business. That insight can come from younger members of the organisation, and can become a win–win situation because leaders benefit from knowledge and employees are given access to senior people, so their engagement level improves. BBC Worldwide uses reverse-mentoring to help share market understanding at many levels. Employees who actively use social media tools are invited to mentor senior leaders about the trends they see. They have a dialogue about possible opportunities for the business, with some leaders regularly connecting with individuals to test ideas. The result is greater insight, and employees who feel valued that they can make an even greater contribution than in their direct role.

Support Investment in People Development

The organisation will create investors if people feel valued as individuals. Senior leaders can exercise influence in this area by supporting investment cases for people development and ring-fencing the associated budgets. In times of turbulence, it's common for organisations to cut training and development budgets. This sends a negative signal to employees about their value to senior leaders. The amount of money that is saved is also usually relatively small. As a senior leader, challenge yourself and think about how you can support investment in people development during difficult times. It may be that the type of development needs to be more creative. For example, you could consider job shadowing in a partner company as an alternative to formal training. However, senior leaders must support investment in staff development if they are to get the best out of people.

Give Line Managers More Space

The reality is that most middle managers have multiple demands on their time and energy, both at home and at work. They are often overwhelmed and unable to devote sufficient time to people management, thinking time, and thus innovation. Processes often get in the way of speedy decision-making, and in large organisations risk consuming even more time for the average middle manager. If leaders want to enable managers to be their best, they need to consider making the lives of managers easier. This means giving them the space to do their jobs effectively. Very often, this comes from making sure that processes are fit for purpose. We discussed the importance of this earlier in the context of the Strategist role.

During 2010–2011, Sony Europe began a major programme to overhaul its back office operations. Simon Ashby, Senior Vice President of Operations, led the eighteen-month transformation. Both he and his colleague Roy White attribute the programme's success to making space for managers to manage their people and be their best throughout an emotionally and practically difficult transformation.

As a senior leader, consider what you could do to create more space for your managers to manage and engage their employees. How can you ensure that managers use that space to actually manage and engage staff, rather than focusing more on the comfort zone of their day job to fill that time?

Support Managers Using Ongoing Dialogue

Senior leaders can support managers in a variety of ways to help them engage their people. The importance of doing this has been highlighted in earlier chapters, but it's worth emphasizing the senior leadership's responsibility to support managers by hosting, facilitating and encouraging dialogue, particularly concerning major change issues. It's difficult for managers to perform their role as Storytellers if they haven't had the opportunity to talk with senior leaders and understand more about what is happening. It's also likely that their understanding will only be at a saver level unless an extensive dialogue is held in a coaching style.

During a period of change, leaders can take practical steps to do this by setting up forums to enable managers to talk with other managers. These offer an excellent way to share experiences and challenges. Gordon Watt used them very successfully when he led the project to close Galileo's Systems Development division at Swindon in the UK and transfer the responsibilities to Denver in the USA. Managers came together once a week in a forum to talk about the issues they were facing in motivating their people during a rapidly moving and unexpected shock, and helped each other to find solutions to their individual challenges. Gordon attended, but as an observer rather than leader. He'd set up the meetings, but wanted the managers to take ownership and gain whatever value they felt appropriate from the forum. It was hugely successful, and provided a simple way to ensure that managers had access to whatever they needed to keep their people focused and engaged. As a manager, you don't need to wait for someone else to set up such initiatives. If you're leading a change programme, use manager forums as a way to keep your key stakeholders engaged. If you're a leader, set one up and encourage managers to take ownership to keep the conversation valuable and relevant.

Innocent has recently started a leadership programme for middle managers across the 280-strong organisation. When engagement results come through each quarter, the executive board involves the various cohorts in discussing the results and what they mean for the business. This offers an opportunity for them to give their own viewpoints, but also to ask questions and gain clarity about areas that are important to their teams. The groups come together over lunch. This is easy to organise, and the result is an engaged leadership team that is well placed to convey greater clarity to their own teams. It also helps leaders to be consistent in their explanations because they've had the chance to explore rationales and messages at a deeper level.

Let People Share their Ideas Directly with Senior Leaders

Leaders have a challenging balance to strike between being seen to deliver versus enabling their people to do great work. The culture of the organisation will dictate how far this balance tips in one direction or another. For example, some organisations expect their leaders to deliver great work. They expect their senior managers to present ideas and progress reports at board meetings even if it's their teams that have done the work. In other company cultures, it's accepted and encouraged that a senior leader sponsors a team member to come and present their work directly to the board. It's important for leaders to understand how to achieve this balance. Engagement comes from empowerment, and this to a large degree involves helping people to do great work, then letting them take the credit for it. Leaders who focus too much on taking credit for delivery often lose great talent because their staff feel suppressed and undervalued. This doesn't benefit the organisation in the long term. For leaders, it's important to give employees access so that their ideas can be heard.

The leadership development programme of a global media company allows participants regular and direct access to senior leaders on the board. As part of the twelve-month programme, each person is asked to progress an idea that will add value to the business, such as accessing a new market or reducing costs. Each person is given a board-level mentor to work with on advancing the initial idea. The first step is to investigate whether it's feasible. They work with their board-level sponsor throughout the year, and gain growth, visibility and insight during the process. The executive board has witnessed some fabulous ideas and been surprised about where some of them have originated. The programme is open to anyone in the business to attend, but is subject to an applications process. Anyone who applies is asked to put forward an idea as part of the process. Those who aren't accepted onto the programme are put in touch with the appropriate managing director in the business so that they can still share their ideas and they aren't lost.

22 *The Senior Leader as Pilot*

Senior leaders must be accessible, authentic and visible if they want to engage people across the organisation. In the role of Pilot, they will already be engaging if they follow the approaches required of a manager as Culture Builder. Senior leaders are obliged to be even more visible, highly authentic and accessible to people beyond their own direct reporting line. They can achieve this in the following ways:

- Be authentic.
- Be visible and accessible across the entire organisation.
- Be open when accepting feedback.
- Value managers for people management.
- Be clear about what's expected of managers.
- Take tough decisions, and share them honestly.
- Live the company's values.
- Role-model.
- Use an appropriate tone when conversing at all levels.

Be Authentic

Senior leaders need to authentic when conducting activity to engage others. If they try to be someone they're not, it will shine through incredibly brightly. Being authentic means understanding more about yourself (as your work to improve your manager as Culture Builder skills will have helped you identify) and how you operate when you are at your best. If you are an extrovert who loves being around others, find ways to engage with others that allow you to be this way. If you feel more comfortable meeting people one-to-one, use engagement approaches that lend themselves to more intimate opportunities that allow you to tell the story and build trust.

Be Visible and Accessible Across the Entire Organisation

Most employees want their senior leaders to be visible and accessible. In some cases, leaders are fabulous at walking the floor and simple gestures such as smiling and talking to others in the corridor. According to Towers Perrin (2008), only 41 per cent of employees agree that their senior managers try to be visible and accessible. This tells us that most senior leaders need to increase their visibility and accessibility.

This can be achieved in a number of ways, but applies to all senior leaders from the CEO down. It starts with spending time with people outside the immediate executive office. This is also true of senior leaders who are not on the executive board. It's very tempting to spend the majority of your time with those more senior than yourself, when you also need to be visible across the entire organisation.

The CEO must spend time with frontline managers as well as the broader employee base. A variety of studies have shown that the managers most responsible for a company's success or failure also happen to be the ones with whom the CEO spends the least amount of time. I have certainly found this from my work. Frontline managers and shop floor supervisors are at the very first level of management across businesses operations, so it's they who must motivate and boost the morale of the staff who ultimately execute any strategy on a day-to-day basis. Frontline and middle managers should be as deserving of a CEO's attention as senior leaders, yet few CEOs realise that it's their job to connect and engage with managers on a regular basis. This mindset needs to change if the environment in an organisation is going to be full of investors rather than savers.

For senior leaders, this isn't a difficult area in which to make a difference. The solution is simply to have dialogues with managers across the organisation on a regular basis. See it as a way to tap into the reality of your markets, not just a motivational exercise where you 'press the flesh' and share strategy.

Leader Top Tip

When you're visiting a location; be visible. How many times do people in a non-headquarters location know that a senior manager has even visited? Are you visible when you visit a location for a short succession of meetings?

Each time you visit a factory, sales office or other location, schedule an extra hour to host a roundtable dialogue with a cross-section of managers. Schedule skip-level meetings or ask a line manager to schedule a team lunch, and make it your business to attend. Be clear that your intention is simply to hear what's happening in the business, what people are feeling and thinking, and that it's a very informal opportunity to say hello.

Creativity and new ideas are what drive leaps in business. Most organisations are constantly searching for the next 'big idea' and expend huge investment in research. Great ideas often come from the most unlikely places in companies, so senior leaders absolutely need to give every person with a good idea or point of view access to senior leaders.

At the Stakis hotel group, major investment was devoted to bringing all employees together on a regular basis to 'press the flesh' with leaders. Line managers were important in motivating and communicating with employees on a day-to-day basis, but leaders saw that they had a significant role to play in spending time with individuals and getting to know them. CEO Sir Rio Stakis went to great lengths to be visible to his people across the hotel group. Employees said that everyone had met Sir Rio, or if they hadn't met him, a close colleague had.

Leader Top Tip

Use management by walking around on a Monday to help with the Monday-blues feeling and create more of a 'Thank God it's Monday' feeling among people in your business. Schedule time in your diary to walk around and ask people how their day is going, what they're hoping to achieve this week, or what excites them about the week ahead.

In a recession it's even more important for managers to feel engaged themselves and understand their critical role in keeping other people engaged. Leaders so often retreat and stop communicating and involving managers. This is dangerous – and the opposite is actually required. Often, tough decisions have to be made in times of economic pressure when locations are being closed, staff are being downsized and the organisation is divesting from areas of the business. During these times there is more operational pressure on managers, so it's important for leaders to show that they still value managers for motivating and caring for their people. Giving them enough information and space and rewarding them for being accessible and professional are vital. For managers, it's essential that they are visible during these tough times.

Be Open When Accepting Feedback

Openness is an essential quality of leadership, and is particularly important when you're trying to engage rather than disengage others. As a senior leader, your behaviour when responding to feedback or questions is critical. Your tone, approach, body language and what you say will be analysed and pulled apart, whether in a formal or informal setting: how you respond to a query or challenge from others, how emotive you become, how much you change your viewpoint, and why. All of these factors are important for a senior leader when accepting feedback. Get it right and you'll influence engagement levels very positively. Get it wrong and you'll risk losing the essential trust that a leader in the role of Pilot needs.

It's easy to lose respect and trust as a leader or manager. One global director told me of a meeting he'd attended recently where another senior leader had given a presentation to a hundred managers from across the world, then invited questions. One individual raised his hand and asked a question. The leader's reaction was to cut the person dead, possibly because the question related to something he'd already answered in his presentation. His behaviour created an immediate bristling reaction in the room, and people visibly disengaged. In one small moment, he'd lost the room and a huge amount of trust from the attendees. To this day, that leader hasn't regained trust among that management group, and this was more than a year ago.

As a senior leader, think about how you react to others. One of the core competencies of the Pilot is to remain composed and authoritative. A great Pilot never loses control of his emotions. Senior leaders need to draw on this skill when responding to questions. Be open to what others are asking, and see it as genuine enquiry rather than a judgement.

At an organisational level, higher engagement will come when large-scale events and roadshows include the opportunity to meet leaders or provide feedback through question and answer sessions. If these are being used, it's important for senior leaders to remember to remain open throughout. This can be tricky when it's a roadshow and each audience asks the same questions. However, for senior leaders, this is a good opportunity to give a consistent response to all audiences and to build on it each time, perhaps commenting that you realise it's an important question for people because it's been asked at each event.

Value Managers for People Management

An organisation has to value managers for their people management abilities if engagement levels in the company are to rise. As I've stated elsewhere in this book, people management is core to any leadership and management role in a highly engaged organisation. Senior leaders need to lead the way by promoting people based on their people management, motivation and engagement track record in addition to their technical experience. When announcing employees' promotions, it's also a good idea to mention this as one factor behind them. For example, in the email announcement congratulating a person on her promotion, include a quote from a senior leader expressing how delighted they are that this individual is being given the opportunity to do more, especially as her ability to create an environment where others can thrive is so noteworthy. Such messages send a strong signal to others in the organisation about what it values.

Be Clear About What's Expected of Managers

Senior leaders need to convey clear, succinct messages and to be explicit about what is expected of managers. This helps to start a chain reaction, because if there's a clear expectation from the top right down through the hierarchy, managers will have a desire to engage their people.

The obvious way to do this is by ensuring that a management objective for everyone, including senior leaders, is that they engage their teams effectively to perform at their best. Senior leaders can explain to the entire company what they expect of each other and how they will measure one another to ensure they are accountable. Starting by saying what you expect of yourself, then of each other, followed by expectations of managers is a powerful structure. It's a simple strategy, but very rarely put into action. Just reflect for a moment. When was the last time you were clear about what you expect from your managers? When was the last time a senior leader was explicit about what was expected from you?

Remember that senior leaders should expect deliverables from their managers, but also allow them to find enough time to reflect and strategise.

With so much pressure on time, it's often hard for managers to give themselves space for thinking and reflection, but in engagement terms, this is crucial. Great engagers are able to spot when someone's withdrawing or when side conversations are starting due to lack of understanding or satisfaction with a situation. They'll spot when performance is beginning to wobble, even in disparate or geographically spread teams. They use their intuition to notice the signs. Most are capable of this to some degree, but for those who do not have this strength, when under pressure, their intuition often fails. Kirstin Furber, Senior Vice President and Head of Human Resources at BBC Worldwide, commented:

I have found that great leaders make time to meditate and disconnect. This is so important, and I certainly know that my antennae are less effective when I'm full-on and don't make space for meditation and reflection.

Take Tough Decisions, and Share them Honestly

Being a leader can be difficult. During turbulent times, there are many storms for leaders to weather. During successful periods, there is often huge pressure to keep up momentum. Senior leaders have to take tough decisions, and that's part of their job. Often, these decisions will affect engagement levels because they have an impact on employees in some way. During such periods, managing change competency in a leader is crucial. All the roles of manager as Culture Builder have to be super-charged for leaders.

As a Pilot, there are two major rules. The first is to take tough decisions even if they're going to be unpopular, uncomfortable and painful for some communities in the short term. A guiding principle for a senior leader is to ask 'What's the right thing to do here?' A tough decision becomes slightly easier when you know that it's the right thing to do, even if it doesn't feel particularly good at the time.

The second rule is to share that decision with context and honesty. Explain why you've had to make the decision at least three times when first communicating. Keep doing so, because that's what people need to know. Even if it's a painful impact for some individuals, the fact that they understand the rationale will help them to navigate through in the long term. A senior leader also needs to be completely honest throughout the process. The Pilot's role involves being trusted and trusting. Trust erodes rapidly if a senior leader isn't honest. Telling people the truth is essential to keep people engaged throughout any difficult change. If the truth is tough, a senior leader then needs to draw on all of the roles of manager as Culture Builder for their own people. He also needs to be even more visible to people, as well as supporting managers throughout the hierarchy. This means giving them regular updates, even if there's no progress to report and involving them wherever possible so that their engagement levels are maximised.

As part of Logica's Programme for Growth, it decided to spend more on its client-facing activities, funded by rationalising its desk capacity and locations, reducing them by nearly 50 per cent, which meant that the headquarters in London was set to close. This was a significant announcement, and directly affected more than two thousand people. Not only was the site to be closed, but a new way of working would be implemented that entailed a major change in Logica's culture. People would be part-client/home workers, and spend a smaller proportion of their time in the office. Two hundred managers gathered in London for a meeting to talk about the company's direction. When, as part of this, it was announced that the old London office would close, immediate applause spread across the entire auditorium. The leadership team was stunned. People said 'Thank you for just making the decision and telling us so quickly.' They could see that the current operating model wasn't sustainable, and were grateful that a decision had been taken and they could move forward by sharing the news and implications with their teams. They spent the rest of the day working together to talk about the consequences of the decision and how to progress it practically. The context set as part of the announcement together with the speed of the decision and the honesty of the leaders meant a message about a major change to peoples' lives was successfully received. The level of dialogue and team-building at the event also equipped managers to go back and share the news effectively with their teams with the minimum amount of disruption.

Senior leaders have to be brave when leading change. Taking major decisions that are unpopular or hurt staff you care about may feel painful, but remember that you may be doing the right thing in the long run. Gordon Lyle, Stakis's former Head of Human resources reported:

> When Hilton Hotels acquired the Stakis hotel group, the leadership team decided to retain a Scottish-based office for Stakis members of staff. The team knew that many valued employees wouldn't move to the Watford-based Hilton office, so it decided to maintain a presence rather than lose great staff. The reality was that eventually the Scottish office closed, and the whole lead-up to it was quite painful.

He felt that sometimes it's better to be brave and make the tough decisions early so that people can move on, and not prolong the agony.

Live the Company's Values

Senior leaders usually set the company's values, so it's important that they live them. If you aren't prepared to live the values, then don't bother to communicate them. Through your work as a Prophet, you will have thought about your own purpose and values. You'll then have worked through how those align with what you stand for in the business. In the role of Pilot, senior leaders must live the values for the entire organisation to see. If senior leaders don't live the values, it signifies disconnection and lack of trust. Both are exceptionally disengaging for the organisation, and will not encourage people to become investors.

Many organisations identify purposes and values. These are displayed on posters and adorn the walls of offices throughout the world. Interestingly, most are common to all businesses. They often remain words, unless leadership and managers truly align activity with the purposes and values proclaimed.

In Diageo, the purpose of 'Celebrating Life Every Day Everywhere' had been established some time before Stuart Fletcher, former President International, and his team realised that it would mean so much more if people were excited and aligned behind a truly rich meaning of the phrase. He and his leadership team placed this organisational purpose at the core of their breakthrough strategy and helped people see how, by living the purpose, the business could become even stronger and more fantastic. They started by ensuring that the International Breakthrough Strategy was created to bring about the realisation of this purpose. In conversations with their teams, they shared their own personal purposes and how these connected to Diageo's purpose, focusing on leading conversations that imbued the organisation with energy, heartfulness and possibility. They brought to life in vivid ways three strategic areas of focus: 'amazing relationships bringing out the best', 'great times, great experiences' and 'enriched communities'.

Role-model

Senior leaders are critiqued like actors in the spotlight on the stage. They have an audience comprising their entire organisation. As soon as a senior leader arrives at the office, he is being observed, talked about and analysed. What he wears, whether he smiles, how he behaves while collecting his coffee – all are watched by employees and form the basis of water-cooler conversations around the organisation. It's therefore imperative that leaders role-model appropriate behaviour.

A great, possibly apocryphal, example of this is the story of Franklin D. Roosevelt, who while entertaining a guest was observed to pour some of his tea into a saucer, along with additional cream and sugar. The nervous guest, wanting to follow convention, immediately copied the president, and was horrified to see Roosevelt place his saucer on the floor for an eagerly waiting pet dog.

We talked earlier about role-modelling in the context of managers as Culture Builders. For senior leaders, it's even more critical because there is often little opportunity to explain actions. Senior leaders also have massive influence across the company. If a manager role-models good behaviour, it causes a ripple in the organisation. Hopefully, there will be enough great ripples that wonderful engagement will result. With senior leaders, role-modelling causes great waves, so you'll want to ensure that they have a positive impact.

In terms of influence over managers' ability to engage others and therefore create investors, senior leaders must lead by example. The way you engage with those who report to you directly will have a great influence on how they, in turn, manage and connect with their people. Employees and managers take their lead from senior leaders, so their behaviour affects the climate, confidence and how others act in the organisation.

Gordon Watt was Director of Service Development at T Mobile. He learnt quickly that it's not what a leader says, it's what they do that speaks to teams:

I had a very long commute, so would leave home before the traffic built up. That meant I'd typically be in the office for 7 a.m. and leave about 7 p.m. once the rush hour was dying down. I noticed that people started arriving earlier at the office after a couple of weeks. I told people that I was only in early due to my personal commute and that I didn't want others to do the same. I would disappear at lunchtime for a swim, but people didn't see this. They saw me present in the office for 12 hours and thought that is what I valued. When I realised that telling people not to work similar hours wasn't going to work, I came up with a new strategy. I would arrive at 7 a.m. and find a coffee shop where I would start my work. At 8.30 I would leave the coffee shop and walk into my office. By role-modelling this behaviour, my people didn't feel it necessary to arrive at 7 a.m. any more. An important lesson in how leaders role-model even when not intending to!

Use an Appropriate Tone When Conversing at All Levels

Tone was discussed as part of the Pilot's role earlier. It's also important for senior leaders to be mindful of tone and to use it appropriately in both formal and informal environments. The right tone can create an engaged audience in a presentation, conference or one-to-one conversation. A less appropriate one can create mass disengagement from which it's hard to recover.

Logica established an 'Ask the CEO' email facility to allow its employees to engage with its CEO. Around two hundred people a year used the opportunity to pose questions. The answers were shared with the originators, and where appropriate, with the wider Logica population. In 2008, on the appointment of a new CEO, the emphasis was changed and a new bulletin board area was set up for people to 'Tell the CEO'. The result was staggering, with 40–50 statements per week being posted. Steve Thorn, Global Transformation Director, puts the dramatic change down to the shift from 'ask' to 'tell'. He believes that people feel they have permission to share with the CEO, and not just ask a question. It's not uncommon to see people 'tell the CEO' about something significant a colleague has delivered or to praise a peer. People ask questions about the rationale for specific decisions, and comment on direction and progress. All questions and comments receive a response that the entire company can see. It's used by some geographical areas more than others, which reinforces the need to provide a variety of ways for people to engage with their leaders when operating globally. Different company and country cultures have different preferences concerning communication style. For example, it's very common to see people from the Logica India businesses contribute to 'Tell the CEO', but less so for French or Finnish business members by way of a contrast.

Changing the tone intentionally is a wonderful skill of great leaders. Naomi Climer spent much of her career at the BBC, and remembers the period under Greg Dyke's leadership very clearly:

> There had been issues for a while regarding bad press about the organisation. Our own journalists were even being critical in their columns in newspapers. But Greg addressed the situation head-on, using a wonderful example of tone. In an all-staff webcast, he said the unthinkable. He said that it seemed the worst critics of the BBC seemed to be its own staff. He reminded us all that we work for the BBC and it pays our salary, so if we couldn't say anything positive, we shouldn't say anything at all. I remember him saying that if anyone felt that critical, they should leave the organisation.

Naomi remembers how her stomach tightened into a knot because she felt so uncomfortable at the change of tone he'd intentionally used. But he was absolutely in control of his message and his emotions, and had courageously used a different tone to make a strong point.

Magnetic Power of Word

Stuart Fletcher, Former President International at Diageo, is a living role model of many areas of the leader as Culture Builder. As part of the Diageo International 'Breakthrough, Every Day, Everywhere, Everyone' programme, he paid huge attention to the 'power of word'. This is a great example of a leader being both a Coach and a Pilot. Stuart explains:

I was always using a huge amount of energy to move people from where they were to align with where we needed to be. My challenge was that I wanted to be putting energy into so many places; I needed to get better at managing myself. I therefore paid significant attention to changing the way I communicated and behaved so that I focused on pulling people towards alignment rather than driving them towards it, expending much less energy in the process. The shorthand for this in my leadership stand was 'magnetic'. I'd use my expression and understanding of others to be more discerning about my message and find ways to land my point most effectively.

At the top of his notebook he'd write 'Judo and Henry Fonda' as a reminder to himself about the magnetic power of word. 'Judo' would remind him that he had to make the maximum impact with minimal effort so that his energy wasn't wasted. 'Henry Fonda' (as in the role he played in the film *Twelve Angry Men*) would remind him not to try to move everyone at once, but to think of and talk to people as individuals. This helped him to deliver real impact and success in the business.

Senior leaders are the Pilots, and communication and human resources professionals have a role to play in helping them to navigate. However, the leaders need to engage the staff from these disciplines who can help them, and invite them to offer their support.

During my research for this book, I was fascinated by the difference in value each organisation and leader placed on the five roles. The majority of companies valued the roles of the Strategist and the Storyteller. A desire clearly existed for more leaders and managers to be Coaches and Prophets. However, most recognised that this was an aspiration rather than a reality. Interestingly, in the John Lewis Partnership it was clear that huge value was placed on the Prophet because the partnership's purpose is central to everything people do. The Storyteller is key, and there is evidence of Pilot and Coach behaviours, because challenges are shared with partners to resolve them, rather than kept as management issues. The Strategist role was less evident. What JLP focuses upon is the value of relationships, sharing responsibility and giving the opportunity for everyone to influence outcomes. It's not surprising, therefore, that engagement levels are high and that its managers concentrate on the roles of Prophet, Storyteller and Coach.

My final message concerns the importance of a blend of all five roles – any one role taken to an extreme will become a negative factor. It's also worth mentioning that the Pilot role underpins the other four. In my research for this book, the leaders I spoke to in organisations that enjoyed high levels of engagement would quickly talk about ways in which their leaders demonstrated them all, used the roles appropriately, and were sensitive to the situation and mood of the organisation when deciding which one to lead with.

Engagement in Action

CHAPTER **23** *Engagement in Action*

Earlier in this book, you'll already have seen some snippets of great engagement in action that I hope will have inspired you and given you rich insights. The pages that follow capture more in-depth, diverse examples of real engagement in action. You'll find instances of organisational engagement, leadership-led engagement and managers playing a key role to make change happen. Many of them are cases where I have been directly involved. Others are exceptional examples gathered through my research. Each one highlights areas to watch for if you're considering replicating an approach. More practical tools and advice for implementation are available at www.TheCultureBuilders.com.

Here's a list of the case studies that follow:

The Leadership Role During Transformation – Sony Europe

Sustaining a Dialogue with Managers – the Pfizer Managers' Forum

Engaging Managers by Building a Restaurant in 24 Hours – Burger King

The Leader and Manager Role During a Merger or Acquisition – HBOS

Engaging the Stakeholders Who Will Have the Biggest Impact on Success – Sony Europe

Increasing Understanding of Strategy through a Focus on Managers – BSkyB

Using Diversity to Engage and Build Team Spirit – MGM Resorts

Embedding New Behaviours through Change Champions – Pfizer Primary Care, Europe & Canada

Engaging and Aligning People with Strategy Using Meaningful Language – Diageo

The Beginning of a CEO-led Transformational Change – UKTV

Using Peers to Engage Each Other During Transformation – Pfizer

Creating a High-performing Team by Focusing on Levers of Engagement – Innocent

Engaging Employee Groups with Specific Approaches – the Sony Springboard Gender Project

Using Management Development to Create a Tipping Point – a Global Media Company

Creating the Right Environment for People to Engage – Sony UK

A Unique Example of Engagement through Attachment and Significance – John Lewis Partnership

Engagement During Transition Resulting in Team Closure – Galileo and Covia

Involving Others to Articulate Purpose and Vision – Sony Europe

Daily Engagement in a Small to Medium-sized Company – Solarcentury

A Culture of Development to Boost Engagement – a Global Media Player

Engaging a Business as a New Leader, and What to Watch For – Sony Audio Europe

The Leadership Role During Transformation – Sony Europe

In 2010–2011, Sony Europe undertook one of the biggest transformations of its history. Every back office team, and thousands of employees, throughout the region felt the impact of more efficient and effective organisational structures, systems and processes being developed and implemented. The need to succeed was paramount, and the importance of keeping people engaged was critical – many teams were the engines that made it possible to deliver to customers.

Simon Ashby was clear from the beginning about his challenge as the leader of this transformation. He volunteered for the role, but asked to lead the vital two-year programme as 100 per cent of his job – not a secondment, but a complete commitment with no safety net.

Simon was passionate about signalling to others working on the programme that it was so important that he would invest his future career in its success. If he failed, he was probably going to be looking for a job outside of the company. As a leader, he wanted to set the tone from the outset that this was a high-stakes programme that needed the best focus, people and management. He handed over the reins of his previous role to the successor he had deliberately developed over previous years, and embarked upon his next huge challenge. Simon explains:

I saw it as my role to be consistently confident from the beginning. I needed to be certain from the start that we could achieve what we promised to the company and this meant spending time with the project teams to coach and mentor at every opportunity. It also meant questioning decisions in a positive vein to be sure we had made them appropriately and with the belief they were right. This ensured I had the arguments ready when challenged by other leaders about why we were going in a certain direction.

From day one, I made it clear to my team that I would trust them to make the right decisions and that I would take accountability for success and failure of what we did collectively as a team. This meant everyone had confidence to act but also understood that if something didn't work, I would accept the consequences. My aim wasn't to cause a reckless culture but actually to create an environment where the team could act with initiative and bring the best of themselves to the job. It worked.

Simon chose the best talent he could find within the business. The staff seconded onto the programme were taken on full-time, and their regular roles were back-filled for the duration of the secondment. This was a factor that was critical to success, as Simon knew he needed total focus, but that the business still needed to function normally. When recruiting a programme manager, Simon enlisted the help of an external recruitment agency and encouraged people from within the organisation to apply. Simon remembers:

The result was even more successful than I had anticipated. I'd seen this as a great opportunity to make visible the aspirations and desires of some great people in our company. I also saw it as a way of key people receiving feedback that would help them develop their careers further. We'd also get a great candidate. This all happened, but in addition we also chose an internal candidate that surprised some people because it wasn't a person well known throughout the business. This gave others hope that there was a chance for anyone with the right skills and attitude to flourish.

Setting the right tone and sending the appropriate messages to his team were important to Simon throughout the programme. He immediately moved his physical location in the building and created a new area for the project team to work together. He sat in that area, away from the other executives.

It was essential for the team to identify early wins to demonstrate that the programme wasn't just a plan and that it would immediately have an impact and momentum. This was particularly important as the transformation programme followed on from many other change projects during previous years. 'Quick wins give momentum and it's important that managers and leaders of programmes remember this is a critical success factor,' believes Simon.

In any change programme, leaders and managers have the constant role of showing how far the business has come and where it's aiming to go. They can also ensure that major milestones are celebrated and recognition is given to key people and teams that have successes along the journey. When fast-paced change happens, it's often easy to forget to stop and take stock of progress to date and to recognise those that have made a significant contribution to achieving it. Keeping a programme team engaged over time is a massive challenge during change, and highlighting those milestones is a tangible way to contribute to motivation and morale.

At the end of large-scale transformations within organisations, there is often a period of anti-climax for those closely involved. The clear sense of purpose and high engagement associated with well-delivered programmes can often leave individuals deflated after they've been implemented. This is particularly likely if top talent have been recruited into change teams. At the end of the Sony programme, Simon saw signs of deflation and people not feeling good about going back to their regular roles. He took immediate action to remind people that they had achieved a huge amount and that their skill set and value in the company (their 'stock') was now much greater than it had been before. He saw this as vital for ensuring that the individuals returned to their roles with decent levels of engagement in Sony, rather than just the programme team.

What to Watch For

- Set the tone from the beginning – show people you're serious as a leader when embarking on a transformation programme. If people see that you're staking a great deal on it, then the best will want to be involved and make it a success.
- Recruit the strongest possible talent to be part of your team (including those who have hitherto been unknown if they're the most suitable fit).
- Advertise positions, ask people to apply, and use it as an opportunity to give valuable feedback to each person who comes forward.
- Physically locate yourself with your team.
- Find quick wins so that early momentum is achieved.
- Recognise key people and teams when significant milestones are successfully reached.
- Be ready for long-term change programmes to take on a life of their own and for teams to make a final push to the finish line if they're highly engaged.
- Work out how you will help people deal with the sense of loss that inevitably comes at the end of a project.

Sustaining a Dialogue with Managers – the Pfizer Managers' Forum

Pfizer places a great deal of importance on maintaining a strong dialogue with its managers. In the UK, the company provides a complementary suite of activities, information and resources to enable this. The important factor for the company is consistency – ensuring that actions are maintained and a schedule is followed, but at the same time balancing this with an assessment of what information needs to be shared and the capacity of the group at any given time to be involved in group activity.

The Managers' Forum covers a range of items, from bi-monthly newsletters to all-manager meetings, relayed around the country via webcasts. All activity has one aim in common – ensuring that line managers feel informed and up to date on key activities and developments within the company. All information, recordings and tools are made available via a dedicated resource website, and information is provided in 'grab and go' formats that help managers to navigate the complexities of working in a 'self-help' organisation.

Activity is steered by a pioneer group of line managers who are used on an ad hoc basis to discuss the activities and requirements of their peer group. This process identifies unmet needs on a regular basis, and ensures that activity is consistent with the wider group's requirements. This group steered the creation of a line manager induction process that focused on seven core activities among their duties, with the aim of giving new managers an initial boost in confidence and capacity to manage.

The Forum takes a local focus, delivering on the needs of the UK group, and ensuring that information and changes are relevant to that group. It sits alongside, rather than competing with, the global management development approaches, which tend to be more developmental in nature rather than process- and information-led.

Ultimately, the Forum has created an 'information-ready' group that understands the value of the Forum's communication, recognises that it only carries important information, and understands how to cascade it further to their own people. Attendance at events and broadcasts is high, as are responses to information and actions. Because the Forum is owned by the managers, in the sense that they steer its content, they regularly provide speakers for the broadcasts and are supported with cascade information, it enjoys a high degree of credibility, and a recognition that it's there to help rather than to add to the workload.

During a period of business change, the groundwork laid down by the Forum was highly valuable in ensuring that managers were kept informed and engaged throughout. The information and update routes were valued, well-used and easily accessible, so managers stayed close to the changes and were fully informed as developments arose or actions were needed.

Pfizer maintains a very open policy towards the Forum – 90 per cent of the information and activity is publicly accessible, meaning that any colleague can access the content. This is an important element in building an inclusive, trusting culture. Hiding all of this information behind restricted sites and 'for your eyes only' documents would be time-consuming, would run against the company ethos, and would ultimately be futile.

The company has taken the view that it's far better to be transparent in dealings with colleagues – a long-held ethos that even dictated glass-fronted meeting rooms when the new UK headquarters was built in the early 2000s.

What to Watch For

- Be consistent and deliver on a schedule of events over the long term – allowing activity to tail off leads to negative perceptions and lowers the group's sense of value.
- Don't just run activities for the sake of it, bearing in mind the first point: where there's nothing new, say as much and use the time or space for something more relevant.
- Allow the group to steer what it does, how, and when. Make sure that you follow up with questions, garner feedback and use input to shape what you do next.
- Think about what the group will find most valuable, and will use the most often. There's no point creating activities and items that will sit on a shelf.
- Avoid the time and expense of trying to secure content from parts of the organisation. Assume that whatever you create will be seen by everyone, and should thus be tailored to avoid this being a problem. Also recognise the value to engagement of having most of your content out in the open.
- Create activities and communications for line managers that can be used for wider purposes – for example, business change communications.

Engaging Managers by Building a Restaurant in 24 Hours – Burger King

During 2001, the business strategy at Burger King was to open many more restaurants in the world – a real push on its development strategy. 'In his role as President, Burger King International, André Lacroix was a fabulous example of a visionary leader that enthused people and made them think anything was possible,' remembers Kai Boschmann, former Senior Communication Director at Burger King International.

Each year, senior managers from across Europe would come together to spend time hearing about the company's direction. These events were always creative and inspiring. However, this time they were looking for a new way to really engage the hearts of managers through an experience. They decided to involve the management group in building a restaurant in 24 hours. Kai explains:

> A hundred and ten European managers built a restaurant in 23 hours and 20 minutes. It was one of the most memorable management meetings ever, and we still regularly mention it. It had a major impact on engagement levels and the level of emotional investment people were prepared to make in the company.

It was a highly experiential way of demonstrating the strategy, and one that used all the senses.

Before they arrived, all the managers attending were asked to submit their shoe size, head size and any medical issues that might prevent them from doing physical exercise. They were invited to fly to Heathrow, travelled on a bus, and then were blindfolded, so there was no opportunity to gather clues about their destination.

The group emerged from the bus in Rotherham, next to a construction site. They were put into teams along with professional construction workers. Their brief was simple: to build a Burger King restaurant within 24 hours.

In addition to this challenge, the building was also the first to be built in a modular form, which in itself was significant for the business. Even though it came in several large pre-assembled units, there was a huge amount to do to achieve success. Further value was gained from the activity by asking each team to keep a video diary. Another camera filmed the whole event, and the footage was later put together as a strategic documentary for use in the business to cascade the messages, some of it also being used parts externally to promote the brand, especially from an employer brand point of view.

'Teams worked for just less than 24 hours and met the challenge. The bond and learning individuals walked away with was like nothing else we'd ever experienced,' says Kai. The restaurant opened several weeks earlier than planned, so the event paid for itself through early sales income. Kai reports:

> Some of those who participated still have their hard hats, the video and many great memories. The team left with a very clear idea about our strategy and what it really felt like. They were able to take back their learning and tell the strategic story in a much more real and enthused way than ever before. People are still talking about it ten years later.

> **What to Watch For**
>
> - Ownership sits with the CEO, and that person needs to be central to the experience.
> - Always ensure that there are pre-work and post-work activities to keep the story alive and ensure it's not just one event that has limited impact.
> - Be clear about the expectation that managers will go back and share the story with their staff.

The Leader and Manager Role During a Merger or Acquisition – HBOS

In 2009, HBOS merged with Lloyds after the financial crisis deepened in the UK. HBOS had its own unique culture, one that believed it was there to always try harder than its bigger and more powerful competitors. The organisation was full of hugely passionate people who believed in the company and enjoyed being part of an inclusive values-based culture.

During the merger with Lloyds, HBOS employees were told that Lloyds found the culture unique and wanted to learn from it as the merger and integration continued. This may well have happened, but employees felt there was little evidence of the intention once HBOS became consumed within its bigger one-time competitor.

During a period of immense uncertainty and anxiety, leaders and managers had a critical role to play in ensuring that people were treated fairly, employees remained engaged and that customers didn't suffer. People felt let down and disappointed by the progress of the merger, but it was important that didn't affect customer satisfaction and business performance.

'The role of leaders at a senior and line manager level became even more crucial,' explains Gordon Lyle, then Human Resources Director for HBOS. As with any change, line managers often feel extremely vulnerable during a state of flux, and having little access to information only heightens their anxiety and frustration at not being able to lead and guide their people. It's important for senior leaders to involve and communicate with managers constantly, with clarity and with consistency. Gordon remembers:

Great leaders in HBOS did this instinctively during the merger with Lloyds. Many line managers bought their people together and talked with empathy about how they understood the merger was causing anxiety but that until we had answers to the big questions, we had the opportunity to feel more positive by channelling our energy into continuing to do what we do, to the best of our ability. It made a huge difference to the way people felt and the performance of the business during a very difficult time.

What to Watch For

- Bring your people together on a regular basis – either formally at a team meeting or informally for half an hour a week over a coffee.
- Start by acknowledging that it's a very difficult time, and ask people to share how they're feeling (be ready for tears, swearing and frustration).
- Move on to sharing any new details or clarity you have about what is happening, and be honest if you don't have any news but emphasise that you're committed to passing it on as soon as it emerges.
- Recognise that you have two choices – you can see the rug as being pulled from under your feet, or see yourself as dancing on it. Ask yourself which choice you will make, and ask your people which choice they want to make too.
- Be brave – take tough decisions early; don't put them off.
- Be visible and accessible – the natural tendency is often to retreat, because it's painful to face your people when you may have no news or bad news. Resist this instinct and remain visible and accessible.

Engaging the Stakeholders Who Will Have the Biggest Impact on Success – Sony Europe

During the late 2000s, Sony Europe developed various programmes to revitalise its business. Some of these focused on growth, and others aimed to increase operational efficiency across the region.

One efficiency initiative aimed to reduce expenditure on air travel and to change attitudes towards it through a variety of methods.

Once appointed, the team used the stakeholder power/interest tool to plot key stakeholders, their current versus their desired positions, and to identify the benefits the project could deliver for each individual or team. This provided clarity about which specific communities would have the biggest influence on the success of the goal of reducing travel. The insight for the project team was that the least energy should be spent addressing Sony Europe's employee population as a whole. This was powerful because it meant the project manager was able to target his efforts on the key stakeholder groups and address them effectively, rather than spreading his energy across multiple employees.

The key stakeholders were country and business unit heads. They had the power to engage their people in the project and work out the best way to achieve its aims. Online meetings were used to share the initial objectives and what it meant for each leader. Sony Europe's President requested each person to attend, and the board-level sponsor outlined the importance of the project to business success. He provided the context before the project manager outlined full details about what it meant for each business leader.

The travel reduction programme was one of a series of efficiency initiatives at the time. Each business unit and country leader was expected to attend monthly updates on the projects via an online meeting. At these sessions, the travel project manager would share progress towards the goals. He used a red, amber and green traffic light system to show where countries and business units were making a contribution to travel reduction or where no real progress had been made. Real names were listed to show which individuals were high spending travellers. This was a cultural shift for the organisation, and felt uncomfortable for many attending the virtual meetings. However, the impact was significant, and this visibility created an acceleration of behaviour change in areas where progress had been slow. One reason for this was the collective understanding of the need to achieve the goal.

In parallel, the travel policy changed and all-employee communications were issued across Europe to update every team on the standardisation of travel policy. A new suite of tools called WorkSmart was also made available to employees. These included Web meeting tools and a cheaper audioconferencing capability.

The project achieved its goals earlier than targeted due to the engagement levels of all key stakeholders. Targeted communication, a clear goal, involvement and thus engagement were critical success factors in sustaining new attitudes towards travel.

What to Watch For

- Map all stakeholders at the beginning of each project.
- Devote energy to engaging stakeholders who will have the biggest impact on success – don't be tempted to divert too much energy to the all-employee group unless it's appropriate.
- Sometimes, making people feel uncomfortable is OK, but offer support and tools to give them answers to the problems you're highlighting.
- Maintain regular communication with all key stakeholders – a frequent forum and schedule is often best practice for projects involving multiple stakeholders.

Increasing Understanding of Strategy through a Focus on Managers – BSkyB

Three years ago, a People Survey highlighted an issue with motivation and strategic understanding among the Contact Centres at BSkyB. The management team focused on two areas to address the issue: communication and management development.

A communication framework was designed that clarified what information staff could expect, how regularly, what managers needed to do with it, and their role in the process. A quarterly conference call took place for all line managers – 600–700 people – to share the latest business performance and direction. Understanding among employees was measured by making calls to a significant sample every four to six weeks. People were asked to comment on the information they'd received, and their knowledge was tested.

Managers were given more clarity about their role and where they fit within the organisation as a whole. Support and development was offered to individuals to enable them to improve their people management skills.

Nick Green, Internal Communication Director, feels the effort was definitely worthwhile. The performance of the Contact Centres turned around considerably, and trust levels increased. If your goal is to change behaviour, make it a long-term commitment, and don't expect a toolkit to change people on its own.

What to Watch For

- If strategic understanding is low, communication alone is not enough – managers need to be properly engaged.
- Ensure that managers understand the strategy, give them tools to help share information, and offer support to sustain them.
- Conduct regular pulse tests to measure improvements.
- When an engagement issue is identified in your organisation, act immediately.

Using Diversity to Engage and Build Team Spirit – MGM Resorts

At MGM Resorts, Diversity Champions are used to help increase levels of engagement among employee groups.

The training initiative began in 2001, and by the end of 2011 more than 11,000 of approximately 60,000 employees had been trained in diversity and inclusion. The individuals go through a comprehensive training programme that reaches beyond the obvious parameters of diversity by helping champions look at themselves, the world and each other. Debra Nelson, Vice President of Diversity at MGM Resorts, explains:

It's a transformational programme. People come from across the world to stay and play at our properties. We want them to have an experience that means they will return again and again. Our employees are very important in this respect since they are the keepers of our culture. They demonstrate this everyday through their engagement and respect for each other and our customers. The agenda of diversity education compels us to look at ourselves and how we show up in the work world. Through self-examination exercises, it also forces us to 'look into the mirror'. Transformation happens when participants are engaged intellectually and emotionally. In effect, our training successfully instils an intellectual and emotional connection to diversity, rather than a theoretical business case-led programme. Employees who complete the program are called Diversity Champions. They return to their workplaces feeling empowered, engaged and wanting to help their colleagues feel more motivated too.

Debra has seen a sharp rise in engagement levels and a desire to make meaningful contributions to the company as a result of this diversity education programme.

Once Diversity Champions return to their posts, they're able to join councils where they work together to support the business objectives of the company and to create community engagement initiatives. These community projects galvanise employees and contribute to morale and productivity.

Each property holds regular Recharge Events where Diversity Champions are reminded of the diversity values they learned in training, such as the importance of treating others with dignity and respect. These events also help keep their hearts and minds charged appropriately. Debra Nelson believes:

When MGM Resorts merged with Mandalay Bay in 2005, diversity was used as a strategy to create a common company culture and a shared vision. At the time, the two companies had different cultures and methods of operation; however, the Diversity education program was used as a platform to bring people together and to accelerate their knowledge and appreciation of each other. The speed by which people began to identify commonalities, and respect and value each other was faster than we could ever have imagined. The diversity programme was a big factor in the success of our integration.

What to Watch For

- When training champions, be as creative as possible in your approach and remember that the emotional experience is more important than the rational reason for being a role-model.
- Re-charge events are critical to maintaining momentum and keeping champions energised.
- Consider linking key business drivers to champions programmes, rather than a purer communication champion approach.

Embedding New Behaviours through Change Champions – Pfizer Primary Care, Europe & Canada

In 2009, the Pfizer Primary Care division continued to look at new ways to engage people in a transforming business.

During May that year, it created a network of communication champions to enable peer-to-peer communication in the face of the challenges of a changing business environment. The network was set up to support the existing top-down and bottom-up communication channels throughout the company.

In each country, around 10 per cent of the Primary Care division staff are part of the champions network – the minimum number of people that Pfizer has found is needed to gain critical mass and action to create a tipping point.

The senior leadership team select people who are great connectors, not just high performers or members of a talent pool. Each is a credible and articulate communicator or someone that enjoys networking – a critical point to remember when choosing members.

Their task is to role-model behaviour, talk to peers about what is happening in the business, tell stories about progress and highlight when action is being taken that isn't congruent with the direction or desired behaviours in the organisation.

Once champions are nominated to take part, they're given training, including how to tell stories in an engaging way to create deep understanding and emotional connection with the information they need to share.

Champions are involved in a regular conference call to keep them abreast of the latest business developments. They're given access to content to help them create an informed dialogue within the various teams and countries in the region. In some cases, a champion may be aware of a development or story before their manager. In many organisations, this creates conflict, where managers may be frustrated because they don't have access to the context and content in order to share and discuss them with their people first. This can feel undermining in some company cultures. The other possibility is that it may cause managers to abdicate responsibility for communicating. Both of these are huge risks with champions programmes, but Nigel's confident that Pfizer hasn't experienced such issues.

The senior leadership team made it very clear at the outset that the champions were there to support other communication channels and to share information in a peer-to-peer fashion.

Champions are currently being used to embed new behaviours. Senior leaders in the Primary Care division have defined the cultural behaviours that are required to drive performance. The champions have been called on to validate those behaviours and to explore how each of them can be demonstrated in their roles.

What to Watch For

- Appointing champions who represent all areas of the business is vital.
- Enlist enough champions to create a tipping point – 10 per cent of the staff is a minimum.
- Maintaining momentum is crucial – regular interaction is necessary.
- Set up forums to allow champions to exchange their progress, challenges and best practices.

Engaging and Aligning People with Strategy Using Meaningful Language – Diageo

In 2003, as President of Key Markets at Diageo, Stuart Fletcher was only seeing 6–7 per cent growth in the business. He knew the potential was much greater, so he decided that action was required. He identified the area in Diageo that was growing most rapidly – the Venture business, which had relatively lower investment and resources, yet was consistently outperforming other areas. He met with its leader to explore the secrets of its success. The result was the development of a breakthrough strategy for the newly created Diageo International region, which he led from late 2004, that has taken the business into double-digit growth and has seen the International Region deliver 70 per cent profit growth for Diageo plc.

In 2003, Stuart gathered the heads of his 12 key markets together for three days and worked through an intensive breakthrough thinking programme. It was a bold move for Stuart because this was the first time he'd pulled his direct reports together: 'I decided to throw my heart and everything into the process and be single-minded to make it work,' Stuart comments.

The programme consisted of four areas. The first was breakthrough thinking, where the team explored the fact that current thinking generates current results, so breaking out of traditional thought patterns to create innovation is necessary. The team was introduced to how extraordinary thinking produces extraordinary results, and how to achieve that process.

The second area they explored was relatedness. This showed the importance of relating to others and a greater cause. People looked at how, with more relatedness, more is possible, increased emotional connections develop, and more freedom is seized upon to act. Stuart remembers:

The importance of 'being there' – being present – was a hugely important part of this module. We were introduced to the value of truly being with each other and the people with whom we lead and interact.

The third module was about 'stand' – what an individual stands for. Each person identified something that was his or her stand – something that wasn't happening or seemed impossible today, but was an extraordinary, unpredictable ambition. This was then turned into an intention that individuals would devote their heart, body, and soul to making happen. Stuart's stand was to make his region's performance fantastic. It wasn't fantastic at that point, and he had no idea whether it was possible, but that was what Stuart wanted to make happen, and he turned it into his intention to succeed.

The last area was alignment. Individuals looked at how they could hold themselves accountable in delivering their own stand, but also support and work with others to achieve theirs. This meant collective ownership. It also meant that if someone 'fell off their stand', the rest of the team were there to help them climb back on.

When the International region was created, Stuart and his team had been investing in growing their breakthrough leadership capability for some time, and now understood the importance of articulating the direction for employees in language that was meaningful to them and outcome-based. The International Executive team met four times for four days on each occasion, and created a rich description of the future it wanted to create – the International Breakthrough Strategy.

The team developed a single 'big picture' that articulated the purpose (Celebrating life, every day, everywhere), destination (the most celebrated business in every market) and key performance metrics (employer of choice, net sales value targets, profit targets, best corporate citizen). It created three strategic areas of focus: 'amazing relationships bringing out the best', 'great times, great experiences' and 'enriched communities'. Behind each strategic focus area was a more in-depth description of the future that outlined the key outcomes intended to make the business a success. Each one was written in emotive language that immediately engaged employees. The leadership team members created it themselves, and therefore had total ownership of the content.

The breakthrough 'Every day, everywhere, everyone' programme was initially shared with the top 70 leaders, and through them everyone else started to be engaged in its delivery. 'Those leaders were given the freedom to tweak the strategy for their markets, but in reality only about 5 per cent of it was changed in most markets,' remember Stuart. The country leaders went on to share the strategy with their local country teams and engage them in the content during either one-, three- or four-day breakthrough sessions. Every one of the 8,500 staff in the International Business were invited to attend, from senior leaders to security and post room employees.

On the third day of his annual leadership conference in 2008, Stuart asked for all operations, including warehouses and manufacturing and customer service centres, to be shut down for 30 minutes so that people could attend via conference call. Seventy-five telephone lines were used to connect 6,500 employees across the world to hear Stuart express his heartfelt appreciation about what had been achieved to date and how essential each individual would continue to be to the future. Before the call, managers were given the key messages so they could schedule team sessions after the call to explore what they had heard in more depth. Some places held events immediately, others waited until the next business day to hold dialogues in teams. The feedback was so personally moving for Stuart that he continued this approach thereafter. In 2010, 8,500 people participated in the call.

The results have been outstanding. The breakthrough strategy was designed during Diageo's 2004/2005 financial year (FY05), and more widely shared with employees during FY06. The business has doubled in size in five years thanks to the launch of the breakthrough strategy. Stuart reports:

It took about two and a half years to reach all employees in all countries. Some markets, like Australia, took the message to employees very quickly and had plenty of conversations around the direction with people so they could see what it meant for them and how their behaviour and work could best align. Others took a little longer because that was more suitable for their market situation. However, I truly believe that the growth would not have been possible without the leadership capability we have developed and the capacity, energy, passion and alignment among our people as a result of a focus to engage.

What to Watch For

- As a leader, look to others who are succeeding, and be curious about what you can learn from them.
- Be courageous and clear about what you stand for as a leader.
- Collectively create the story of strategy as a leadership team.
- Demonstrate the importance of messages by giving everyone access to hear them.
- A short shutdown sends a clear signal about the importance of understanding strategy and how much people are valued in your business.

The Beginning of a CEO-led Transformational Change – UKTV

UKTV is one of the most important and successful multi-channel television providers in the UK. Formed in 1997, it is an independent commercial joint venture between BBC Worldwide and Scripps Networks Interactive. It's well known for its television brands in the entertainment, lifestyle and factual genres: Watch, GOLD, Dave, Alibi, Eden, Blighty, Yesterday, Home, Really and Good Food.

When Darren Childs arrived as CEO in 2010, the business was experiencing similar challenges to other media organisations:

> *The economic downturn was having an impact across the sector and there was a need to be more savvy about future business. UKTV had been without a CEO for a long period, and people were feeling uncertain about direction and strategy. Frustration was evident in some areas because there wasn't a clear values framework, so people didn't have a foundation to drive effective ways of working together.*

Darren was clear about the need to engage people, set a clear direction, lead by example and demonstrate the values he believed were necessary to continue and accelerate UKTV's success against the backdrop of the changing market. However, as he began his work, his attention was diverted to a potential change of shareholder, the need to move the offices from central London to a more cost-effective location, and a number of other significant business issues. 'The impact was that I had to stall the work around strategic clarity and engagement while I gave my energy to managing some big issues and ensuring the best possible future for our business,' he explains.

With those issues under control, Darren knew that he needed to understand more about the climate before he started any significant engagement activity. He sensed that greater understanding was needed about the imperative to be commercial rather focusing on creativity at the expense of everything else.

He commissioned an employee survey, thus giving a quantitative measure of engagement levels. This was run in parallel with listening sessions where everyone in the company was invited to attend in small groups and talk about what was good and what could be better in the business. Exit interviews were reviewed to identify trends and areas for improvement. Darren also scheduled small breakfast sessions with groups of 12 people. At these, he listened to issues that people raised and started to give the staff more strategic clarity.

The feedback was honest and candid. The passion for the business was immense, but people wanted more strategic clarity, leadership, creative focus, career development, reward and recognition for achievements.

This feedback was shared with the executive team, honestly and using direct non-attributed quotes. The take-away was clear: despite Darren's belief that people understood the major challenges in the business and the reasons for focusing on them, the message hadn't permeated through the staff. People were asking for more investment, risk and innovation because they felt these had stalled – yet the executive team had overseen more investment and taken greater risks than ever before, most of it sponsored by them. It was clear that a disconnect existed between what was happening at a senior level and the visibility of what, why and how elsewhere in UKTV.

Leadership team members immediately took responsibility. The day after the results were shared with the executive team, they cleared their diaries for the following week and developed a robust action plan.

One week later, Darren hosted a day where everyone in the company was invited to hear the results and then participate in a dialogue about them. Unlike similar engagement survey workshops, the focus was not on asking teams to come up with ideas and workstreams to solve the problems. Darren wanted to take ownership of the issues that had been raised, and not abdicate responsibility to other teams. He comments:

> We were completely open about what people had said and the impact of that was hugely significant. People said afterwards they felt slightly uncomfortable hearing the feedback summary but that they had massive respect for us because we treated them like grown up's and didn't hide or spin the results.

The executive team realised that it was important to put the record straight about some of the incorrect perceptions that had surfaced through the feedback sessions before it could press the reset button and outline its commitments. It identified the common issues and asked people from across the business to say a few words about the reality. For example, some felt that investments weren't being made, so the Acquisitions team explained how much had been invested in new product during the previous month.

The executive team also shared its initial commitments for action: 12 were agreed and shared, with an executive sponsor for each one. There was a mix of short, tangible commitments that would give immediate fixes to problems with longer-term commitments that involved looking more fundamentally at the way business was conducted and focusing on values as a framework for working together better. Darren explains:

> I wanted to kick-start innovation because it is so important for our business, so one of our actions was to introduce an innovation pot for work that wouldn't require the same return on investment justifications as other investments. This was a big step in helping people to see that we needed creativity and commercial focus within the business; and that they weren't at odds with each other.

Perhaps the most powerful factor during the day was Darren's humility. When he opened his response to the feedback, he started by looking his people in the eye and saying: 'I've heard what you've said; I wasn't here for you as much as you wanted me.' He explained the reality of the business challenges that had consumed so much executive time and energy, and people immediately began to understand the issues he'd been dealing with. He talked positively rather than defensively, then explained that he didn't want to have to run surveys or feedback sessions in future to understand the climate. He was now in a position to spend even more time day-to-day with each team, and was excited about doing exactly that. The courage and honesty of Darren's words did more to reset the attitude and climate in the business than any action plan or engagement plan could ever have achieved.

After the one-hour feedback, myth-busting and commitment session, people were asked to meet in their department teams and talk about what they'd heard. Darren joined for the last 15 minutes of their one-hour conversations to hear conclusions about what excited them about the commitments, what questions remained, and what action the teams felt they wanted to take as a result of what had been said. Darren observes:

> It was like speed-dating the whole company. Every group had a different perspective, yet there was great commonality across the departments. I really enjoyed hearing what they had to say and being able to answer questions directly. I was able to meet everyone in our business face-to-face that day. It was a tremendous experience.

Prior to the feedback sessions, a leadership group was formed and department managers were invited to attend a two-hour briefing meeting – the first time this community had been bought together and involved in a proactive way. This happened the day before the all-employee gathering, and enabled Darren to convey the key messages that would be shared on the day. They saw the feedback and heard Darren's message about the reality of the business challenges, his personal commitments, and the executive commitments for change. One of those was to bring the community of managers together regularly to keep them aware of business progress, context, and to give them an opportunity to be involved in decision-making about the future of the business.

The format for the dialogue sessions was shared and the managers asked to facilitate their conversations after the formal feedback session. They were fully tooled up with the information, process, and confidence to host a true dialogue with their people.

In parallel with the feedback process, Darren also placed attention on aligning the executive team. Members discussed the business direction, culture and the need to be a guiding crew. He instilled the importance of communicating with their teams at all levels, and set out the need for all individuals in the business to embrace the balance between creativity and commerciality – that one couldn't happen without the other.

Time and energy were directed to articulating the purpose and strategic direction of UKTV, with the involvement of all colleagues. Middle managers played a particularly important role in shaping the story.

The executive team collaborated to provide a framework of direction, and represented it in a visual big picture (see Figure 5.3). Workshops then took place with middle managers to give input and challenge the initial work. This resulted in a final version that managers felt they had created, fully understood and owned. It was challenging to articulate the final statement of UKTV's purpose, so this was left as an 'essence' at first, with a selection of words rather than a clear articulation.

An off-site session with all employees was held to introduce the strategic direction and create emotional connection by exploring what it would feel like when UKTV was truly living its purpose. A picture of the future was constructed, covering what the business would be saying, feeling and doing when it got 'there'.

A small team of middle managers created the final purpose statement using input from the away day and across the business. The result was that the statement in Figure 5.3 was fully understood by all the employees, who felt passionate about living it.

With a new mood within the business, the executive team worked further on the desired values framework for the company. It reviewed the input from earlier listening sessions and engaged middle managers to talk about what they believed UKTV valued today and what it *should* value if it was to achieve its goals. Darren says:

During the dialogue sessions, people had healthy debate and challenged one another. The exercise of involving people in this way led to behaviours that truly represented the values we wanted to live. The process itself didn't just define values, it helped people to embrace and live them as they discussed the topic.

The final list of desired behaviours was introduced to the middle managers during a day out of the office. Small groups explored each value and talked about where they saw it in action today, where they could live it more fully in their teams, and where they could take it from an aspiration to a true behaviour in their own everyday working lives. 'Making it real helped people own the behaviours we needed,' believes Darren. 'I saw real change immediately, and that wouldn't have happened if I'd just communicated a set of desired values.'

The morning after the off-site session, the executive team and middle managers presented the values to the entire staff. They used real examples to bring them to life, then met with their teams to explore them in depth. A bank of 'values in action' examples was created during the same week, based on the team discussions. Within days, the appraisals process began and each individual was encouraged to discuss the values further. Everyone devised a personal objective to increase one behaviour to bring the values to life. They had their own business objective, and one concerning one UKTV behaviour.

The values are now embedded through recognition, reward, recruitment approaches and much more. Darren concludes:

It took nine months from starting the survey through to introducing the values framework and integrating it within areas such as our performance management. The shift in the business has been dramatic. People are clear on our direction and decision-making is aligned. There are defined lines of responsibility and people are living our values, which are not aspirational but are real behaviours that help people work well together. This is all contributing massively to a growing business, and at the end of 2011, less than a year after we started this work, we had our best year yet. It's absolutely clear to me that an engaged organisation drives business performance, and that this is influenced hugely by middle managers. Our work continues.

What to Watch For

- As a new CEO, take the temperature within the first 90 days so that you develop a true picture about the climate early on.
- Understand the values framework of the company, how people interact, and whether that framework will deliver the results you need for the business.
- Be honest and open – don't spin results from a survey. You'll gain more trust from being upfront about the issues than from spinning to cover things up.
- Use an external group to research and share data – this is more credible than the human resources department or CEO sharing what they've heard.
- Conversations about the results and action planning by departments are very worthwhile, but consider whether you may want to have a more macro conversation first, where people start to take ownership for the big cultural issues rather than jumping straight into tactical solutions planning.

- Involve managers and get them to take ownership of the problems and solutions – share survey results with them first (the day before) so they are well-equipped to deal with questions and concerns among their teams.
- Follow through – as a leader and manager, people will be excited by your commitments, but will want to see rapid action.
- Provide updates about progress on each commitment on a regular basis – let it form an ongoing part of your communications.
- Engage with people in emotional, fun ways.
- Encourage people to imagine the future for themselves.
- Pay attention to your middle managers – they're the key to creating any cultural shift.
- Integrate desired behaviours (values) into the entire fabric of the organisation – the language, leadership behaviour, performance management, bonus and reward schemes and recognition are just some of the areas that help embed them.

Using Peers to Engage Each Other During Transformation – Pfizer

In 2006, Pfizer embarked on a major restructuring of the organisation to create a leaner and more competitive company. Nigel Edwards was Communications Head for the UK company. He was responsible for ensuring that people in the business were taken on the journey through transformation and could look to the future with a positive mindset. The changes meant new responsibilities for many, especially in the field-based workforce.

He led a series of interventions to take people through the change, and is still using many of the successful techniques in his wider European remit today. His aim was to use the opportunity to create more open and dynamic culture of communication.

The new structure was in place by July 2007. Nigel planned a sales conference for the following September where the entire organisation would come together for the first time in history. This was to be a defining moment where people could look to the future and be excited about working together in a new way. The conference would communicate the context, direction and goals for the coming years. However, this left a gap of three months that needed to be plugged to ensure people weren't left behind in the journey of transformation.

One way to close this gap was to involve people in telling their stories as a way of sharing experiences and emotions.

Three months before the conference, ten people in the field force were selected to be involved in sharing their experiences. The ten were chosen from the areas of the UK where most change in job roles had occurred. They were each given a tripod and camcorder and asked to record the personal journey they went on as the changes began to take effect over the three months leading up to the conference.

Between the July launch and the September conference, internal communication produced five episodes covering a different range of the video diaries. The first set of episodes was delivered to employees' homes on a DVD. The next was placed on the intranet a few weeks later, so remote field employees could watch it. Then, just before the September conference, the whole series was placed on a DVD and distributed to each employee. These weren't stage-managed videos, scripted or constructed around presentations, or captured in formal business settings – they were down-to-earth conversations between employees and a camera lens at the end of a hard day, conducted from the comfort of their own homes. Nigel explains:

> *We didn't lose anything in professional quality terms, though, because professional quality would have undermined the whole thing – they had to be real, because people had to recognise them as being 'like my situation'.*

This approach was designed to let the impact of peer empathy guide employees through the change:

> *If we'd had regular updates from the director saying, 'Well, we started on July first and we're making real progress. These are truly exciting times for the business,' – and all the while people on the ground are actually going through several levels of emotional confusion, with all manner of uncertainty and disillusionment constantly running through their heads – what legitimacy does this have? It doesn't really have any. It's just PR. Whereas, during a big and unsettling change like this, the learning comes from seeing people like me, doing the kinds of jobs I do, resolving the same queries I have, at the same rate. That's the real power. And that's what we set out to do.*

One manager became known for making her entries sitting in a chair, in her dressing gown, drinking a cup of coffee in the early morning before getting ready for work. Another video diary would frequently feature children running around in the background.

The approach was not moderated, and was authentic. People watching could see the real fears, uncertainty and positive factors their colleagues were experiencing throughout the change.

Staff entered the September conference in a stronger emotional place, already having an understanding of the implications of transformation from a plethora of angles.

Figure 23.1a   Still from Pfizer video
Source: Copyright Melcrum and reproduced with kind permission.

Figure 23.1b   Still from Pfizer video
Source: Copyright Melcrum and reproduced with kind permission.

Figure 23.1c   Still from Pfizer video
Source: Copyright Melcrum and reproduced with kind permission.

Figure 23.1d   Still from Pfizer video
Source: Copyright Melcrum and reproduced with kind permission.

What to Watch For

- Find ways to plug a time gap between engagement interventions during transformational change.
- Involving employees in sharing their personal stories is incredibly powerful as long as the content is authentic.
- Keep the approach un-moderated.
- Give people freedom to be themselves if they're involved in creating content.

Creating a High-performing Team by Focusing on Levers of Engagement – Innocent

Innocent is well known in the UK for its fresh approach to food and drink. The business has grown hugely over the last few years. Founded by three best friends from university in 1999, it now employs over 280 people across different business areas. Its clear purpose and values attract high-quality talent to work in the organisation, and ongoing engagement is seen as a key driver of performance.

Every quarter, Jo Huddie, Innocent's Learning and Engagement Manager, takes a pulse check of engagement levels across the entire business. Three questions are asked concerning employee advocacy, motivation and excitement. Jo explains:

> Measuring each quarter gives us constant visibility of engagement levels and allows us to see the warning signs of any areas of the business where teams may lack clarity, motivation or understanding.

An annual survey also takes place to take a deeper look at engagement levels. Key driver analysis is carried out to identify the areas that make the biggest difference to engagement levels.

In 2009, the engagement survey highlighted issues in one of the teams most critical to business growth. Scores for questions relating to whether individuals felt their opinions counted and whether they were in control of their workload were particularly poor. The results coincided with a new leader entering the business. He saw that the business success depended on his re-engaging people in the team, so he made this his priority.

He first set about appointing the best team for the upcoming business challenges. He put the right people in the right roles, and recruited new skills and capabilities where needed. The result was a team where 70 per cent of people were new and the whole group had a high desire to be engaged.

The team began the 'Fresh Start' initiative to engage, give clarity and ensure maximum performance.

The leadership team started by spending three days with each other off-site to build a stronger team and improve their leadership skills. An external facilitator conducted video interviews with members of the team and wider business that were shared with the leadership at the start of the event. Jo reports:

There was something about seeing the feedback on video that made it really impactful. It set the tone for the group's time together to consider how they were going to best lead the new team and take the business forward.

This was followed by a two-day session involving the whole team where members explored the key area the leadership team had identified for success: How we want to work together.

The result was a purpose that the team was passionate about and believed in. Members had agreed behaviours and ways of working together that would enable them to be consistent and successful.

In order to ensure that the session had a practical impact on life at work, there was an open and honest discussion addressing the factors contributing to low engagement that people wanted to change. Five key areas were addressed, from agreeing how to live and breathe the team purpose to defining a better decision-making framework and holding more effective meetings. Jo explains:

It was the basic frustrations that stop people doing their very best that we wanted to address. People felt that if these could be addressed they would be able to contribute more.

Team members took on leadership of different workstreams to improve the five issues identified. This meant that there was real ownership among the entire team and engagement wasn't seen as a management issue. They turned each set of intentions to change into a very specific action plan that was extremely visible. Progress was reported and heroes celebrated each month to demonstrate the importance of living the team purpose. Jo observes:

The way changes happened was very practical and innovative. They developed a 'golden rules' toolkit for meetings that included an ear that people could hold up if they didn't feel others were listening. Their measure of success was when they no longer needed the toolkit because they were adopting all the desired meeting behaviours. They could then burn it! As it was designed by the team themselves, it fit with our culture and was more effective as a result.

One year into the change, engagement scores had improved and the leadership remained focused on maintaining momentum. It continues to perform beyond expectations.

What to Watch For

- Have clear goals for any engagement initiative.
- Don't see the answer to increasing engagement as being a one-off off-site session – it's important to attack issues from different angles.
- A shared sense of team purpose is vital, and should be the first stage for action when you want to increase engagement for performance.
- It's important not to miss the basic blockers to performance – for example, this team found that more effective meeting etiquette made a big difference to both how people felt and their effectiveness.
- Conduct a diagnostic exercise beforehand so that problems are understood before any off-site session – this means that the quality of solutions will be higher than if too much discussion takes place.

Engaging Employee Groups with Specific Approaches – the Sony Springboard Gender Project

Sony Europe is one of many organisations with a strong focus on ensuring diversity, and gender is one key component. The Professional Solutions Europe (PSE) division is one area of the business that has seen its customer profile change, with more women in key positions. It's therefore keen to ensure that women with the right skills are also considered for key roles in Sony.

Val Elliott, Head of Commercial Engineering at Sony Europe, championed and implemented the Springboard programme across Sony UK. It started in 2011, and continues to work with women across the organisation to increase their confidence, profile and value in the company. Val says:

> We have great learning and development across Sony Europe and our senior female managers have the opportunity to participate. However, we also want to be sure we are providing the best environment to attract high performing women into senior roles here. We also wanted to grow the confidence of women across all levels of Sony and to do this we worked with Springboard to develop a development programme for our ladies in non management positions.

Val understood from research that it's common for women to feel less confident when returning from maternity leave. She could see trends that often women return to work in lower-grade roles, either due to a lack of confidence or because they need more flexible working patterns. She also knew that there were women in administration roles who assumed that they wouldn't progress any further in their careers, but actually had huge potential.

The Springboard programme was designed to build confidence and give women a space to talk openly about business issues, personal issues and challenges. The four-day programme ran over four months, with learning groups in between to enable staff to offer support to each other and build networks. 'We talked about values, what people wanted to get out of life, and introduced the idea of personal brand,' explains Val.

Some of the women believed that they'd be promoted simply by virtue of being on the programme, so expectations were managed carefully – it was more a question of helping participants to think about what they wanted out of their lives.

The result has been that individuals have taken on projects they wouldn't have considered before. They're more confident in putting ideas forward, and feel more comfortable sharing opinions than they did before attending the programme. Val reflects:

People feel different about the company. They're clearer about what they need and I'm really noticing that individuals are going out of their way to do something extra. Managers have noticed the difference too. They are telling me how much more contribution they see from individuals and asking for spaces in future programmes for other team members.

The programme wasn't set up to be an engagement lever, but has clearly increased levels of engagement and created a propensity to invest rather than save among many of the participants. Val explains:

There was some resistance from managers to sending individuals on the programme at first, but that was due to a lack of understanding. There are now plenty of examples of more confident women in our divisions, so managers are really seeing the benefit of a more capable, confident and engaged set of individuals.

What to Watch For

- Don't underestimate how much effort is needed to help managers understand why such a programme exists and the benefits to them.
- Be ready to manage expectations of individuals who assume that a promotion will be waiting for them after the programme.
- Consider how to keep it alive after the formal programme finishes – for example, by setting up an alumni programme.

Using Management Development to Create a Tipping Point – a Global Media Company

In the past, a particular international media organisation had invested in its senior leaders and top talent, and high-performing leaders had continued to grow even stronger. However, investment in middle managers hadn't been as significant. The Head of Organisational Development believed passionately that the middle management layer made a huge difference to performance and engagement. He wanted to create a tipping point in the culture by ensuring that all managers had the right level of development so that they could bring the best of themselves to work each day. He also knew that investing in this community would contribute to turning them, and those around them, from savers to investors. He knew that it's managers who have the power to influence the top talent but also pull their own people into new levels of performance.

The business case was put forward and agreed to provide a management development programme that covered the fundamentals for individuals to strengthen their people skills. For some, this acted as a useful refresher, and for others it ignited new capabilities.

Managers were invited to participate in face-to-face focus groups to explain to the Human Resources department what areas they would like help in strengthening. People were very honest, talking about areas where they struggled and requesting help to refresh their skills.

As a result of the input, a curriculum consisting of two modules was created. By October 2011, nearly 300 managers had experienced the programme and given glowing feedback about its relevance and value to them in their people management roles. The first module covers the fundamentals of good management. The group explores what strong people management looks like. It covers specific areas such as delegation, contract setting, appraisals, feedback and coaching, using open questions. People always have interesting examples to share of bad management and good management. As individuals begin by sharing their own experiences, they start to see for themselves where their strengths lie and where more work may be required. It's a great way to help people see where they have blind spots that need attention. Once they've identified the areas they need to develop, they're given the tools during both modules to help them.

The second module takes participants through how to handle poor-performing individuals and difficult conversations.

The results have been amazing. Individuals have transformed their style of management and had a variety of successes across the business. One individual excused himself immediately after the session on delegation, explaining that she'd delegated something that morning and now realised what a disaster could occur as a result of her style. She wanted to go and rectify it immediately. Another manager completely transformed relationships and performance with IT contractors by using contract setting to understand their needs better and work out more effective ways to collaborate in an environment where their official managers were in another company.

Managers are currently being trained so that they can deliver components of the programme. This faculty will help to keep the learning current and build a management community that has higher engagement levels. The aim is that by keeping the content up-to-date, the managers involved will continue to grow and model great behaviour.

What to Watch For

- Secure commitment for all managers to experience the development programme – sending a very strong signal to the organisation about what leadership values.
- Gain input from managers about their needs in advance. This gives insight and ensures there is an appetite for what is created and offered.
- Involve managers in delivering the programme so that they become stronger investors themselves and keep building their own capabilities.
- Ensure that all senior leaders go through the programme in one of the first tranches.

Creating the Right Environment for People to Engage – Sony UK

During 2010, Sony UK received its employee engagement survey results and identified that action was needed to increase motivation in most areas of the business. The leadership team asked the employee council to suggest actions to boost motivation, and a series of ideas emerged. However, one of the most significant breakthroughs came from an initiative in the Basingstoke location.

Managers in the Basingstoke Management Forum wanted to take significant action to boost morale in their divisions. They decided to involve their teams and ask for ideas that would create a greater feeling of being valued among teams and individuals.

The result was the birth of 'The Bridge'. Val Elliott, Head of Commercial Engineering at Sony Europe, explains:

> We have a large number of technical and engineering communities at our Basingstoke site, and we decided a series of technical taster sessions would be hugely motivating to showcase the communities' skills. A group of local managers and non-managers took ownership and created a forum where people could talk about projects going on, see new technology ideas from different divisions and talk together about their impact and advancement. It appeals to the group because they are getting their hands on new technology and have a place to talk about new ideas. It also gives the business a benefit because some of the ideas are really exciting – so much so that we are having to bring our Intellectual Property expert into some conversations.

By the end of 2011, 60–70 people were involved in the scheme from across Sony. Despite being focused on technical teams, it's now attracting sales and marketing people too. Val believes:

> We created a new level of engagement because people in our engineering community feel more valued by the organisation and their peer group. As leaders, we created the environment for people to consider what would make them feel most valued. We then sponsored it. Those that run the group recognised that engineers like to feel valued for the skills they have and that this kind of initiative would do more for motivation than a staff away day or party' she adds.

The approach is already becoming part of the 'way we do thing around here' rather than a special initiative. 'It's having a big impact on how people feel,' says Val, 'and I look forward to seeing it get even stronger.'

What to Watch For

- Consider the different types of employee groups and how different 'being valued' looks for each one.
- Create an environment that allows groups to come up with solutions themselves – they'll very often own them and believe in them more.
- Use networking at the end of the sessions.
- Make sure the feedback loop after discussions is short, to maintain momentum.

A Unique Example of Engagement through Attachment and Significance – John Lewis Partnership

While sitting in the reception area of the John Lewis Partnership in London, I was struck by the words hanging on the wall:

> *In 1914, John Spedan Lewis laid the foundations for a different kind of business. His vision was of a great commercial enterprise where success would be measured by the happiness of those working in it and by its good service to the general community.*
>
> *We carry forward that ambition in today's John Lewis Partnership, the UK's largest and longest living example of employee ownership and a leading force in UK retailing.*

In conversations that followed with Patrick Lewis, the Partners' Counsellor, it was obvious that unlike many corporations, these words were the fundamental belief of JLP's leaders and owners. They weren't simply an aspiration. JLP's purpose – unusually – is not to maximise profit.

Levels of engagement are extremely high in the business, and it's success is well documented – a great example of attachment and significance in action.

The John Lewis Partnership is an organisation that has a clear sense of purpose and ownership structure that creates investors rather than savers. Patrick explains:

> *The ownership model drives engagement and performance. We are a partnership, and that means that any person joining the group becomes a partner. This immediately creates a different dynamic in the attitudes people have about the organisation. Within our recruitment conversations, we make it very clear that we expect more of each other than in many organisations. We expect people to give more to the partnership, but in return they get a significant return. This means we tend to attract and retain people that have a desire to give as well as receive as part of a long-term relationship rather than a short-term career move.*

Partners are co-owners of the business, and therefore have a deeper attachment right from their first day. Levels of engagement are high because partners have a desire to engage and see success. The lack of annual short-term shareholder financial pressure means more long-term investment in people, the working environment and career development. For example, in many retailers, middle manager induction includes one day working in-store. In JLP, it's more likely to be two weeks. Leaders spend considerable time ensuring that partners understand the purpose of the organisation and what it means at every level. There are many social and special interest partner groups that are funded by the partnership – for example, a choir, orchestra and numerous sports clubs.

While JLP's business model is rare, and almost impossible to implement in an existing corporation or organisation, the principles espoused are nonetheless valuable as learning points. Simple questions starting with 'What if …?' make colleagues think in very different ways – What if this was *your* company, What if we were about to spend *your* money? These are powerful openers. Ultimately, highly engaged companies don't even need to state ownership – the workforce already assume it through the ways they are asked to make decisions, create new value and treat each other with respect and equality.

Engagement During Transition Resulting in Team Closure – Galileo and Covia

Four years after Galileo had merged with Covia, Gordon Watt, then Vice President of Systems Development and Senior Executive in Europe, received a call from the Chief Operating Officer in the USA informing him that the Systems Development division in Europe would close and its work be transferred to Denver. Gordon was given a deadline of twelve months, but instinctively knew that keeping his team engaged for that length of time would be challenging and unfair. When he discussed this with his senior managers, they collectively decided to cut the expected transfer time down to just three months: one month for planning, one month for handover, and one month to offer support once handover had taken place.

The American team had issues with passports, so the planned handover in the UK was held up. Gordon decided the best answer was to fly the team to Denver and hand over there. This would mean that his people were still able to meet the deadline and move on with their lives.

Gordon knew that he needed a focus and an emotive rallying cry for his team members to ensure they would give their all and stay engaged throughout the three months. He decided it would appeal to them if they 'did something faster' than the new American parent had ever imagined or was capable of. This was hugely motivating – people saw it is a chance to prove their value.

However, he knew that this alone wasn't enough. It was natural that everyone would be worried about their futures and how they would pay the bills. The Human Resources Account Manager came up with an ingenious idea. She decided to hold a jobs fair and invite all the relevant IT companies to come and hear more about the staff and how they were embracing the challenge. All the companies she invited attended. Ninety-eight per cent of the team had jobs lined up before the end of the first month. This ensured that people knew their future was secure and could turn their attention to making the transition a success.

At the beginning, Gordon brought all of the managers together and shared the three-month plan that he and his senior managers had developed. He asked them 'What do you think?' and gave it to them to refine – really giving them ownership for the mammoth challenge ahead. He set them the mission, but gave them control over execution.

After this, managers came together once a week in a forum. They talked about the issues they were facing with motivating their people and helped each other to find solutions to their individual challenges. Gordon attended, but as an observer rather than a leader. He'd set up the meetings, but wanted the managers to take ownership and gain whatever value they saw appropriate from the forum. It was hugely successful, and a simple way to make sure that managers had what they needed to keep their people focused and engaged.

In addition, Gordon sponsored an open forum that took place once a week. Typically, 150–200 people would attend, and the purpose was to offer an opportunity for people to ask for more information about anything at all that was concerning them.

Throughout the project, key milestones were represented on a staircase and displayed up the stair well in the building. This was important in allowing people to see that momentum was being maintained and that they were making tangible things happen. Recognition was a big lever of engagement during this transition. If Gordon saw an individual had done something great from a weekly progress report, he'd find them and congratulate them personally:

> I would say well done, but also inquire what had helped them make it happen. I was interested, but also wanted to show that it wasn't just a pat on the back: I really understood the gravity of what had been delivered.

Other communication devices sprang up unofficially. An 'underground' newsletter started, and Gordon recognised that he had an opportunity to embrace this rather than seeing it as a threat. He offered content for it, and the former CEO wrote an article for the last edition expressing his pride in what the teams had achieved.

The team took on their own mission to maintain momentum and keep each other engaged. They organised social events each time a key milestone was reached. 'Go-karting was a favourite,' Gordon remembers. At the end, the team arranged a huge party at the Imperial War Museum repository, among the Spitfires and Lancasters. They invited their former CEO to join them, and all of those attending celebrated and recognised each others' incredible achievements.

Gordon says that the biggest lesson he learnt throughout the transition was to cover the basics of making people feel secure about the future. Then, it's important to motivate and keep people engaged throughout the journey. He knows that the initial jobs fair was a vital foundation for engaging people for the rest of the journey.

What to Watch For

- Be a role model – treat people as individuals.
- Make people feel secure as quickly as possible.
- Define a 'call to arms' that will rally people and help them feel fired up.
- As a leader and manager, be brave and do the right thing. For example, Gordon opted to aim for three months not twelve months before closure.
- Find people who have done great things on the journey. Congratulate them personally and be interested in how they did it, what they learnt and what made them proud.
- Involve managers at the beginning and give them ownership – provide them with a framework and let them populate it.
- Managers' forums are essential for sharing experiences and overcoming issues.
- Give people access to you – hold open forums with no agenda to help people feel heard.
- Don't be afraid if teams set up informal communication methods – embrace them and their input.
- Celebrate milestones regularly.
- Give managers as much face-to-face time and opportunities to share experiences as you can possibly create.

Daily Engagement in a Small to Medium-sized Company – Solarcentury

Solarcentury is a renewable energy company with approximately 120 employees across the UK, Italy and France. The company enjoys high levels of engagement and phenomenal performance from its people, which in turn has created an incredibly profitable business.

Its CEO, Derry Newman, joined after spending his career in corporate environments. He had a great passion for the company and wanted to play a part in taking it from a start-up to a successful commercial entity. Derry has always believed that engaging people is the key to success, and has created an environment at Solarcentury where the role of managers in engagement is different from that in a large corporate.

Every three months, all employees gather off-site for a quarterly update. Anyone who wants to share news about their project is invited to present. Some people use visual aids such as PowerPoint presentations, some make passionate speeches, often without notes. Everyone uses humour and openness to get their point across.

Senior managers never review the presentations prior to the event – each contributor is trusted to put together content that is relevant for their peers. People talk about their projects, their pride, how they cracked challenges, and recognise those colleagues who played a part in making them happen. Derry believes:

> The peer-to-peer recognition is a very important part of the success of these quarterly updates. It creates a huge degree of shared ownership and pride among the whole company. The projects are really interesting for people to hear about, such as the person who led the project to build a solar power system on a disused tin-mine in Cornwall. He talked about what it took to make the work happen, and people could really understand the complexity of our work and how diverse it can be.

Often, people use photomontages to tell their stories at the meetings. They take pictures throughout the lifecycle of the project and aim to capture the emotion of a customer and/or the team at various stages in its progress. 'It's a definite case of a picture paints a thousand words,' says Derry.

Quarterly meetings are sometimes held at customers' sites so that people can see the impact of the work that has been done, as well as hear from colleagues about their progress.

In between the quarterly sessions, all employees come together for an hour every month for a shorter update where they receive a business overview and share progress. Derry is proud that these events aren't planned weeks in advance. The date is in the diary, but the content is shaped on the day: 'That way, it's totally in tune with the speed of our market and is more authentic than a selection of speeches created in advance.' He devises the agenda on the train to the office on the morning of the event. At 9.10 a.m. the company gets together and hears a business performance update. New starters are introduced, then individuals are asked to share news about projects, issues or initiatives:

> One week we could be talking about safety on a construction site in our industry and reminding people of health and safety issues to protect our own people. The next we could have a team member showing us how we are innovating new materials and processes to make solar products that are simple to fit and maintain. The content is totally diverse and current. We don't use

PowerPoint or scripts. I ask people on the day to comment and they do so, unrehearsed. The consequence is that we break down barriers between teams, people feel accountable for what they do, and we engender a huge sprit of openness.

Derry also believes that the monthly and quarterly sessions boost individuals' confidence and skills. They learn from their colleagues' stories because they are often expressed in an emotional and personal way. They gain confidence from presenting their own stories.

The format of having little preparation has encouraged people to become more articulate and to think on the hoof. It also means time isn't spent unnecessarily on creating PowerPoint presentations.

At a project-based level, project leaders will send out communications at the beginning of a new initiative that clearly show how they would like to work with others to achieve success. They'll send a 'what I need from you' message to all those connected with the project and make explicit what they require. This ensures that everyone is aware of what is needed, takes ownership, and buys into the action required. A simple example could be the IT group needing to upgrade systems. It would send a 'what we need from you' message to all colleagues to explain what is happening, why, and that what it needs is tolerance and patience during the unavoidable two-hour outage.

One of the core principles for Solarcentury is to be open and honest in their communication. It's not unusual to hear the Chairman or CEO say: 'We're telling you this even though most companies wouldn't …'. The result is a high degree of trust and engagement levels.

This best practice has also reduced the dependency on middle managers to communicate business direction to their staff. 'If companies have great cross-company communication, they don't need to use up more time trying to cascade messages,' reflects Derry.

This frees managers up to coach, train and develop their people in addition to their operational responsibilities, and is something that larger organisations could do well to find ways to replicate.

What to Watch For

- Openness and honesty are crucial, and fundamental to all communication.
- More short, sharp communication is almost always needed.
- Move away from scripted presentations where too much time is devoted to preparation. Encourage people to tell their story from the heart.
- Use short meetings between senior leaders and middle managers to update them on the latest news, followed by dialogue to ensure a deeper level of understanding.

Involving Others to Articulate Purpose and Vision – Sony Europe

Sony Europe experienced a number of business challenges during the last decade. Just like its competitors, it faced increasing competitive pressures, shrinking margins and rising consumer expectations. This created a need for the organisation to become faster, more efficient and customer-centred.

Fujio Nishida, President of Sony Europe, wanted to develop more capacity to differentiate within the organisation by unlocking greater creativity among teams and individuals. He knew that to do this, he needed to engage people and take them on a journey.

Fujio believed that it was essential for Sony Europe to be clear about its core purpose as a first step to creating a more creative culture. He knew that a clear purpose would provide the anchor needed for people so that 'being more creative' had a context. He also recognised that he needed to involve others in defining the purpose.

A senior leadership development programme had existed for a couple of years, so many high-potential employees had already been identified as a talent pool. Fujio tapped into this community and appointed six senior managers to design an approach to involve others in defining the purpose.

The project team held one-to-one conversations with senior leaders across the business, and used their input to design a two-day workshop for the top 50 people in the business. They came together and explored the purpose of Sony Europe and why it existed for its stakeholders.

Stimulus materials were provided to each attendee in advance of the workshop. This included examples of previously articulated purpose statements for business units within the organisation. It also featured the best and most meaningful purpose statements from other organisations that the team could find. One page in the preparatory reading contained a consolidated collection of the values of all senior leaders and members of the talent pool. This was designed to stimulate thinking about the values of the business and how they fit with personal values of leaders.

At the workshop, the project team became facilitators and led the group through a series of dialogue sessions to explore the strengths, personal perceptions of the purpose, and to share insights. There were team discussions and personal reflection time. The result at the end of the two days was a shared view about the essence of the purpose. The group also defined the culture it wanted to create to truly live the purpose, and the behaviours required to unlock more creativity.

A small group agreed to draw up the purpose based on the output of the two days and create a final statement that could be shared with the total organisation. A draft was created and reviewed with the entire group via a series of online meetings. The final purpose was then agreed.

Fujio took the inspirational purpose to the broader organisation through a series of roadshows. He acted as a Prophet and Storyteller to introduce the essence of Sony Europe to every employee in each office across Europe. This was done through personal stories from Fujio, inspirational video material and dialogue. Fujio asked the audience for examples of the purpose in action, and to think about how they could live the value of creativity more fully in their everyday work.

Each roadshow was tailored to the size of the group and its culture. In each case, he put the message into context and used local examples where possible. The senior leaders in each country were asked to take a role in sharing their perspectives of the purpose in action so that the story was also owned by local leaders.

Senior leaders and managers developed their own local approaches to continue embedding the purpose, and Fujio measured his direct reporting managers on the associated values. Employee communication around the story underpinned its introduction

---

What to Watch For

- Providing great examples helps to stimulate conversation and a better-quality conversation among teams defining their company's purpose.
- Involve talent pool members in designing and facilitating engagement programmes – it leads to excellent results, and those individuals will be more highly engaged, become ambassadors for the change and tell the story as a result.
- A consolidated picture of leader/manager values provides interesting insights and an opportunity to deepen engagement levels.
- Underpin purpose and values work with communication, and integrate it into performance measures for individuals.

A Culture of Development to Boost Engagement – a Global Media Player

The leadership development programme in a certain global media company is open to all employees. Twelve places are allocated each year to the staff members who qualify. Anyone who wants to participate is asked to submit an application, and then attends a one-day assessment. The organisation makes it very clear that the programme is open to all, and so far has seen an excellent spread of level and diversity among those who've put themselves forward.

The assessment involves exercises centred around the company values, a presentation about a business project that the individual would like to launch, an interview about their reasons for wanting to take part in the programme, and a written test about a business conundrum. This exercise alone provides huge value to those who apply. Each candidate is given personal feedback, and individuals learn a great deal by going through the assessment process. For those who are not accepted onto the programme, the programme co-ordinators ensure that their business project proposals are shared with the appropriate managing director in the business, and each individual is given the chance to connect with them to share their ideas. This means they gain extra visibility among senior executives, and in some cases are invited to be involved in taking the project to the next level. The result is that anyone who applies but isn't successful still becomes more engaged and has an increased chance of being an investor rather than saver.

Those who are successful go through a year's course of eight modules, including finance, project management and communication skills.

In between modules, participants work on a self-defined business project. This can be anything an individual feels would make a difference in the business. Some projects have involved innovative ideas for growth, others have explored ways to make the business more efficient.

Each person is allocated a board-level sponsor and mentor who supports them throughout the project and helps them prepare a final presentation to the full executive board at the end of the course. Both the board members and the individuals on the programme gain huge value from the mentoring process. The ideas are treated very seriously, and some have even been taken forward before the end of the programme because it makes sense to progress quickly to gain the benefits.

Individuals on the programme also work-shadow others and participate in a corporate social responsibility project. The work-shadowing tends to relate to the project each individual has defined so that it has a connection to their passion and interest areas.

The result is a group of people who are highly engaged in the business. Participants' skill and confidence levels increase, and this permeates through to have an impact across the organisation. There are cases where individuals have been promoted more than one level, and others where personal assistants have inspired the executive board to take action in new areas.

What to Watch For

- Opening up the programme to everyone sends a really clear message to the organisation about the value it places on development. With the right application process, this means passionate people of all levels can participate.
- Board-level mentors give the programme credibility and an opportunity for great ideas to gain sponsorship.
- Where individuals aren't selected for the final programme, they should leave feeling highly engaged because they've gained other benefits through the process. It's a good idea to involve their managers at this point so that they have a strategy to keep engagement levels high and ensure that effective career plans are put in place based on the feedback.

Engaging a Business as a New Leader, and What to Watch For – Sony Audio Europe

During 2008, Sony was experiencing significant market challenges, driven by the move to a digital world, emerging competitors and eroding margins. Every area of the business needed to think differently to create competitive advantage. One such area was Audio Marketing Europe (AME), and when Andreas Ditter joined as Vice President at the time, he found a business that was not hitting the numbers and had undergone numerous organisational changes. He immediately decided that he needed to focus on boosting business performance and creating a culture for sustainable growth.

He set about meeting every individual in AME one-to-one to build a picture of how people were feeling and where areas for improvement existed. In parallel, he conducted an engagement survey so he could see which levers could be pulled for the greatest impact.

Andreas didn't just understand the internal view, he also talked to his internal customers to understand how they could work together better to deliver more business and increased value to all.

The survey showed that AME was below the benchmark for similar organisations. In particular, levels of senior engagement were low. The values were understood throughout the business, but weren't lived, and staff felt a lack of purpose.

His predecessor had introduced a programme called 'Fun-damentals'. This aimed to help people think about how they engaged with each other in daily business life. It had made a difference to how people worked, and Andreas continued to sponsor it and look at how he could use it to engage his people more effectively and create responsible managers who acted as leaders. Andreas remembers:

When I entered the business, I realised the secret to success was going to be capable people that were well led, managed and engaged. I made engagement and growing the leadership capability my mantra. I kept a journal at the time, and remember writing 'people development is a major key to motivation and satisfaction – I will make it my priority' in it.

He adopted an approach involving:

* creating a more cohesive leadership team;
* understanding, developing and engaging talent through a clear people and communication strategy;
* equipping staff with the right skills and capacity to perform at their best.

A MORE COHESIVE LEADERSHIP TEAM

Andreas took the bold step of working with a trusted provider to develop a highly challenging, highly experiential event that would put his senior team in a position where they began to build a strong set of shared stories, perspectives and lines of respect for each other. The result saw his management team spend two days living in snow caves on a glacier in Norway. Team members were given simple equipment to enable them to build the caves, eat and survive. It was an extreme experience drawing on every skill each individual possessed.

The result was increased respect among team members, and a deeper understanding of each other and how to best work together. Andreas explains:

I remember a true breakthrough in building trust. One of my team was absolutely exhausted and was struggling to keep pace. Without really thinking, I took his skis and carried them for him. He was stunned, and I realised that such a simple act had given us a stronger bond that paid dividends later.

The event combined self-understanding with team development, and pushed the group into a shared, unfamiliar environment in which they were reliant on each other to succeed. Creating 'clans' to encourage them to compete ultimately became a cohesive factor, the trials set along the way constantly demonstrating that only through total collaboration would the group succeed.

PEOPLE AND COMMUNICATION STRATEGY

The management team worked with Human Resources to assess key positions and people. They identified where gaps and development opportunities existed, and put a strategy in place to address them. Each leader was given a development plan, and Andreas invested in relevant training to support them.

The leadership team worked on defining the core purpose, vision, goals and values of the business. They helped colleagues to explore these through a series of quarterly meetings and team discussions.

The purpose was identified as 'SMILE – to put a smile on people's faces'. The business recognised that it was all about helping people to have experiences and feel emotions through audio. It felt that a smile was an indicator of a good time, and thus the primary purpose of the business. It was a clear engagement vehicle that everyone could identify with and talk about with pride. Andreas explains:

> Audio products are all about entertainment, therefore a smile can be used as a key performance indicator to identify if people are having a good time – both consumers as well as internal customers. It's also obviously a very catchy name.

Andreas believed that the values of professionalism, ambition, clarity, enthusiasm, customer focus and ownership were hugely important to driving sustainable business success. He coached his managers to live these values at every opportunity, and measured their success in doing so.

Ownership was particularly important, and Andreas used the budgeting process as a way to build collective ownership and buy-in:

> Before I joined, the numbers were given top-down. When I joined, we engaged all stakeholders and built them together. This meant people bought into them, and was a big contributory factor to us hitting the numbers.

A CAPACITY FOR STAFF TO PERFORM AT THEIR BEST

AME invested in a three-day programme to help individuals sustain high performance. This focused on empowering people to live and work in ways that would serve them best. It was a great lever for engagement, with people feeling valued and invested in.

The result was a business that over-performed:

> We missed our budgets by a mile just before I joined, but we were over-achieving as a result of this work. I feel proud that the focus on empowering people to manage and engage better made such a difference to our business performance. At the beginning, my management team were sceptical, but when they realised the power of the work we were doing, they engaged at the highest possible level and carried on the work once I moved on to take on another challenge.

Andreas moved to Germany and took a role as Managing Director of Sony Home Entertainment. Looking to repeat the success at AME, he decided that culture and people were areas he would focus upon to strengthen the business. However, the environment was so different that some of the techniques he'd used in his previous role weren't as successful. He explains:

> I learnt very quickly that I needed to adapt my style and approach to fit the different culture I have here. Rather than a total focus on culture, I've had to keep a balance between empowering individuals to make change through tightly focused business projects that are easy to understand, and more conceptual behaviour change areas. It's a great example of how flexible a leader needs to be and how openness is required to change an approach to fit the culture.

What to Watch For

- Find out what pain points exist in a team when you arrive, and work with them.
- Have a clear purpose as a leader and for the business – communicate it, make it emotional, and keep it simple so that people can engage with it.
- Give people the space to grow and you will be surprised at the results.
- Be willing to focus on business-related projects *and* cultural projects to create engagement and performance.
- Work with others to make yourself successful as a leader – a great coach or human resources colleague can be a good sounding board and guide.
- Invest in awe-inspiring experiences, and ensure that you derive maximum benefit from them.
- Take care not to get frostbite when using an ice toilet!

More practical tools and advice for implementation are available at www.TheCulture Builders.com and join in the conversation at www.facebook.com/TheCultureBuilders.

References

Accenture (December 2008) 'An Accenture Point of View on Employee Engagement – What It is, Why It Matters, How You Can Change It' (unpublished), cited in MacLeod and Clarke (2009).

Barber, L., S. Hayday and S. Bevan (1999) *From People to Profits*, London: Institute of Employment Studies, cited in MacLeod and Clarke (2009).

Black, Dame Carol (2008) *Working for a Healthier Tomorrow: Review of the Health of Britain's Working Age Population*, London: The Stationery Office, www.lge.gov.uk/lge/dio/2108899, accessed 27 April 2012.

Business Link with the Department for Business, Innovation & Skills (2011) *Become a More Engaging Manager*, London: Business Link, www.businesslink.gov.uk/bdotg/action/layer?r.l1=1073858787&r.l2=1084688832&r.s=tl&topicId=1084696772, accessed 27 April 2012.

CBI-AXA (2007) *Annual Absence and Labour Turnover Survey*, cited in MacLeod and Clarke (2009).

CIPD (2006a) *Reflections on Employee Engagement*, London: CIPD, www.cipd.co.uk/NR/rdonlyres/E8C71850-FB75-4CAB-901B-00D2363F311E/0/reflempengca.pdf, accessed 27 April 2012.

CIPD (2006b) *Right Management: Measuring True Employee Engagement*, London: CIPD.

CIPD (2011) *Management Competencies for Enhancing Employee Engagement*, London: CIPD, www.cipd.co.uk/hr-resources/research/management-competencies-for-engagement.aspx, accessed 27 April 2012.

Corporate Leadership Council, Corporate Executive Board (2004) *Driving Performance and Retention through Employee Engagement: A Quantitative Analysis of Effective Engagement Strategies*, Washington, DC: Corporate Leadership Council, www.mckpeople.com.au/SiteMedia/w3svc161/Uploads/Documents/760af459-93b3-43c7-b52a-2a74e984c1a0.pdf, accessed 27 April 2012.

Fleming, J., C. Coffman and J. Harter (2005) 'Manage Your Human Sigma', *Harvard Business Review*, July.

Gatenby, M. et al. (2009) *Employee Engagement in Context*, London: Chartered Institute of Personnel and Development.

Harter, J.K. et al (2006) *Gallup Q12 Meta-Analysis*, as cited in MacLeod and Clarke (2009).

Hassan, Fred (2011) 'The Frontline Advantage', *Harvard Business Review*, May.

Hewitt Associates (2004) *Employee Engagement Higher in Double Digit Growth Companies*, Research Brief, Lincolnshire, IL: Hewitt Associates.

Ipsos MORI and Improvement & Development Agency (2006) *Lessons in Leadership*, London: Ipsos MORI and IDeA, www.ipsos-mori.com/DownloadPublication/1224_sri_localgovt_lessons_in_leadership_122006.pdf, accessed 27 April 2012.

Kipling, Rudyard (1902) 'The Elephant's Child', *Just So Stories*, www.kipling.org.uk/rg_elephantschild1.htm, accessed 27 April 2012.

Loehr, Jim and Tony Schwartz (2003) *The Power of Full Engagement*, New York: The Free Press.

MacLeod, David and Nita Clarke (2009) *Engaging for Success: Enhancing Performance through Employee Engagement. A Report to Government*, Kew: Office of Public Sector Information, Information Policy Team, www.bis.gov.uk/files/file52215.pdf, accessed 27 April 2012.

Melcrum (2004) *Making Managers Better Communicators*, London: Melcrum Publishing, www. melcrum.com/offer/catalogue_reports/mmbc/index.html, accessed 27 April 2012.

Melcrum (2011) *Developing a Communication Toolkit for Managers*, London: Melcrum Publishing, www.melcrum.com/offer/CTM2011/, accessed 27 April 2012.

Thibodeau, P.H. and L. Boroditsky (2011) *Metaphors We Think With: The Role of Metaphor in Reasoning*, Cambridge and San Francisco, CA: PLoS ONE, http://dx.doi.org/10.1371/journal.pone.0016782, accessed 27 April 2012.

Towers Perrin (2008) *2007–2008 Towers Perrin Global Workforce Study*, www.towersperrin.com/tp/getwebcachedoc?webc=HRS/USA/2008/200802/GWS_handout_web.pdf, accessed 27 April 2012.

Towers Perrin-ISR (2006) *The ISR Employee Engagement Report*, New York: Towers Watson.

Watson Wyatt (2009) *Continuous Engagement: The Key to Unlocking the Value of Your People During Tough Times*, 2008–2009 WorkEurope Survey Report, London: Watson Wyatt, www.watsonwyatt.com/research/pdfs/2008-EU-0617.pdf, accessed 27 April 2012.

Whitmore, John (2005) *Coaching for Performance*, London: Nicholas Brealey.

Wiseman, Liz and Greg McKeown (2010) 'Bringing Out the Best in People', *Harvard Business Review*, 88(5), 117–21.

Index

Page numbers in **bold** refer to figures and tables.